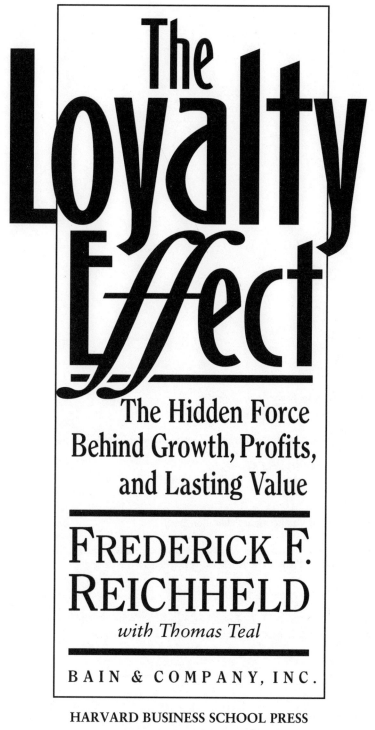

The Loyalty Effect

The Hidden Force
Behind Growth, Profits,
and Lasting Value

FREDERICK F. REICHHELD

with Thomas Teal

BAIN & COMPANY, INC.

HARVARD BUSINESS SCHOOL PRESS
Boston, Massachusetts

Loyalty-Based Management℠ is a registered servicemark of Bain & Company, Inc.

Printed in the United States of America
00 99 98 97   10 9 8

Library of Congress Cataloging-in-Publication Data
Reichheld, Frederick F.
    The loyalty effect: the hidden force behind growth, profits,
and lasting value / Frederick F. Reichheld with Thomas Teal.
        p.   cm.
    Includes bibliographical references and index.
    ISBN 0-87584-448-0
    1. Customer relations.   2. Consumer satisfaction.   3. Job
satisfaction.   4. Labor productivity.   5. Loyalty.   I. Teal, Thomas
A.   II. Title.
    HF5415.5.R438   1996
    658.4—dc20   95-39972
                                                                      CIP

The paper used in this publication meets the requirements of the American National Standard
for Permanence of Paper for Printed Library Materials Z39.49-1984.

This book is dedicated to my family,
who taught me the value and the virtue of loyalty.

Contents

Preface

The ideas in this book began to come together in the mid-1980s when I and a group of my colleagues, all of us consultants at Bain & Company, were struggling with a series of growth-and-profit riddles. Traditional models of competitive strategy did not fit the marketplace realities we observed in industries where knowledge and intellectual capital comprised the critical assets. Initially, we were trying to make sense of some striking disparities in performance among various companies in the insurance brokering industry, and the usual strategic factors—market share, scale, unit cost, and the like—had failed to explain the wide range of results. Eventually, however, we noticed one previously unexamined factor that did seem to make sense of the situation and the numbers. Firms that earned superior levels of customer loyalty and retention also earned consistently higher profits—and they grew faster as well. Closer study enabled us to quantify this loyalty-based advantage and nail down its connection to superior profit and growth, at least in insurance brokering.

A short time later, another consulting team I worked with extended this new economic framework to the credit card industry. We constructed the lifecycle economics for credit card customers and measured retention performance among competitors. Once again, retention explained relative growth and profits with remarkable accuracy. We then turned our loyalty laser on a third business in which intellectual capital comprised the key strategic asset—our own consulting business—with much the same result. Bain's profit margins over time were closely linked to variations in customer loyalty.

Over the past decade, Bain's loyalty practice has studied dozens of industries and developed practical tools—described in this book—to help our clients find and keep the right customers. In the process, we learned that customer loyalty is inextricably linked to employee and investor loyalty and that major improvements in the one often require improvements in the other two. We will discuss this subject at length, because once a company understands the ways in which customer, employee, and investor loyalty are linked, its management team can use loyalty to shine a new light on its value creation process and reexamine and improve the fundamentals of its core strategy.

As intellectual capital assumes greater and greater competitive weight in more and more industries, we expect the loyalty-based business paradigm to grow steadily more compelling. Over the next decade, thousands of businesses will come to realize that their most important assets are their human assets—their customers, employees, and investors—and that to build winning strategies, they have to find ways to attract and develop the right human assets and earn their loyalty. A number of companies recognized the precious nature of their human assets long ago and built their business systems accordingly. We call these companies loyalty leaders, and we use many of them as practical case studies of how a business can be managed to earn superior loyalty. And as you will see, their impressive track records argue persuasively that Loyalty-Based Management[SM] is not some futuristic theory about the increasing importance of intellectual capital but rather an established formula for growth and profit that has worked reliably in the past and continues to deliver outstanding results even in today's supercompetitive world.

Given the increasing importance of the knowledge that resides in human assets—and by extension, in their loyalty—it is reasonable to wonder why ours is the only major consulting firm to include loyalty among its core practice areas. The answer can be found in several of Bain & Company's unique characteristics and operating principles. To begin with, Bain's consulting approach includes a passionate focus on concrete, sustainable, and *measurable* client results. We have found that using short-term earnings as the only rigorous measure of performance leads many companies to place too much emphasis on reducing costs and too little on investing in the assets (usually human) that generate growth. Loyalty is a practical way of measuring the efficacy of those investments and, of course, of predicting the duration and value of the human assets themselves. Chapter 8 shows that for businesses where intellectual capital is critical, profits and loyalty together provide a clearer and more balanced scorecard than short-term earnings.

A second distinctive Bain principle is the emphasis we place on partnership. We have always found that the most fruitful consulting relationships grew from collaborative partnerships with clients, and we learned long ago that partnership is the best way to shepherd our own company through good times and bad. Over the years, in short, we've discovered that partnership is one of the pillars of productive loyalty and therefore of loyalty-based management, a subject we discuss in depth in Chapters 5 and 10.

Another Bain tradition is close analysis of the microeconomic forces that drive a company's cash flow, primarily because a rigorous, fact-based study of these forces can help paint a clear picture of competitive threats and opportunities. Loyalty economics, the focus of Chapter 2, is one of the analytical frameworks we have found especially useful. The analytical rigor in all the economics sections of this book is representative of the Bain approach.

A fourth hallmark of the Bain approach that bears on loyalty is our constant effort to understand what customers value and how well competitors are delivering that value. Since we often find satisfaction surveys and the other standard tools of market research inadequate to this task, we have developed several tools of our own. One of these is failure analysis, especially as it applies to customer and employee defections. Another is the defector matrix. Both are described in Chapter 7.

Loyalty as we conceive it is critically important as a measure of value creation and as a source of growth and profit, but we stop well short of claiming it to be a cure-all or a magic bullet. Bain's practical, results-based orientation has made us enormously skeptical of management fads and of the consulting based on them. We have been around long enough to see an awful lot of fashionable business ideas come into vogue then fall into disrepute. As a result, we train our case teams to use the tools that best fit the job and never to rely entirely on any single approach, including loyalty. The goal in every case is to develop a rigorous and thorough understanding of an entire business system and to identify the forces that drive competition today and those that will drive it tomorrow. Loyalty is often an important element in this picture, but it is rarely the only element.

One of our most unusual opportunities at Bain & Company comes from the proximity of Bain Capital, a separate private equity investment firm formed by several Bain consulting alumni in 1984. Our ongoing interactions with Bain Capital and with some of its portfolio companies have given all of us a bit more insight into which tools and analytical structures really do make money for shareholders and not merely for the consultants who promote them. In addition, many of us have invested substantial portions of our savings with Bain Capital, as limited partners. We too have come to understand that the consultant's view of value creation may sometimes differ sharply from the pupil-dilating perspective of investors with their own money on the line.

Bain Capital has reinforced our skepticism toward many popular management concepts. The firm has made some of its most successful investments in companies jettisoned by large corporations because top managers saw a poor "strategic fit" or a mismatch with the corporation's overall "core competence," or because the business was not earning its "risk-adjusted" cost of capital. In case after case, Bain Capital was able to help create enormous value despite the popular theories, and these experiences have been a rich source of learning for Bain & Company consultants.

Learning and intellectual capital are of course at the heart of consulting—perhaps the purest form of an intellect-driven business—and some of the most important lessons I have learned about loyalty came from observing our own company. In my nearly twenty years at the firm, I have seen it grow from one small office on Boston's waterfront into a company of fifteen hundred employees spread across twenty-three offices around the globe. In my opinion, the key to the firm's success has been its loyalty to two principles: first, that our primary mission is to create value for our clients, and second, that our most precious asset is the employees dedicated to making productive contributions to client value creation. Whenever we've been perfectly centered on these two principles, our business has prospered. Our most difficult times have been those few periods when we inadvertently drifted off center. In each such instance, however, the reaffirmation of our loyalty to primary principles produced a remarkably swift return to the path toward growth, profit, and lasting value.

ACKNOWLEDGMENTS

Obviously, the lessons I have learned from the firm's clients and from my colleagues have shaped my thinking about business. However, I want to make it clear that I, not Bain & Company, wrote this book. It is principally a product of my own experience, of the lessons I have learned from family, friends, and teachers, and of the inner dimensions of personality and spirit that have caused me to seek the truth in my own peculiar way. My partners have given me enormous latitude to say what I think, and I am deeply grateful to them. I hope the final product is worthy of their confidence.

In addition, I want to thank the executives of the companies we have identified in this book (and in the articles that preceded it) who generously contributed their time and their insight. These include Mitt Romney, Josh Beckenstein, Bob White, and Mark Nunnelly of Bain Capital; Bill Lynch of the Leo Burnett advertising agency and Phil Scaff, formerly of Leo Burnett; Dick Chitty, Fred Arnow, Don Esmond, George Borst, and Dave Illingworth of Toyota/Lexus; Charlie Cawley, David Nelms, and Craig Schroeder of MBNA; Steve Robinson and Dan Cathy of Chick-fil-A; Ed Rust, Jr., Vince Trosino, Chuck Wright, Kurt Moser, and Sandy Colee of State Farm; Ben Edwards of A. G. Edwards; John Wilson and Tod Krasnow of Staples; General Robert Herres, Herb Emanuel, Staser Holcomb, and Paul Ringenbach of USAA; Jim Ericson, Bob Carlson, and Dick Hall of Northwestern Mutual Life; Carl Sewell of Sewell Village Cadillac; and Royce Yudkoff of ABRY Communications.

I especially want to thank Tom Tierney, Bain's managing director, for his encouragement and support over the past two years. A number of Bain partners were kind enough to read portions of the manuscript at various stages of its development, and their suggestions and criticisms have improved it greatly. They include Bob Bechek, John Donahoe, Dave Johnson, Charlie Jones, Louise O'Brien, and Chris Zook. Important external perspectives were added by Bob Charpie, Royce Yudkoff, and Ralph Willard. Finally, the criticisms offered by Tom Jones and Christopher Lovelock in their capacity as reviewers for the Harvard Business School Press were extremely helpful.

That very few of these criticisms were directed at the writing itself is thanks in great part to the excellent job performed by my editor, Tom Teal. Formerly a senior editor at the *Harvard Business Review,* Tom identified fuzzy thinking in more than a few of my early drafts, and his writing skills have helped to make the manuscript far more readable than I could ever have managed on my own.

John Nichols, minister of the Unitarian-Universalist Society of Wellesley Hills, helped me think through the nonbusiness dimensions of loyalty. His network of Unitarian minister colleagues provided a unique intellectual resource in the form of a stack of sermons on loyalty.

I am also indebted to Earl Sasser, a friend and former teacher at the Harvard Business School, for encouraging me to write about my work and for helping to launch my writing career by coauthoring an article for the *Harvard Business Review* in 1989.

A great number of Bain colleagues around the world—more than I could possibly list here—have contributed to the Loyalty Practice over the years. This book could never have been written without their outstanding work, and I am deeply grateful. Many of the research gaps were filled by Jessica Colvin, who also updated, rationalized, and organized the work of various Bain case teams into the economic model described in Chapter 2. I owe a tremendous debt of thanks to my assistant, Linda Polmear, who not only dispatched a fabulous assortment of jobs associated with the creation of this book but also managed to juggle the various dimensions of my professional life (client work, practice administration, speaking engagements, etc.) so I could continue to function as a consultant and still concentrate substantial effort on thinking and writing at my satellite office in South Natick.

Finally, and most importantly, I want to thank my wife, Karen, for her love, patience, understanding, and encouragement. She has been my constant sounding board for these ideas as they made their way from dinner-table conversations into a series of articles, essays, and speeches and finally into this book. Her wisdom has shaped my thinking enormously. I could never have hoped for a more wonderful and loyal partner.

1

Loyalty and Value

LOYALTY IS DEAD, the experts proclaim, and the statistics seem to bear them out. On average, U.S. corporations now lose half their customers in five years, half their employees in four, and half their investors in less than one. We seem to face a future in which the only business relationships will be opportunistic transactions between virtual strangers.

But are the experts right? Has the time really come to abandon hope and enter the world of fast-money speculators, job-surfing careerists, disposable employees, and fickle customers? Even more important, can companies succeed by embracing opportunism as a way of life? The answer is no, not if they care about long-term growth and profits. Experience has shown us that disloyalty at current rates stunts corporate performance by 25 to 50 percent, sometimes more. By contrast, businesses that concentrate on finding and keeping good customers, productive employees, and supportive investors continue to generate superior results. Loyalty is by no means dead. It remains one of the great engines of business success. In fact, the principles of loyalty—and the business strategy we call loyalty-based management—are alive and well at the heart of every company with an enduring record of high productivity, solid profits, and steady expansion.

With rare exceptions, CEOs have enough experience and common sense to understand what nonsense it is to speak of loyalty's demise. They know, for example, that a strong customer franchise is critical to business success, and that doing business with people you trust and understand is more predictable and efficient, and thus more profitable, than doing business with uninvested strangers. Yet if CEOs are wise enough to see the power of loyalty, why are defection rates so high? How do they manage to lose half their companies' customers every five years? The answer is that most of them don't measure defections and have no idea they're losing customers at such a rate. Or, if they do suspect the truth, they see it as a problem for the marketing department.

But customer loyalty is too important to delegate. It has a crucial effect on every constituency and aspect of a business system; it drives business success and therefore CEO careers. The responsibility for customer retention or defection belongs squarely on the CEO's desk, where it can get the same kind of attention that is lavished on stock price and cash flow. Consistently high retention can create tremendous competitive advantage, boost employee morale, produce unexpected bonuses in productivity and growth, even reduce the cost of capital. Conversely, persistent defection means that former customers—people convinced the company offers inferior value—will eventually outnumber the company's loyal advocates and dominate the collective voice of the marketplace. When that moment arrives, no amount of advertising, public relations, or ingenious marketing will prop up pricing, new-customer acquisitions, or the company's reputation.

In the mid-1980s, when a group of consultants at our firm began helping clients to improve their customer retention, we believed it was a practical way of increasing growth and profits, and as a kind of bonus, that it would enhance employee motivation and pride along the way. The truth was a good deal more complex. We found we could not progress beyond a superficial treatment of customer loyalty *without* delving into employee loyalty. We found that there was a cause-and-effect relationship between the two; that it was impossible to maintain a loyal customer base without a base of loyal employees; and that the best employees prefer to work for companies that deliver the kind of superior value that builds customer loyalty. We then found that our concern with employee loyalty entangled us in the thorny issue of investor loyalty, because it is very hard to earn the loyalty of employees if the owners of the business are short-sighted and unreliable. Finally, predictably, we found that investor loyalty was heavily dependent on customer and employee loyalty, and we understood that we were dealing not with tactical issues but with a strategic system.

Customer retention is a subject that simply cannot be confined within narrow limits. We came to understand that business loyalty has three dimensions—customer loyalty, employee loyalty, and investor loyalty— and that they are far more powerful, far reaching, and interdependent than we had anticipated or imagined. Loyalty has implications that extend into every corner of every business system that seeks the benefit of steady customers. Tempting as it may be to delegate customer retention to marketing, what can marketing do to stem the outflow of employees and investors? It is unrealistic to expect any single function to achieve fundamental improvement. Retention is not simply one more operating statistic, it is the central gauge that integrates all the dimensions of a business and measures how well the firm is creating value for its customers.

Here we strike bedrock, because creating value for customers is the foundation of every successful business system. Creating value for customers builds loyalty, and loyalty in turn builds growth, profit, and more value. While profit has always occupied center stage in conventional thinking about business systems, profit is not primary. Profit is indispensable, of course, but it is nevertheless a *consequence* of value creation, which, along with loyalty, makes up the real heart of any successful, long-lasting business institution. The more consulting work we've done over the years, the more clearly we've seen that the only way to achieve *sustainable* improvements in performance is by building *sustainable* improvements in value creation and loyalty.

Stemming the customer exodus is not simply a matter of marketing; it demands a reconsideration of core stategy and operating principles. Loyalty provides the unifying framework that enables an executive team to modify and integrate corporate strategy and operating practices in ways that will better serve the long-term interests of customers, employees, and investors. Even more important, perhaps, the loyalty framework permits a set of practical measures that executives can use to manage the company's value creation process, the upstream source of all profits and growth.

ACCOUNTING—LOYALTY'S PUBLIC ENEMY NUMBER ONE

Today's accounting systems often mask the fact, but inventories of experienced customers, employees, and investors are a company's most valuable assets. Their combined knowledge and experience comprise a firm's

entire intellectual capital. Yet these invaluable assets are vanishing from
corporate balance sheets at an alarming rate, decimating growth and
earnings potential as they go. In a typical company today, customers are
defecting at the rate of 10 to 30 percent per year; employee turnover
rates of 15 to 25 percent are common; and average annual investor churn
now exceeds 50 percent per year. How can any manager be expected to
grow a profitable business when 20 to 50 percent of the company's most
valuable inventory vanishes without a trace each year? It's a nearly
impossible challenge.

A few companies—we'll call them loyalty leaders—have decided to
forgo this challenge by plugging the leaks in their balance sheets. These
firms have discovered how to acquire the long-term loyalty of customers,
employees, and investors and so have changed the fundamental economics of their businesses. While competitors struggle to generate growth
and cash flow, these companies thrive.

How do they do it? To begin with, loyalty leaders avoid snapshot
accounting. The business pictures they study are time exposures. Second,
they see people as assets rather than expenses, and they expect those
assets to pay returns over a period of many years. Loyalty leaders choose
human assets carefully, then find ways to extend their productive lifetimes
and increase their value. Indeed, loyalty leaders engineer all their business
systems to make their human inventories permanent. They view asset
defections as unacceptable value-destroying failures, and they work constantly to eradicate them.

By diligently improving value and reducing asset defections, loyalty
leaders have lowered their inventory losses to a mere trickle, and their
resulting performance has been astonishing. By decreasing defection rates
in all three groups—customers, employees, and investors—they have
achieved prodigious growth in profits and cash generation. They have discovered that human capital, unlike most other assets, does not depreciate
over time. Like good wine, it actually improves with age.

Reducing inventory losses is no easy matter, but there is a secret to
success. You cannot *control* a human inventory, which of course has a
mind of its own, so you must *earn* its loyalty. People will invest their
time and money loyally only if they believe that their contributions to
your company will yield superior returns over time. The secret is therefore
to select these human beings carefully, then teach them how to contribute
and receive value from your business system—or better yet, give them
incentives to learn these lessons for themselves. The key to decreasing

inventory losses and growing profits is to manage a virtuous cycle of loyalty, learning, and value creation. As you will see in some detail in the course of this book, each compounds the other two.

Most managers simply don't realize how much value the loyalty of human assets creates. They are used to husbanding more traditional types of inventory. What would a car dealer do, for example, if he discovered that a brand new stereo system was missing from his parts inventory? He would probably turn the dealership upside down. And what would he do if he lost a loyal customer? Most would shrug their shoulders. Yet the probable annuity value of that customer's purchases exceeds the cost of the stereo ten times over.

Few business people think of customers as annuities. Even fewer look at employees and investors this way. But the difference is exactly the difference between a snapshot and a time exposure, between a publicity still and a full-length feature film. When managers begin to understand the long-term economic consequences of loyalty, they will begin managing their businesses with the goal of zero defections.

LOYALTY—THE LITMUS TEST OF CORPORATE PERFORMANCE

The zero-defections approach to human-inventory management implies an altered theory of business. The current approach might be called the profit theory. All business skills and competencies stand or fall on their capacity to contribute to profits. The new theory sees the fundamental mission of a business not as profit, but as value creation. It sees profit as a vital consequence of value creation—a means rather than an end, a result as opposed to a purpose. In addition, the value-creation theory of business helps to unify the disparate perspectives of investors, accountants, marketers, and human resource managers.

The new theory also makes loyalty a truer litmus test of corporate performance than profits ever were or could be. Profits alone are an unreliable measure because it is possible to raise reported short-term earnings by liquidating human capital. Pay cuts and price increases can boost earnings, but they have a negative effect on employee and customer loyalty and so shorten the duration and worth of those assets. Since the only way a business can retain customer and employee loyalty is by delivering superior value, high loyalty is a certain sign of solid value creation.

It may sound as if loyalty and profits are in conflict. If business were a zero-sum game, that would be true; any given pay increase or price reduction would be a tradeoff against increased profits. Investors could make more money only at the expense of customers and employees, and vice versa. But business is not a zero-sum game, and the putative conflict is a misunderstanding. To resolve it, we have to break out of the snapshot mentality and recognize that there are two kinds of profit. Call the first kind *virtuous:* it's the result of creating value, sharing it, and building the assets of the business. The word for the other kind of profit is *destructive.* Destructive profit does not come from value creation and value sharing; it comes from exploiting assets, from selling off a business's true balance sheet. This is the kind of profit that justifies terms like *profiteering,* gives business a black eye, and actually shortens the life expectancies of the businesses that seek it.

When profit is a company's goal and purpose, virtuous and destructive profits serve equally well. But once you see profit as a means to, and a consequence of, the sustained creation of value, then only virtuous profit will do. Unfortunately, it's not always easy to tell them apart. For example, accounting reports won't help, because on a profit-and-loss statement, the two look identical. The complete answer to distinguishing between them will be one of the subjects of this book. But briefly, the best way to differentiate between good profits and bad is by measuring the loyalty of your most valuable assets: your customers, employees, and investors. If defection rates are low and decreasing, then profits are virtuous. If not, you are probably liquidating your balance sheet—and destroying long-term value.

MIRACULOUS CASH FLOW

This book is not theoretical; it's about a practical process that helps managers create so much value for customers that there's plenty left over for employees and investors. It can help you generate superior profits and cash flow by showing you how to improve customer acquisition; how to hire better employees, compensate them more effectively, increase their productivity, teach them to learn from their failures, and motivate them to offer superior value to customers; and finally, by showing you how to build better investment and ownership structures. We call this integrated approach to business loyalty-based management.

The basic principles of loyalty are not something we invented. They have been around for centuries. Loyalty-based management is merely our codification of a phenomenon we observed and analyzed over the course of more than ten years' work, studying the problems and successes of a wide variety of companies and their competitors. Again and again as we pored over the numbers, profits, strategies, and tactics of different firms and industries, we came across companies that were generating mystifying levels of free cash flow. The reason stared us in the face, but we only gradually came to understand its true significance.

What distinguished these unusually successful companies from their competitors was a measurable advantage in customer and employee loyalty. Each time we found a performance record that was hard to square with the traditional economics taught in business schools, we also found a company with superior loyalty. Each time we found a company with outstanding loyalty, we also discovered a company that was delivering superior value to its customers and employees, and at the same time generating inexplicably strong cash flows to fund internal growth.

For example, we looked at the Leo Burnett advertising agency and found it was generating surprising cash flow levels. In fact, Leo Burnett has grown to become the largest single agency in the world—with sixty-three global offices and $600 million in revenues—without ever having had to raise capital by issuing stock, and with little or no bank debt. Furthermore, the firm's compensation is among the best in the industry (which ought to squeeze cash flow), and it holds pricing to competitive levels. And nevertheless it has the highest cash generation in its industry. The explanation of this apparent miracle is that Leo Burnett creates so much value for its clients that they stay with the company year after year. In the late 1980s, for example, only 2 percent of Burnett's customer revenues were lost to competing agencies each year.

Chick-fil-A, of Atlanta, Georgia, is another good example. Over the past five decades it has grown from a single diner to a chain of more than six hundred quick-service restaurants by means of superior loyalty. The company hit our radar screen when we discovered that its turnover in store operators ran at 4 to 6 percent per year in an industry where average turnover runs 40 to 50 percent. Then we found out that Chick-fil-A's store operators earn an average of 50 percent more than the operators at other fast-food chains. Pricing in the fast food business is quite competitive, so we expected the difference to squeeze cash flow. On the contrary, Chick-fil-A has financed its tremendous expansion mostly by means of internal cash flow, along with some minimal debt tied to real estate. As a private company, it has never issued stock, and each store operator puts up only $5,000 in earnest money. So where did the cash come from?

In the coming chapters, we will look at more than a dozen companies which, like Chick-fil-A and Leo Burnett, have earned the highest loyalty in their respective industries. These loyalty leaders not only hold a retention advantage over their competitors; in all but one or two cases they also enjoy a faster rate of growth. We use a disproportionate number of insurance companies as examples, but it happens that insurance is one of the few industries that has measured retention with some rigor for decades, and it thus offers a unique opportunity to study loyalty over time. Readers who think the insurance industry is overdone should note that we also include examples from industries as diverse as automobiles, advertising, telecommunications, tractors, truck wheels, banking, fast food, computer software, retailing, and local television broadcasting. Several of the loyalty leaders we highlight will be unfamiliar to readers, principally because they are not public companies and have therefore escaped the attention of media writers and security analysts. Since genuine loyalty-based businesses are hard to uncover, we have had to use the examples we could find—small ventures and corporate giants, relatively young companies and companies that have pursued loyalty for more than a century.

When we delved into the operations of these loyalty leaders, we uncovered business systems extraordinarily well designed to create and deliver superior value to customers, employees, and investors. Perhaps we should have anticipated exactly this discovery. All through history, the builders of great companies with enduring records of success have striven to deliver superior value, to customers first and employees second, so that investors could profit over the long haul. But we were really surprised by the levels of growth and cash flow we found. To understand their mysterious source, let's take a quick look at a company that is one of the true marvels of loyalty-based management: State Farm Insurance.

THE ROYALTY OF LOYALTY

State Farm is a mutual company, owned by its policyholders, so it has never issued stock. It insures more than 20 percent of the nation's households, and its lead in market share continues to increase. State Farm's concentration on customer service has resulted in faster growth than at most other multiple-line insurers; but where growth consumes the earnings of some companies and saddles them with debt, State Farm's capital has mushroomed to more than $20 billion—all of it internally generated surplus. This is more capital than AT&T or General Motors commands. In fact, this is the largest capital base of any financial services company in North America, and it puts State Farm in the top tier of all companies in the world. State Farm has the lowest sales and distribution costs among insurance companies of its type, yet its agents generally make much more money than agents who work for the competition. By means of careful customer and employee selection and retention, State Farm is often able to price below the competition and still build the capital necessary to protect its policyholders in years like 1992, when it incurred $4.7 billion in catastrophe losses.

All these impressive achievements can be traced to State Farm's superbly designed loyalty-based system, which puts measures, incentives, agent selection, training, career paths, customer acquisition, product line, advertising, pricing, service levels, and all other company functions into the service of value and loyalty. As a result, agents stay with State Farm more than twice as long as they stay with its competitors, and they achieve productivity levels 40 percent higher than the industry norm. Customers receive such a potent mix of service and price that retention rates exceed 95 percent—the best performance of any national insurer that sells through agents. And despite the generous helping of value it allocates to customers and agents, the company itself has retained sufficient surplus cash flow to accumulate those $20 billion we mentioned earlier. All in all, State Farm's performance has been so consistently stellar that *Fortune* magazine has called it the U.S. financial services industry's most successful corporation—"indeed, one of the nation's great businesses."[1]

We'll see more of State Farm later in this book, but the question that springs to mind immediately is why more companies haven't followed its example. There are very few secrets in insurance. Agency contracts are widely known, pricing must be filed with every state government, and regulatory agencies publish and disseminate financial and statistical data about every company. In any case, State Farm has made no secret of its business philosophy and strategy. Founder George Mecherle often named customer persistency and devotion to agents as the keys to State Farm's success.

Mecherle's explanation was probably as clear as an explanation could be, but few companies have tried to follow the advice that produced

$20 billion in internally generated surplus. It's hard to see why. One possible answer is that unconsciously, most organizations have developed (or received) a fundamentally different picture of the cause-and-effect relationships that govern business systems. We all use mental models to sort out relevant information from noise and then organize that information into useful patterns. When these models are accounting paradigms, managers quite simply cannot grasp the economics of learning and loyalty that sustains State Farm's success. They may listen to Mecherle's words, but they fail to hear his message.

A good example of this difference in paradigm arose in the aftermath of Hurricane Andrew, which produced such large insurance claims in 1992 and 1993. The need to keep losses under control led many companies to cover the claims required by their contracts in South Florida, then refuse to renew customer policies to avoid future losses. State Farm took a radically different view. It had no intention of canceling customers it had expended so much energy and expense to acquire and maintain, most of them for many years. Indeed, as State Farm sees the world, it would be economically irrational to destroy the value of the company's investment in a large block of high-quality customers. Most important, disloyalty to its customers would be philosophically unacceptable. Loyalty is a two-way street. Moreover, loyalty must be *seen* to be a two-way street. How could State Farm possibly expect its customers and agents to remain loyal if the company did not demonstrate loyalty when the chips were down?

When Andrew blew the roofs off houses because contractors had not properly anchored them to their frames, State Farm paid its customers *more* than their policies required in order to bring the houses up to code. When a *Wall Street Journal* reporter asked why the company was willing to overpay, C. A. Ingham, then State Farm's general counsel, replied, "We will be insuring the homes in the future, and we don't want them damaged in the future."[2] State Farm expects its customers to stay with the company for years, so this approach will save everyone money in the long run.

There is a kind of business manager who reads this story and thinks, "What a gimmick! What clever public relations!" But there is a sound strategic and economic rationale to State Farm's behavior, which conventional management thinking simply misses. The driving force behind State Farm's low costs is not parsimony or PR but loyalty, a systematic approach to keeping revenues up and expenditures down over the very long term of the customer lifecycle.

State Farm is not the only company that has prospered by managing its human capital inventory according to the principles of loyalty. Let's go back to Leo Burnett for a moment. The Chicago-based advertising firm that created the Jolly Green Giant, the Friendly Skies, and the Marlboro man has treated customers and employees as its most valuable assets since its founding in 1935. Advertising firms are notorious for high turnover. Prodigious client churn goes hand in hand with the kind of employment policy that alternates between layoffs and frenzied hiring. But at Leo Burnett, layoffs are rare, and so are client defections. The company invests enormous sums in recruiting and training. It pays new hires well above the industry norm, and since 1943 has failed only three times to contribute the legal tax-deductible maximum (currently 15 percent of salary and bonus) to every employee's profit sharing plan.

Leo Burnett is organized so that senior account managers spend the vast majority of their time on a single client, so they get to know their customers and their customers' businesses. (The arrangement also makes it very clear who is accountable for the success of each customer's advertising.) Productivity at Leo Burnett is the highest in the industry, 15 to 20 percent above its principal competitors.

Above all else, however, Leo Burnett is dedicated to client retention. Over the four-year period from 1986 through 1989, 98 percent of each year's revenues came from repeat accounts—the highest retention rate in the industry. When the Oldsmobile account was up for review in 1993, the company closed one office entirely and moved dozens of employees to Chicago to consolidate its Oldsmobile staff in a single, integrated location. To top it off, the CEO resigned his executive position so he could concentrate on his role as chief creative officer, which among other things meant giving more time and energy to the Oldsmobile account. If the whole thing was a grandstand play, it worked. But it seems unlikely. For Leo Burnett, dramatic change and expenditure for the sake of delivering superior value—and keeping an account—is the essence of good business. The CEO was simply continuing the tradition established by Leo Burnett himself, who founded the firm on loyalty-based principles. When Burnett retired, he made a speech that is still an important part of the firm's training program. In it, he told his colleagues he will demand that his name be taken off the door when the day comes that they "spend more time trying to make money and less time making advertising—our kind of advertising."

THE NEW CALCULUS OF LOYALTY

Companies like Leo Burnett seem to march to a different drummer. They certainly live in a different world from today's business schools, which emphasize profits and shareholder value to the virtual exclusion of all other overarching goals. But let's look at the economics of the advertising business and see who's got it right. Figure 1-1 shows, on the vertical axis, the relative productivity of each major advertising agency in the United States in 1989, and on the horizontal axis, the average annual customer retention rate for the three years from 1986 to 1989.

Leo Burnett, all alone in the upper right hand corner, enjoys the highest customer retention rate, 98 percent, as well as the highest productivity, about 20 percent above the industry average. The other firms seem to line up on a fairly neat diagonal, the poorest retention coinciding with the lowest productivity.

Figure 1-1   The Relationship Between Customer Retention and
                   Productivity in the Advertising Industry, 1986 to 1989

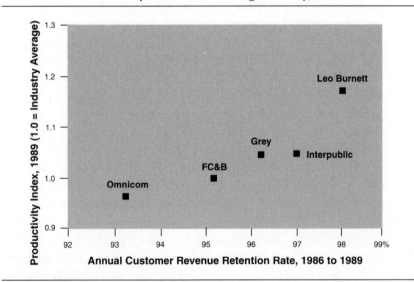

Sources: Productivity, *Advertising Age;* Customer Retention, Bain Analysis.

Of course, the remarkable thing about this exhibit is that a single variable, the customer retention rate, seems to correlate almost exactly with relative productivity, and may even explain it. We noted earlier how well loyalty works as a litmus test for value creation. Here we see a strong suggestion of an equally intimate link to profits. A shift in retention of as little as 5 percentage points—from, say, 93 to 98 percent—seems to account for more than a 20 percent improvement in productivity. Because Burnett is a private company and does not report its profits, we can only speculate about how this productivity advantage translates into profit. But in a business like advertising, it should increase profit potential by 50 to 100 percent. That other drummer that Leo Burnett, State Farm, and other loyalty leaders march to apparently beats out a whole new economic calculus.

We find the same kinds of patterns in other industries. Figure 1-2 shows the largest U.S. insurance brokers in terms of their profit margins and customer retention rates. Once again, the firm with the best retention rate, Johnson & Higgins, has the highest relative profits, while Frank

Figure 1-2 The Relationship Between Customer Retention and Profitability in the Insurance Brokerage Industry, 1983–1988

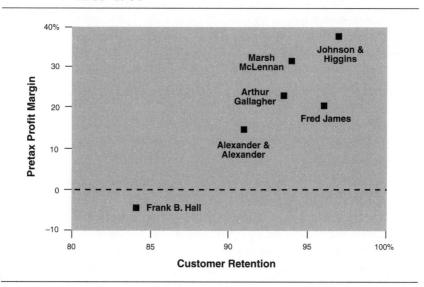

Sources: Annual reports, Bain estimates.
Note: U.S. operations only.

B. Hall, with the lowest retention rate, trails in profitability. In other words, the relationship between performance and retention is very much what we found in advertising. Improving retention by five percentage points doubles the profit margin. Not surprisingly, Johnson & Higgins places great emphasis on customer loyalty. One of the company's most senior executives interviews every client of any significance who defects, to help the firm learn from failure and improve its performance.

Among stockbrokers, the company with the highest retention is A. G. Edwards, and once again, the loyalty leader also leads in profitability. This company heads everyone's list as a provider of value to customers; it leads the industry in broker retention, and it still has enough money left over to put a broad smile on investors' faces. In this notoriously cyclical industry, where most firms are lucky to earn a 10 percent return on equity over the course of a market cycle, A. G. Edwards has averaged better than 18 percent for the past ten years.

We have repeated this analysis across a wide variety of industries, and the results hold steady. Despite the obvious fact that other variables also drive profit differences, and though the pattern in Figures 1-1 and 1-2 is more pronounced in some industries than in others, superior retention consistently creates at least the potential for higher profits.

As we'll see in later chapters, Lexus, the luxury division of Toyota, is poised to establish itself among the royalty of loyalty. Although Lexus is the first brand ever to win all three of the industry's customer satisfaction awards in the same year, the division is not content with mere satisfaction. Dave Illingworth, the first general manager of Lexus U.S., stated emphatically, "The only meaningful measure of satisfaction in this industry is repurchase loyalty!" [3] Accordingly, Lexus has built a new business system, engineered from the ground up on the principles of loyalty-based management, and is now on its way to setting record levels of customer loyalty in the auto industry. Toyota does not report Lexus results publicly, but industry experts have estimated that in recent years, the Lexus division accounts for just 2 percent of Toyota's unit sales but delivers one-third of the corporation's operating profits.

Another practitioner of loyalty-based management, MBNA, started out as the credit card division of Maryland National Bank in 1982. Instead of leaping precipitously into the new-account feeding frenzy in the industry's formative years, MBNA chose to market credit cards through affinity groups like the National Education Association. Gradually it customized its entire business system to earn the loyalty of such groups and their members. MBNA was one of the first credit card companies to measure retention. It learned which affinity organizations had members with high inherent loyalty, then focused its investment on those potential customers. It tailored its backroom systems to the individual needs of each group, and then based employee bonuses not on profits but on measurements of factors that drive customer loyalty. In MBNA's entire history, the company has suffered only a handful of defections from its thirty-seven hundred groups. By 1994, its individual customer base had grown to more than 14 million cardholders.

As in other cases, customer loyalty has done wonders for investors. Since becoming a separate company in 1990, MBNA's return on equity has approached 30 percent after taxes, and earnings per share have grown at 18 percent per year. Since 1982, MBNA has surged from thirty-eighth to second place in total bankcard balances, while profits have increased more than twentyfold. To what does Charlie Cawley, MBNA's founder, attribute this extraordinary performance? The answer is printed in large letters on the cover of his annual report: "Success Is Getting the Right Customers . . . and Keeping Them."

BLINDED BY THE FLASH OF SNAPSHOT ACCOUNTING

Right there on the cover of Cawley's annual report, in other words, is one of the great secrets of business success. In fact, the cover of that report probably has more lasting value than the financial statistics inside. The odd thing is that most managers know this but can't make it work. Customer retention has become a hot topic at industry conventions, and MBNA has a wide reputation as a company that has mastered the art and science of loyalty-based management, but most managers look at MBNA's motto and fail to grasp its full meaning. Instead of systematically revamping their operations with customer loyalty in mind, most managers adopt ad hoc programs. They try to copy one or two of MBNA's practices. They set up recovery units to save defecting customers who may or may not be worth saving. Or they borrow MBNA's policy of delivering employee paychecks in envelopes labeled "Brought to You by the Customer," but fail to base bonuses on the enhancement of customer value and loyalty. Not surprisingly, the payoffs never materialize.

Building a highly loyal customer base cannot be done as an add-on. It must be integral to a company's basic business strategy. Loyalty leaders like MBNA, Chick-fil-A, State Farm, and Leo Burnett are successful because they have designed their entire business systems around customer loyalty; because they recognize that a company earns customers' loyalty by consistently delivering superior value; because they understand the economic effect of retention on revenues and costs and can therefore intelligently reinvest cash flows to acquire and retain the most valuable customers and employees.

The real trouble is that many, perhaps most, executives today have adopted a paradigm which at its heart is inconsistent with loyalty-based management. Press them, and few will insist that the primary mission of their companies is to create superior value for customers and employees so investors can prosper. On the contrary, they believe their primary mission is to maximize profits or shareholder value. And if they ever felt any ambivalence about that mission, the LBOs and hostile takeovers of the 1980s drove it into hiding.

In fact, however, the drift toward investor-centered management began much earlier. It began at the turn of the century, when absentee owners delegated executive responsibility to professional managers. One of everyone's first essential tasks was to develop financial accounting systems to keep absentee capitalists informed about the value of their investments. Business people perfected measurement systems to serve the needs of capital markets, and federal regulators enforced their reliability and uniformity.

The founders of the great industrial companies understood perfectly well that in order to prosper, a business had to deliver value to customers and employees as well as to investors. To quote Henry Ford, "Business must be run at a profit . . . else it will die. But when anyone tries to run a business solely for profit . . . then also the business must die, for it no longer has a reason for existence."[4] Strong, intuitive managers like Ford knew when to ignore the investor-oriented numbers generated by their profitability measurement systems. They were close to the action and could make intelligent tradeoffs between the needs of investors, employees, and customers. Successful owners of *small* businesses still can. Small business owners deal face to face with their true assets every day, and they are deeply and constantly involved in the effort to improve the flow of value to and from their customers and employees. Their understanding of the principles of loyalty-based management is experiential and intuitive. They don't use accounting statements to run their businesses; they use them only to calculate their taxes or deal with bankers.

But as large industrial organizations grew bigger and more complex, new rules and realities took over. For one thing, management layers proliferated. GM eventually had twenty-eight. For another thing, more and more managers were left with no direct access to customers or top executives, so they began to lean more heavily on financial accounting systems for help in making day-to-day decisions. The trouble is that with little or no feedback from customers, such measures take on immense importance: they communicate what top management values and what the company stands for. And when all measures are financial, the architecture of the organization's shared reality comes to rest entirely on profit, usually on short-term profit at that. Promotions and year-end bonuses are tied to the annual profit plan, so managers zero in on managing those numbers, one year at a time. For several generations of managers, the link between a company's long-term fortunes and the loyalty of its customers, employees, and investors has become invisible. The resulting mismanagement of human capital has thwarted progress in many large companies and is at least partially responsible for the setbacks and failures that seem to plague so many modern businesses.

NEW ASSUMPTIONS

There is plenty of evidence that *something* about the current business paradigm is wrong. For example, the good old solid and dependable advantages of market share, cost position, and service quality no longer guarantee success. General Motors, instead of reaping the spoils of market share leadership, is struggling to pull itself out of a downward spiral. A low-cost manufacturer like Caterpillar suddenly finds itself at a cost disadvantage in key markets. A service-quality blue chip like Delta Airlines is downgraded to junk bond status. None of our received business wisdom seems as constant as it once did. Companies like Wang and IBM are profiled as case studies of excellence one day and as management turnarounds the next. The nation's front pages trumpet the Baldrige Award as the competitive standard in the crusade to reassert American quality leadership; then a Baldrige winner files for bankruptcy, and the year's awards are hidden on the fifth page of *The Wall Street Journal*.

And how the solutions proliferate! Total quality management was once a magic bullet; now we're to shift that energy to the reengineering of all our core business processes. A professor announces that empowered learning organizations are the key; weeks later another professor finds that strong leadership is what really counts. On Monday, market share and core competence are the essential strategic assets; by Friday they take a back seat to time, the new competitive frontier. Business thinkers career from guardrail to guardrail. Is business really so complicated? *Must* business success be so fragile and transitory?

Or is it just that management science is still in its infancy, and we don't yet understand the fundamental laws that govern business systems? Before Copernicus and Kepler, people thought the sun revolved around the earth. Today in business, we are satisfied that success and survival revolve around profit. Maybe our profit-centered world is as skewed and counterproductive as the concept of an earth-centered universe. That is not to say that profit doesn't matter. Putting the earth in its proper relation to the sun didn't make the earth less important, or the sun more so. What it did do was make sense of the mechanics. Profit does not have to occupy the center of the business solar system in order to be indispensable.

It would be surprising if there weren't some basic flaws in our mental models, since nearly all our thinking on the subject is quite recent. Business schools are inventions of the twentieth century. Harvard, for instance, was nearly three centuries years old before it added a school of business in 1908. Large corporations themselves are a relatively new phenomenon, and unlike scores of cultural, political, and religious institutions the world over that have lasted for centuries, the average Fortune 500 company expires in forty years. Most are outlived by their employees! So it's no wonder the science of business survival is chaotic. We have so little data and so few long-term survivors to work with that we resort to rhetoric and gimmickry in the absence of scientific observation and analysis. And of course short corporate lifespan *itself* suggests some flaw in our current profit-before-value paradigm. Today's layoffs, reengineerings, and restructurings may be our generation's version of Ptolemaic astronomy. Until we reach a better understanding of cause and effect in business, we seem doomed to speculation, confusion, and inconsistency.

One of the more important arguments this book will make, mostly by implication, is that the practice of carefully selecting customers, employees, and investors and then working hard to retain them—in a word, loyalty-based management—represents precisely the kind of objective, scientific insight into the fundamental laws governing business systems that we have been lacking. Certainly the success loyalty leaders have encountered, and in some cases maintained over decades, tends to support this hypothesis. The forces at work here are powerful and have been poorly understood. For example, the enormous swings in cash generation that grow from a relatively small improvement in customer retention are hard to explain in traditional economic theory. How does customer retention drive such swings in profit? Can its effect be quantified and measured? We have begun to answer these questions, and as a result we have begun to view the nature of business from a new perspective.

THE NEW MODEL

The implicit business model behind most present-day strategic plans and budgeting procedures begins with a profit target and works backward to arrive at required revenue growth and cost reduction. We have spent some ten years studying loyalty leaders and their business systems, and what we have learned has radically altered our view of business economics and led us to develop a very different model, rendered graphically in Figure 1-3.

What drives this new model is not profit but the creation of value for the customer, a process that lies at the core of all successful enterprises. Value creation generates the energy that holds these businesses together, and their very existence depends on it. The physics that governs the interrelationships and energy states of a business system's elementary particles—its customers, employees, and investors—we call the *forces of loyalty*. Because of the linkages between loyalty, value, and profits, these forces are measurable in cash flow terms. Loyalty is inextricably linked to the creation of value as both a cause and an effect. As an effect, loyalty reliably measures whether or not the company has delivered superior value: Customers either come back for more or they go elsewhere. As a cause, loyalty initiates a series of economic effects that cascade through the business system, as follows:

1. Revenues and market share grow as the best customers are swept into the company's business, building repeat sales and referrals. Because the firm's value proposition is strong, it can afford to be more selective in new customer acquisition and to concentrate its investment on the most profitable and potentially loyal prospects, further stimulating sustainable growth.

Figure 1-3   The Loyalty-Based Cycle of Growth

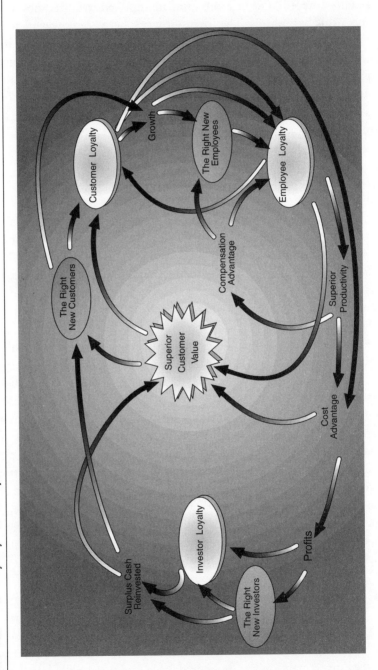

2. Sustainable growth enables the firm to attract and retain the best employees. Consistent delivery of superior value to customers increases employees' loyalty by giving them pride and satisfaction in their work. Furthermore, as long-term employees get to know their long-term customers, they learn how to deliver still more value, which further reinforces both customer and employee loyalty.

3. Loyal long-term employees learn on the job how to reduce costs and improve quality, which further enriches the customer value proposition and generates superior productivity. The company can then use this productivity surplus to fund superior compensation and better tools and training, which further reinforce employee productivity, compensation growth, and loyalty.

4. Spiraling productivity coupled with the increased efficiency of dealing with loyal customers generates the kind of cost advantage that is very difficult for competitors to match. Sustainable cost advantage coupled with steady growth in the number of loyal customers generates the kind of profits that are very appealing to investors, which makes it easier for the firm to attract and retain the right investors.

5. Loyal investors behave like partners. They stabilize the system, lower the cost of capital, and ensure that appropriate cash is put back into the business to fund investments that will increase the company's value-creation potential.

Profits are not central to this new model, but they are nevertheless critically important, not just for their own sake but also because they allow the company to improve its value creation, and because they provide an incentive for employees, customers, and investors to remain loyal. Still, the source of all cash flow, including profit, is the spiraling pool of value that springs from the creation of superior value for customers.

VENDORS AND VIRTUAL CORPORATIONS

The new model just described has one feature that may seem an oversimplification. It concentrates on customers, employees, and investors and ignores vendors, distributors, local communities, and all the other obvious stakeholders in a business. Vendors seem especially important now that so many companies are outsourcing more and more of their work. Moreover, the information revolution has made it possible for more and more employees (and vendor employees) to work at remote locations, linked to one another and the company only by computer. These two trends have convinced many people that we are headed toward a future of virtual corporations—companies comprised primarily of vendor relationships, with few employees of their own.

We believe this vision of the future is probably quite valid. We also believe that loyalty-based management is highly relevant to the evolution of such companies. However, we approach the subject by looking first at the most fundamental building blocks of business physics. If we think of businesses as atoms, with customers, employees, and investors as their subatomic particles, then we will study the way those basic components interact to create higher levels of stability and value creation. We can then apply the same descriptive framework to the chains of atoms that collaborate to form value-creating molecules. But our focus here is the atom's internal physics. Surprisingly, a great deal has been written about links at the molecular level—the bonds *between* atoms—while the more basic bonds *within* each atom have gone largely ignored. How many books and articles have you seen about strategic alliances with vendors? How many about the most fundamental strategic alliance of them all, the partnership of customers, employees, and investors?

Yet the vendor relationship is only an artificially isolated instance of our basic subatomic model, which applies equally well to vendors, lenders (a special class of vendor), and all the other companies that form critical links in the value chain, from raw material source to the consumer's home or factory. In fact, every vendor relationship can and should be seen as a customer relationship, because it is the vendor's responsibility to create value for its customer, not the other way around. Using our basic model, we will demonstrate the relevance of loyalty down the whole chain of interdependent companies. We will describe Lexus and its relationships with its dealers and its ultimate customers. We will tell the story of Accuride, the largest manufacturer (and vendor) of truck wheels, which grew even larger by redefining its loyal partnerships with its customers. We will show how Leo Burnett forms effective vendor partnerships—or from the agency's own point of view, customer partnerships—with clients.

This same logic applies to the employee, who is in essence a vendor selling his or her time to the company. It is each employee's responsibility to create superior value for the customer. But many employees misunderstand the social compact between employer and employee, believing that as long as they go on showing up for work, the company will go on rewarding their "loyalty" with lifetime employment. They are deeply shocked when the company lays them off. The truth is, no company can afford to keep employees who fail to create enough value for customers to more than cover their own compensation. Loyalty leaders have managed to minimize these shocks by treating their employees more like partners. Whether they use independent employee teams or their logical extension, vendor partnerships, the same principles of partnership apply. The key is to compensate partner-employees by sharing the value they help to create for customers.

The principles of loyalty will be even more important in the management of relationships in the virtual corporation, where the line between employee and vendor grows increasingly blurred. Most managers will find they can build real vendor partnerships only with companies they've done business with for years. People in each organization will need the kind of knowledge about the other business, its customers, systems, and decision making, that only a long-lasting collaboration can produce. Similarly, long-term employees are in the best position to become virtual employees, working out of a home office.

In short, long-term partnerlike relationships will be even more relevant in the future than they have been in the past. Loyalty-based management is about building and managing the relationships—all the relationships— that comprise a business system. It is about value-sharing partnerships in which stakeholders—distributors, vendors, communities—share in the value they help to create. These are the principles that enable companies to build effective relationships today and pursue the virtual realities of tomorrow.

CHAOS, FRICTION, AND CHANGE

The loyalty-based business model effectively explains success and failure in the business world. In most of the industries we've studied, the companies with the highest retention rates also earn the best profits. Relative retention explains profits better than market share, scale, cost position, or any of the other variables usually associated with competitive advantage. It also explains why traditional management techniques often backfire in chaotic ways.

Consider how a traditional company typically responds to a slowdown in revenue growth. It may hire more sales staff; it may raise commissions to encourage more aggressive selling; it may drop its price to new customers; it may add new products. And the result? In the order mentioned, it acquires more inexperienced salespeople (lower productivity at higher cost); more dissatisfied customers (who bought under pressure and later regret the purchase); more customers of the wrong kind (price shoppers and buyers with no interest or stake in the product, service, or company); and finally, the escalating costs of a more complex product line.

When it comes to costs, the conventional approach is to redesign processes or lay off employees. But either one is likely to demoralize the work force and impair customer service, which will decrease customer retention and send costs through the roof. The vast majority of cost reductions are carried out for the benefit of shareholders only, and they usually destroy value. But cost reductions passed on to the customer in lower prices or shared with employees to enhance motivation can *increase* value.

While the techniques of loyalty-based management may seem intuitive, they represent a radical departure from traditional business thinking. As we have learned more about the forces of loyalty and their interaction, we have come to view business strategy in a new light. Its objective, we've concluded, is to bring together a well-matched set of customers, employees, and investors and hold them together at least long enough for them to learn how to create and consume value to their mutual benefit. However simple this may sound in concept, it represents a shift in business thinking as fundamental as the shift to a Copernican sun-centered solar system was for astronomers. Customer value assumes the position of the sun; profit and shareholder value fall into orbit around it. All three benefit from the increased clarity of their relationship.

There is a mechanics as well as an astronomy of loyalty systems. Just as friction steals the energy from a mechanical system, defection steals the energy and knowledge from a business system. Without knowing it, managers have engineered enormous friction into their businesses in the name of maximizing shareholder value. This friction destroys value for everyone involved, including shareholders.

The opportunity to reduce friction in most businesses is immense. As we pointed out earlier, shareholders look on their holdings as short-term speculations and turn them over at a rate of more than 50 percent per year. Employees change jobs with increasing frequency; annual turnover of 15 to 25 percent is common. And customers defect at the alarming rate of 10 to 30 percent per year. With this much friction, it's no wonder productivity and economic growth are languishing. Business is conducted among strangers, trust is low, and energy dissipates rapidly.

To make the new model work, most businesses will have to make fundamental changes in their business practices, ranging from refined customer targeting to revised hiring strategies to new ownership structures. They'll need new measurement systems and incentives. And they'll need new criteria for allocating value among stakeholders so as to focus and sustain the value creation process. These changes may cost real money, but there is hard evidence of the enormous financial and systemic advantages they can produce. For one thing, the new model allows organizational stakeholders to make sense of the successes and failures around them and learn practical lessons that can increase value to themselves and everyone else as well. This is not a zero-sum game. For another thing, the players may actually get to know and trust one another, which could permit a real and final victory over chaos, speculation, and uncertainty.

THE DEATH OF CORPORATE LOYALTY

For the moment, chaos seems the odds-on favorite. The world may now be too competitive for loyalty. There is something very appealing about the notion of loyalty, but the appeal is nostalgic. As *The Wall Street Journal* recently pronounced, "The social contract between employers and employees, in which companies promise to ensure employment and guide the careers of loyal troops, is dead, dead, dead."[5] On hearing my plans for a book on business loyalty, one friend assumed it had to be a novel. Even the editors of the *Harvard Business Review* found my documentation of loyalty's positive effects so contrary to conventional wisdom, they made it the lead article for the March/April 1993 issue. And when they had to choose artwork for the cover, the only icon they could find for loyalty was a man wagging his finger at a dog. Loyalty strikes most of us as an attribute of a bygone age, as difficult to take seriously today as honor or fortitude or chivalry.

And yet the purpose of this book is to take the subject very seriously indeed and to persuade you, the reader, to take it seriously as well. As mentioned at the start of this chapter, we began our study of loyalty with a study of customer retention and might have written an entire book about getting and keeping the right customers. But customer retention is too narrow and perhaps too mechanical a subject. Worse yet, although customer retention is the single most important element of business loyalty, broadly considered, it is by itself no more likely to produce business success than marketing or sales or manufacturing alone. So this is a book about business systems that incorporate customers, employees, and investors in a single constellation of common interest and mutual benefit. The word that covers this whole galaxy of goals, strategies, policies, and attitudes is *loyalty*—however old-fashioned it may sound.

My advice is to forget the old-fashioned sound. As you read on, you will find a book about practical business approaches to practical business success, which means cash flow, profit, growth, and long-term survival. Focus on the explicit business message, which if we're right, is not subject to fashion, new or old.

At the same time, however, this book contains some underlying themes and implicit assumptions on a slightly grander social, philosophical, and scientific scale. They help to make sense of the practical advice and company descriptions, and to hold it all together. There are just three of these, and they need to be mentioned briefly here.

POINT ONE—LOYALTY TO PRINCIPLES

Though the word loyalty has an inherently virtuous and artless ring, loyalty can be a complex subject. For example, there are clearly good loyalties and bad ones. The good variety might include sticking with an employee who is injured on the job, even though productivity will suffer. Bad loyalty would certainly include the obedience of a subordinate who followed his boss's orders no matter how dishonest. Just as clearly, loyalty is relative. In fact, we all experience conflicting loyalties to relatives, self, friends, career, and country, and we regularly weigh one loyalty against another on a variety of scales.

The intellectual benchmark on the subject of loyalty is a book called *The Philosophy of Loyalty*, written in 1908 by Josiah Royce, a professor of philosophy at Harvard. For Royce, loyalties arranged themselves in a hierarchy. At the lowest level was loyalty to individuals. Next came groups. At the highest level he placed practical devotion to a set of values and principles. In Royce's view, loyalty per se cannot be judged as good or bad; it is the principles one is loyal to that can and should be judged. And it is devotion to those principles that tells us when and if the time has come to end our loyalty to an individual or group.

As a rule, people dismiss the relevance of loyalty in business. They associate loyalty exclusively with life's finer institutions—family, church, school, community—and since business is a matter of transient, competitive, and self-interested relationships, see it as unworthy of loyalty. But the loyalty Royce defines and characterizes is at least as relevant to business as to any other activity, perhaps more so. Business is always a matter of finding a balance among conflicting loyalties to customers, investors, employees, the nation, oneself. And business is always a matter of managing the interplay between cooperation and competition. The fact that some businesses and business people show themselves loyal only to their own short-term (and, as we shall see, short-sighted) advantage, or that some make poor and even immoral judgments, doesn't alter the fact that loyalty is relevant to nearly everything they do.

The ultimate subject of loyalty-based management is precisely the arrangement of priorities in accordance with Royce's hierarchy. Loyalty-based management is not just about loyalty to individuals or groups; it's about loyalty to a set of principles that will enable a business to serve all its constituents well through time. The guiding business principle of loyalty leaders seems to be a commitment to creating so much value for customers that there will be plenty left over for employees and investors. Loyalty leaders don't see profits as the primary objective, but as an essential element in the well-being and survival of the three principal partners to every business system, customers, employees, and investors. The top executives of these firms are of course very well compensated, but compared to management teams at other companies, they tend to put personal wealth a little lower on the scale of priorities, and the long-term health and success of the business a little higher.

Loyalty leaders naturally prefer long-term partnerships and seek out customers, employees, and investors with the same predilection. Since they expect to be together for a long time, they select their partners carefully. They try to maximize character and integrity in their pool of partner candidates while setting a reasonable threshold for raw talent— which is very different from the more common practice of maximizing raw talent and setting a reasonable threshold for character. What this means in practice is choosing partners with a healthy respect for human dignity, who will seek and find the elusive balance between self-interest and team interest; partners who want to win but are not willing to win at the team's expense.

In their dealings with people, loyalty leaders tend to ignore modern management theory in favor of a code of behavior that is close to the

Golden Rule, or as we will see in the case of several hugely successful companies, the Golden Rule itself. These companies demonstrate that loyalty to principles is a critical element of success even in today's super-competitive environment.

POINT TWO—LOYALTY AND PEOPLE

The coming chapters will repeatedly make the point that loyalty-based management is a rational, viable strategy for generating cash flow, profits, and growth. But in all the talk about customer inventory, human assets, coefficients of loyalty, and cash generation, we mustn't lose sight of the fact that loyalty-based management is about people. In the first place, it is about people in the literal business sense. It is about motivation and behavior, not marketing or finance or product development. And as we keep repeating, it is about customers, employees, and investors, all of whom are people.

In the second place, loyalty-based management is about people in a more abstract sense. It is about humanistic values and principles of the kind people devote their lives to, outside work and sometimes on the job as well. People have always been far more motivated to devote energy to organizations with a service goal than to organizations that exist exclusively to make a buck. This is obviously the case, since in churches and civic organizations, most work for no other reward. But there is no good reason to suppose we can't serve other people in business as well, and there is every reason to do just that. Yet corporate leaders lose sight of the fact. They can't understand why the troops won't rally behind a mission statement that places the maximization of shareholder value as the highest corporate and ethical goal.

Even more surprising is the fact that so many individuals lose sight of the deeply personal opportunities a well-run business can offer them. Choosing whom we work for and with are two of the most important decisions most of us make. The choice of a work community defines our lives and identities more powerfully than our choice of a suburb or a senator or even a house or vacation destination. Yet many people look on a job only as a necessary evil, the unavoidable means of achieving a desired standard of living. They don't expect principled management, just a generous paycheck. The don't expect to get meaning and spiritual sustenance from a job, just to spend by far the greatest part of their waking hours working at it.

But talk to employees at one of the companies we call loyalty leaders, and you will get a very different picture. Employees are proud that they and their colleagues treat customers and each other the way they themselves would like to be treated. They see their work experience as more than a selfish, competitive game. Their pursuit of self-interest is balanced by the organization's dedication to serving others. Partnerships are structured to reinforce the idealistic but still practical ethic that only in serving others well can we serve ourselves well.

Work that is congruent with personal principles is a source of energy. Work that sacrifices personal principles drains personal energy. Loyalty leaders offer people a fulfilling work experience and pride in their loyalties, which are based on values rather than on mercenary convenience. This pride is a powerful source of motivation and energy, and it redoubles the economic advantages inherent in a loyalty-based system.

POINT THREE—LOYALTY AS A SCIENCE

Having made quite a point of the virtue and idealism of loyalty-based management, we will now complete the circle and make the point that brings the discussion back down to earth. The historic performance of companies like State Farm, Leo Burnett, A. G. Edwards, Chick-fil-A, MBNA, Lexus, and others shows that loyalty to practical humanistic principles is *not* a substitute for profit. On the contrary, it is a vital component of the strategies these firms have used to achieve their extraordinary levels of growth and profitability.

Loyalty is neither a substitute for profit nor a gimmick for making easy money. Unless you're willing to grant these two points, at least for the sake of argument, there's little point in reading this book. But the records of the companies just named, and a dozen more, should be reason enough to read on. Given the business results and the inherent motivational appeal that a loyalty-based approach offers, the real question is why more managers haven't followed the loyalty leaders' example. At least part of the answer is that the science of management as presently practiced not only fails to incorporate the forces of loyalty; its short-term, snapshot mentality also appears to put loyalty at odds with profits. Indeed, even the managers at our loyalty leaders have understood the economic and motivational links mostly on an intuitive level. Their wisest decisions have been guided more by strong leadership and cultural tradition than by analysis. Very few of even the best companies have raised loyalty-based management to the kind of objective, scientific system that the less intuitive and the less well led might follow. Different companies have advanced different parts of the framework, but no one has pulled all the pieces together into a science.

The company that has come the closest is USAA, the San Antonio insurance and investment management firm that serves active and retired military officers and their families. Under the leadership of General Robert F. McDermott, USAA's recently retired CEO of twenty-three years—who always insisted that, as he put it, "Customers and employees are both precious resources"[6]—USAA grew from $207 million of assets under management twenty-six years ago to more than $34 billion today. But with this hundredfold increase in assets, the company's employee base has expanded by a factor of only five. Employee defection rates have shrunk from 43 to just over 5 percent, and customer retention is the best of any business we have ever found—within one percentage point of zero defections!

It may have been McDermott's background as a professional educator that prompted him to turn the principles of loyalty-based management into an applied science. Treating employees and customers as precious resources was a good basis for better decision making, but the organization needed loyalty-based *tools* as well as a loyalty-based philosophy. As a first step, USAA invested $130 million in the technology to enhance service and loyalty and to create a whole new family of measures to monitor progress. The company worked hard to understand the economics that underpin loyalty-based management and built that understanding into its decision-making processes. It refined its ability to learn from failure (from customer and employee defections) and to achieve continuous improvement in the creation and allocation of value.

Unfortunately, USAA's solutions are unique to USAA. Loyalty-based management is a science in the sense that it works along clear lines of cause and effect, but enterprises are so complex that the solution for each company is different. There are no simple cookbook answers. Loyalty leaders have all taken different paths and built different business systems. Still, there are a number of general lessons to be learned from their various approaches. What your company has to do is customize these general lessons to fit your specific business, your strategy, your competitive situation, and your aspirations.

The overall goal is to find a way of plugging the human-asset leak in your corporate balance sheet in order to improve your productivity, cash flow, growth, and profits. But you must do it economically. It costs money to raise loyalty, and some of the necessary investments are enormous. So even if you are certain that the principles make sense for your business and are consistent with your mission, you must be able to answer an important question: Exactly how much is it worth to your particular company to increase growth, productivity, and profits? To answer this question in the rigorous cash-flow terms that your CFO would use to evaluate any other investment decision, you need analytical tools that you almost certainly don't yet have. Chapter 2 will provide the scientific, economic framework you'll need to develop such tools for your business.

2

The Economics of
Customer Loyalty

LOYALTY-BASED MANAGEMENT is a Sunday school teacher's dream come true—an ethical approach to business that pays so well it puts the unscrupulous approaches to shame. It calls for companies to create tremendous value for their customers, to share value expansively by giving managers and employees a partnership interest in their work, and to deliver exceptional value in the form of profits to the investors who made the business possible. But where does all this value come from? Can a business really acquire the wherewithal to deliver more to everyone by, well, delivering more to everyone? The Sunday school answer is that loyalty-based business systems perform a kind of miracle of the loaves and the fishes. The more you give, the more you have to give. In one sense, as you'll see, that's not a bad answer. Sharing value really does create value. In another sense, of course, it's a very bad answer, because it doesn't help you to understand how the system works and how the miracle takes place.

For instance, we discovered some years ago that raising customer retention rates by five percentage points could increase the value of an average customer by 25 to 100 percent. In 1989, we published our study in an article in the *Harvard Business Review,* and our numbers made a deep impression on a lot of the managers who read it. Today, however, remarkably few of those managers really understand the arithmetic behind that study or its true implications for business management, beyond the breathtakingly obvious fact that in general, retaining customers is a good thing to do—which, as it happens, is not invariably true. (In the case of certain customers, increasing customer retention can actually *decrease* profits and *destroy* value. In other cases, the increase in value creation can far exceed 100 percent.)

The goal of this chapter is to demystify the value creation associated with loyalty. Loyalty-based management, ethical as it is, does not work by miracles. It works by the laws of economics and human behavior, which means there are practical, objective, mathematical answers to questions such as: Just exactly how much value does loyalty create (and vice-versa)? How do we quantify the link between loyalty and profits? What's the actual cash advantage of holding onto a good customer for one additional year, or five years, or ten?

It turns out that the economics of this ethical business philosophy are very attractive. But few companies are going to make loyalty-based management their applied philosophy—their basis for daily decision making—until they can see the cause-and-effect relationships that tie together value, loyalty, and long-term profits. This chapter will try to explain these economic relationships in concrete language and so make the transition from Sunday school to Loyalty Economics 101.

Regrettably, some readers may find this material difficult. We'll be taking up accounting methods, cash flow, net present value, and probability, along with a dash of systems dynamics, and you may find yourself sorely tempted to skip some sections or move directly to Chapter 3. If you do, you'll miss the conceptual framework that turns loyalty-based management into a science. We considered placing this chapter farther back in the book so as not to put anyone off with an early dose of arithmetic, however mild; but the fact is, most subsequent chapters are based on the ideas and economic principles developed here. In any case, the *basic* concepts are intuitive and simple.

To manage customers as assets, you must be able to value them as assets. This means you must be able to quantify and predict customer duration and lifecycle cash flow. The goal of what follows is to make the analytical process compatible with the financial systems you currently use to allocate resources and run your business, and to help you decide which investments you should make to improve long-term profits and customer loyalty—and which you should scrap. Finally, while this chapter deals exclusively with customers, you will see later that the analogous approach to employees and investors is almost perfectly parallel.

THE LANGUAGE OF LOYALTY

That loyal customers are a good thing is self-evident to every business person. Yet the vast majority of companies don't know the cash value of customer loyalty, and most don't know they don't know. They look at their sales figures or at average customer tenure, and they draw a series of inappropriate or inaccurate conclusions.

The fault lies with the basic language of business, accounting, which at present has a limited vocabulary for evaluating loyalty. Accountants have developed sophisticated techniques for appraising capital assets and their depreciation; they have learned how to monitor the constantly changing value of work-in-progress; but they have not yet devised a way to track the value of a company's customer inventory. They make no distinction between sales revenue from brand-new customers and sales revenue from long-term, loyal customers, because they do not know or care that it costs much more to serve a new customer than an old one. Worse, in most businesses, accountants treat investment in customer acquisition as one more current expense, instead of assigning it to specific customer accounts and amortizing it over the life of the customer relationship.

The result is that generally accepted accounting principles actually *hide* the value of a loyal customer, an impressive feat of concealment given what loyalty can do for the great majority of companies. If you chart comparative profits in most industries, loyalty leaves its footprints everywhere. We saw in Chapter 1, for example, that customer retention explains most of the differences in productivity among the principal advertising agencies. We also saw that in the insurance brokering industry, a five-point improvement in retention translates into a doubling of margins. This kind of difference is normally hard to disguise. As a rule, doubling profits gets a lot of attention, but somehow the economics of *loyalty* are still lost in the shadows of traditional accounting.

Of course, it could be that the effects of loyalty have gone nearly unnoticed because they only make themselves felt in a few odd industries like advertising and insurance. We studied a wide range of industries to test for this possibility, and we found that the forces of loyalty produce quite spectacular results in businesses as varied as banking, publishing, and industrial laundering. Figure 2-1 shows the increase in the net present value of an average customer in a number of different industries when the customer retention rate increases by five percentage points. If a credit card company, to take one example, can hold onto another 5 percent of its customers each year (increasing its retention rate from, say, 90 to 95 percent), then total lifetime profits from a typical customer will rise, on average, by 75 percent.

It is surprising, to say the least, that previously unidentified factors can have such impact. Actually, the economic forces at work here have two different dimensions, and we need to consider them separately if we're to understand the new loyalty model well enough to measure its components and develop its new calculus of profit. The first dimension

Figure 2-1   Impact of a 5-Percentage-Point Increase in Retention Rate on Customer Net Present Value

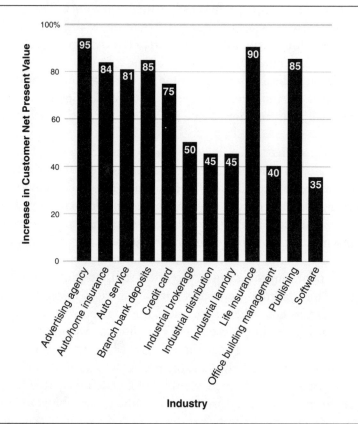

deals with the impact of loyalty on the growth of a firm's customer inventory. This is the customer volume effect. It could hardly be more straightforward, yet it's surprisingly powerful over time. Say you steadily add new customers to the top of your inventory, but old customers are steadily vanishing from the bottom. If you could slow the defection rate, the new customers you gained would increase the total at a much faster rate. It's like a leaky bucket. The bigger the leak in your bucket of customers, the harder you have to work to fill it up and keep it full.

Imagine two companies, one with a customer retention rate of 95 percent, the other with a rate of 90 percent. The leak in the first firm's customer bucket is 5 percent per year, and the second firm's leak is twice as large, 10 percent per year. If both companies acquire new customers at the rate of 10 percent per year, the first will have a 5 percent net growth in customer inventory per year, while the other will have none. Over fourteen years, the first firm will double in size, but the second will have no real growth at all. Other things being equal, a 5-percentage-point advantage in customer retention translates into a growth advantage equal to a doubling of customer inventory every fourteen years. An advantage of ten percentage points accelerates the doubling to seven years.

Not bad these days, when most companies find growth so challenging. Yet this customer volume effect is small change compared to the second dimension of loyalty economics, the profit-per-customer effect. This is harder to see than the customer volume effect, but it often makes an even bigger difference in profits.

In most businesses, the profit earned from each individual customer grows as the customer stays with the company. Figure 2-2 shows what this lifecycle profit pattern looks like in several representative industries. Clearly, the economic consequences of losing mature customers and replacing them with new ones are not neutral. In businesses like auto insurance, life insurance, or credit cards, firms actually lose money on first-year customers, so no number of new prospects can fill the void left by a seasoned customer who defects. In most other industries, new customers contribute to profits right away, but it still takes several new-comers to compensate for the loss of one veteran.

In addition, the consequences of customer retention *compound* over time, and in ways that are sometimes surprising and nonintuitive. While a change in defection rates may have little effect on *this* year's profits,

Figure 2-2   Customer Lifecycle Profit Patterns in Selected Industries

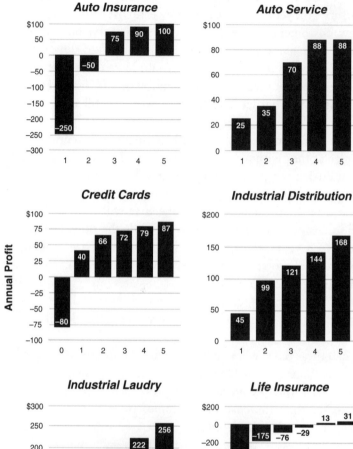

even a tiny change in customer retention can cascade through a business system and multiply over time. The resulting effect on long-term profit and growth can be enormous.

DISCOVERING THE COMPONENT PARTS OF LOYALTY

To understand the economics of customer retention in your specific business, the first step is to quantify and profile the entire lifecycle of the profits you earn from your customers. Today's bookkeeping systems, trapped in period accounting, completely fail to capture these patterns. Fortunately, you can learn to do the calculations for yourself. It takes some experience, a certain amount of rigorous analysis, and perhaps a little help, but you can borrow the only tools you'll need from cost accounting and standard financial analysis. The trick is to identify all the significant differences between new and mature customers that affect the cash flows of your business. Every company is unique, of course, but we have found that the generic model laid out in Figure 2-3 captures most of the important economic effects of customer loyalty: acquisition

Figure 2-3 Why Loyal Customers Are More Profitable

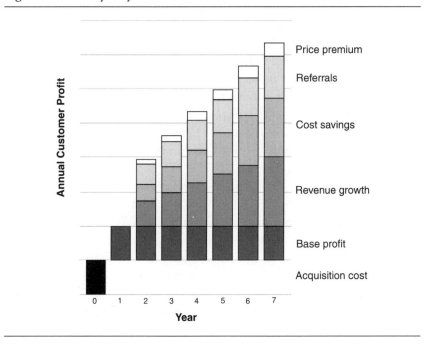

cost, revenue growth, cost savings, referrals, and price premium. We will discuss these effects briefly one by one, but first let me tell you how we discovered and learned to quantify them.

Our first struggle with the economics of the customer lifecycle came in the insurance brokering business. We had been asked to find the root cause of big disparities in profitability among several leading competitors. Insurance brokering is an industry where price levels vary little among competitors. Brokers are paid a standard commission rate on all the insurance they place, usually 10 percent of the entire insurance bill. Nevertheless, profit margins varied hugely among the companies in question, from 35 percent at Johnson & Higgins to a loss at Frank B. Hall.

We began by examining factors like relative market share and market segmentation, and found that these traditional profit drivers accounted for little if any of the discrepancy. Then, since uniform commissions mean that companies with higher profits *must* be spending less money on each sale, we focused our attention on costs. The primary cost at an insurance brokerage is salaries, yet we found that the companies with the highest profit margins seemed to be paying the highest salaries as well. That didn't make sense.

After pursuing a number of false leads, one of our consultants was interviewing customers to discover what led them to switch from one broker to another. His assignment was to question at least twenty-five customers who'd defected from each brokerage, but he was finding, to his frustration, that the most profitable brokerages hardly ever lost a customer. In the case of Johnson & Higgins, a hundred phone calls yielded only three defectors; at that rate, it would take him another 733 calls to reach his quota. When the rate held steady—a second hundred calls turned up only three more ex-customers—the consultant paused to reconsider the assignment.

Johnson & Higgins' high customer retention was clearly a problem for anyone searching out defectors, but for Johnson & Higgins itself, customer retention might just be the big advantage we'd been looking for, the edge that explained the company's higher profits. Our consulting team turned its attention to finding and quantifying whatever economic advantage this high rate of customer retention might yield. We took a closer look at front-end sales commissions. We studied the process of selling and setting up new clients. We compared the administrative costs of new and old customers. We scrutinized broker cost structures. We conducted new interviews and reexamined old ones. We tried to measure every important relationship between customer duration and cash flow. In the end we were able to chart the flow of new accounts into each of the brokerage firms and to build up a customer lifecycle profit pattern for the industry—something no one, to our knowledge, had ever done before. When completed, our model explained most of the previously baffling differences in reported profits.

Over the course of the next five years, we went on to analyze customer profit patterns in a wide variety of industries and with dozens of clients. In Europe, one of our case teams took on the task of helping an industrial laundry service determine how much it might profitably invest in a service quality program aimed at greater customer retention. Among other things, we found unexpectedly large cost and efficiency differences between delivery routes that served mostly stable, long-term customers and those that served more than their share of new and temporary accounts. It turned out that route drivers learned valuable shortcuts when their customer books were stable.

In the Midwest, a case team investigating customer profit patterns for an industrial supply house found not only that new customers bought less than old ones but that orders from newer customers took twice as long to process, included a much greater proportion of nonstandard items (with higher handling costs and lower margins), and led much more often to collection problems and bad debt.

On the East Coast, consultants to a residential homebuilder were trying to determine why the percentage of prospective customers who actually went on to buy a house differed so greatly from one regional office to another. They learned that closing rates depended on referrals, and therefore indirectly on customer satisfaction. While it's pretty rare for anyone to buy a second house from the same builder, satisfied customers do recommend the builder to friends and relatives, and closing rates for referral prospects are significantly higher than closing rates for walk-in customers. It was the difference in referral rates from one region to another that explained the greater effectiveness—and therefore the higher profits—of some sales offices. And the variation in referral rates? That seemed to depend in large part on whether salespeople and troubleshooters were in the habit of responding promptly and effectively to buyer complaints in the first ninety days after people moved in.

Referrals turned out to be a critical driver of profits and growth in the auto service industry as well. So we incorporated the referral effect in our customer lifecycle analyses to help explain variations in profit and growth rates at different outlets for a leading national chain. We found that at Northwestern Mutual, the loyalty leader in life insurance, agents are trained to sell only through referral. Their yield rate for referral selling is one closing for every ten referrals contacted. Yield rates on nonreferral selling are so much lower that pursuing them makes no economic sense.

As our consulting teams discovered and rediscovered these different economic effects, we gradually developed the model in Figure 2-3 and began to use it as a checklist and guide for teams studying customer lifecycle economics in businesses of every kind. In the beginning, such studies took us six to nine months, sometimes longer. Experience and refinement have since reduced the time by more than half, but we find there is no simple, universal formula. To build an accurate picture of customer lifecycle economics in any business—and to produce cost and pricing analyses rigorous enough to support substantial investments—analysts have had to construct entirely new databases and to use existing ones creatively. At the moment, very few companies have the necessary data or the requisite analytical systems, and they don't come cheap. Yet without a means of quantifying the economic value of loyalty, it inevitably falls back into the investment category called "nice, but unnecessary."

Let's consider each of the components in Figure 2-3 separately.

Acquisition Cost

Almost every business has to invest money up front to bring new customers through the door. Most of these costs are easy to identify: advertising directed at new customers; commissions on sales to new customers; sales force overhead; and so forth. To take one concrete example, the first big expense in the credit card business is the cost of direct mail. With a response rate of 2 to 3 percent, a company has to mail out thirty thousand to fifty thousand solicitations to get just a thousand applications. Add credit evaluation, card issuance, and the cost of putting a new account into the bank's data-processing systems, and you wind up with a pricetag for each new customer of $50 to $100.

Not all the costs of customer acquisition are equally obvious. In industries like advertising and consulting, senior managers make the sales proposals, so their time is an investment in customer acquisition. So is the cost of wining and dining prospects, whether they ultimately sign up or not. In retailing, customer acquisition costs include the expense of opening a new store (including its losses before reaching breakeven volume) as well as the cost of loss-leader pricing to draw new customers.

Whatever your industry, you must tally up *all* your customer acquisition expenses, hidden and plainly visible, to find the true up-front cost of landing new business. At most of the companies we've worked with over the years, the number was higher than management expected.

Base Profit

All customers buy some product or service, or we wouldn't call them customers. With rare exceptions, moreover, the prices they pay are higher than the company's costs. This basic profit on basic purchases, unaffected by time, loyalty, efficiency, or any other consideration, is what we call base profit. Obviously, the longer you keep a customer, the longer you will earn this base profit, which makes your acquisition investment look better and better.

Per-Customer Revenue Growth

One advantage of holding onto your customers is that in most businesses, customer spending tends to accelerate over time. In retailing, for example, customers become more familiar with the store's full product line. The man who repeatedly buys shirts eventually notices that you also carry shoes. In auto service, new customers may come in for a wheel alignment or an oil change, but if they like the service and the value, they'll likely move on to more expensive items like tune-ups and tires. Average annual revenue per customer in auto service triples between the first and fifth year.

In personal insurance, the average premiums of loyal customers grow at a rate of 8 percent a year. A typical family's increasing affluence accounts for part of this increase. Insurance on the new Lexus costs more than it did on the old Toyota. An addition to the house means more coverage, and so does the vacation home. Another part of the 8 percent average derives from the fact that long-term customers also tend to consolidate their insurance policies, so that a single long-term agent or company picks up auto, home, and life. At Northwestern Mutual, 55 percent of new sales come from existing policyholders.

Of course, some businesses see no revenue growth from older customers. Snow-removal services find that not even their most loyal customers add new driveways. Laundry customers soil clothing at the same old rate, no matter how long they've been with you. Cellular phone companies see an unusual pattern. New customer revenues surge in the first thirty days, then diminish sharply as the novelty wears off and the first bills arrive. Still, over the long term, customers tend to install phones in additional cars in the household, so the pattern starts high, falls steeply, then slowly rises again to yield ultimate revenue growth from loyal customers.

One word of warning about the revenue-per-customer growth effect: it's easy enough to understand but can be difficult to measure. To get a precise reading, you have to track the annual revenues from each entering class, or *cohort*, of customers separately. Few companies today are equipped to do this. Instead, they take a shapshot of their present customer base, divide it into groups by tenure, and measure the year's revenues from each group. The resulting bar chart—a long row of progressively longer columns showing per-customer revenues for each successive customer class—can be deceptive. Statisticians have a term for this approach—they call it estimating a time series with cross-sectional data—and they caution against it.

The problem is, the bar chart seems to imply a revenue growth pattern for the entering class, but each bar represents a *different* entering class. That fact can mislead the unwary in three ways. First, different customer classes often have slightly different characteristics. There can be age differences, demographic differences, and differences in the marketing promotions that attracted them, to name a few of many possibilities. Second, the older the class, the smaller it has become. This fact can be hugely deceptive if you're trying to project future revenues from a thousand new customers and forget how few of them will still be around in ten or twelve years.

Third, there is always a danger that the defectors from any class are quite different from the customers who stay. For example, if customers who purchase less also happen to be less loyal, then the snapshot approach—based exclusively on customers who stick around—will suggest revenue growth that is far too optimistic, and mislead managers trying to project the consequences of higher customer retention. In this situation, every saved defector would drag down the average rate of revenue growth per customer.

It is not enough to correlate customer tenure with annual purchases and then use the implied growth pattern for everyone. What you have to do is analyze the behavior of defectors as well as that of loyal customers, then estimate growth separately for each customer segment that demonstrates a different underlying behavior pattern. If you are using cross-sectional customer data, this warning applies equally to all the other economic components that drive lifecycle profits.

Perhaps the most important piece of advice we can give about revenue growth over the customer lifecycle is to point out that you can do more than estimate it; you can manage it. A leading credit card firm, for example, discovered it could accelerate its loyal-customer lifecycle, and with it the profits of loyalty. It used rewards and pricing to encourage cardholders to consolidate their use of plastic more quickly, and found it could bring customers to mature sales and profit levels just a few years after signing them up. Bankers too have found they can accelerate the growth of customer balances beyond historic patterns by automatically registering new customers for checking, savings, investment, and credit card accounts, all bundled together in a single statement.

Operating Costs

As customers get to know a business, they learn to be very efficient. They don't waste time requesting services the company doesn't provide. Familiarity with the company's products makes them less dependent on its employees for information and advice. In some businesses, these cost effects are obvious. In financial planning, for instance, planners log about five times as many hours on a first-year client as they do on a repeat customer. Much of this is simply the time it takes to understand a new client's balance sheet, tax status, income profile, and risk preference. Meanwhile, the client is learning to communicate with the planner and the company. Over time, this collaborative learning between client and planner can create enormous productivity advantages that translate directly into lower costs.

The cost benefits in this simple situation are obvious, and so are the cost penalties that go along with employee turnover. Every time a planner quits, a new person has to recapture all that client knowledge. So while customer loyalty has a powerful capacity to lower costs, employee loyalty can be equally vital if the savings are going to persist.

In the auto service business, to take another example, the advantage of customer retention comes partly from knowing the customer and partly from knowing the car, its repair history, and in the case of a persistent problem, the solutions that have already been tried. Repeat customers are also cheaper to serve because they call in advance for appointments and are more flexible on scheduling. New customers drive in off the street, typically at lunchtime or during rush hour, when the business is already operating at capacity. Keeping service bays utilized is one of the keys to running a profitable auto service business. Loyal long-term customers make that job a good deal easier.

In some industries, productivity gains never translate into cost reductions, because employees harvest the gains for themselves. Telephone repair people work like mad to meet productivity standards early in their careers, but as they gain experience, they find they can finish a job schedule that used to take eight hours in six. Unless crew members derive some benefit from achieving superior productivity, they will fill the other two hours with coffee breaks, lunch, and shopping trips.

Even where the incentives and benefits are clear—as they are for insurance agents, stockbrokers, and others who work on commission— productivity gains tend to flatten out after the first five or ten years as people begin to trade extra income for free time. Even here, however, the company benefits. Experienced agents write fewer bad policies, and experienced brokers create fewer problems for their branch managers.

In most industries, the cost benefits of loyalty spiral directly from the way long-term customers and long-term employees interact and learn from one another. Repeat customers tend to be pleased with the value they receive, and their satisfaction is a source of pride and energy for employees. Motivated employees stay with the company longer and get to know their customers better yet—which leads to still better service, builds still greater customer satisfaction, and further improves the relationship and the company's results. This human factor, personal loyalty, is powerful. Brand loyalty often pales by comparison. After all, the customer can get to know a brand, but the brand can never get to know the customer, so it's no surprise that customers are much more loyal to individual employees than to the logos on caps or business cards. What's more, customers will give employees they know a second chance to correct a problem, which has its own benefits for customer retention and productivity.

Still, the powerful logic of a loyalty-based cost advantage will not quantify your cash flow. To *measure* the benefits of loyalty, you have to find productivity and expense efficiencies that you can link directly to experienced customers. Let's look at a couple of examples of how this is done. At a software company, managers noticed that most calls to the customer-assistance center came from new customers, so they began tracking call frequency by customer tenure. When they found that two-thirds of all calls came from new customers, they began assigning two-thirds of the phone center's costs to the new customer accounts. The old practice of allocating the whole cost of the assistance center in proportion to customer revenues put most of the burden on older customers, since there were more of them and they bought more—thus skewing management's perception of how the money was being spent.

Digging deeper still, managers then discovered that some older customers called much more often than others. It turned out that regular users who ran their software daily needed very little assistance, whereas infrequent users like hobbyists often called for advice when they forgot procedures between work sessions. This discovery allowed the company to refine its understanding of customer lifecycle economics another notch and then focus new product development on frequent users, who were cheaper to serve and support.

Consider another example: a catalogue sales operation tracked the time and cost of processing several hundred new-customer orders, then compared the results to a similar number of orders from mature customers. To managers' amazement, they found that processing orders for customers who'd been with the company less than two years cost *twice* as much as processing orders for older customers. There were three key differences. First, new customers didn't know which items were kept in stock, and so were much more likely to request nonstandard items. Second, credit evaluations and losses drove up the general overhead for new customers. Third, new customers were much more likely to order at peak-volume times of the day, which stressed the system and created more errors.

The operating-cost advantages of customer loyalty are particularly strong in retailing and distribution. A shop selling to a constantly shifting set of customers needs a lot more inventory than a shop serving the same people year after year. The former has to guess which fashions, colors, and sizes will appeal to a group of total strangers; the latter knows its customers, their needs and tastes, even their waist sizes. A stable set of customers can help to streamline inventory management, minimize markdowns, and simplify capacity forecasting. Even in manufacturing, no matter how isolated from the ultimate consumer by wholesalers and retailers, a stable set of customers can reduce operating costs by mitigating the uncertainties of new product development, capacity forecasting, product mix, and logistics.

Referrals

A third important benefit of long-term customer retention is that satisfied customers recommend the business to others. Lexus gets far more new customers from referrals than from any other source. Good insurance agents pick up the vast majority of their new customers from recommendations. (Really good agents take the trouble to find out who gave the referral, then try to discover—and repeat—whatever they did to earn it.) Referrals are a vital source of new customers in homebuilding as well, and the best builders have learned how to track the sources and causes of customer recommendations.

Referrals are relatively unimportant in some industries, especially those where customers can sample the product without risk or expense. In credit cards, for instance, an economic model of the customer lifecycle can ignore the referral effect. In other businesses—auto service, for one— referrals are the main source of new customers, so an accurate picture of lifecycle economics must track referrals to their source. A simple way of doing this is to sample a group of new customers for referrals, get the names of the old customers who recommended the business, then find out how long each of those old customers has been around, by calling and asking if necessary.

A final point to remember is that customers who show up on the strength of a personal recommendation tend to be of higher quality—that is, to be more profitable and stay with the business longer—than customers who respond to conquest advertising, sales pitches, or price promotions. One insurance company tracked customers who came in through the Yellow Pages and found their retention rate and profitability so miserable that management encouraged agents to drop the ads. Customers who come on a recommendation, however, are likely to be there for the right reasons. Veteran customers paint a more accurate picture of a business's strengths and weaknesses than advertisements or commissioned salespeople. In addition, since people tend to associate with people like themselves, chances are good that referred customers will fit well with the products and services the company offers. Though businesses are often quick to give the credit for good growth to sexy advertising, brilliant marketing campaigns, or skilled salespeople, the chances are their profitable growth is driven by referrals.

Intuit is a maker of microcomputer software whose flagship product, *Quicken,* lets consumers and small businesses write checks and track their finances on a personal computer. According to *Inc.* magazine, "*Quicken* is probably the most successful personal financial management program ever written, holding a market share estimated at 60%."[1] Though Intuit competes with large corporations employing hundreds of sales reps, the company has sold more than a million units a year through retailers all over the country with a salesforce of just two people. How have they done it? Founder and CEO Scott Cook explains, "Really, we have hundreds of thousands of salespeople. They're our customers." He pauses. "And if you can't please your current customers, you don't deserve any new ones."[2]

Price Premium

In most industries, old customers pay effectively higher prices than new ones. This is sometimes the result of trial discounts available only to brand-new customers. Retailers, magazine publishers, lawn services, custom-shirt makers—all use special introductory offers of this kind (sometimes to the consternation of established customers, who feel they're the ones who deserve to be rewarded). More often, however, the price difference is self-selected. A bank promotes special CD rates from time to time but finds that long-term customers rarely take advantage of them. A retailer offers a coupon to all customers but finds that mature customers are less likely to use it. The so-called loss leader in retailing works on the high probability that customers who come in to get the bargain will buy other products with higher margins, but studies show that loss leaders make up a smaller fraction of an old customer's shopping basket.

Customers who've been around long enough to learn a company's procedures and acquaint themselves with its full product line will almost invariably get greater value from a business relationship. So it's not surprising that they're less price sensitive on individual items than new customers. Unfortunately, few accounting systems capture the information needed to estimate this price premium effect. Even companies that have customer profitability systems generally miss the full impact, because most such systems merely reshuffle information originally gathered to measure product-line profitability. That is, they tote up profits product by product, then calculate the profit from a particular customer or group of customers on the basis of the products customers buy. This approach ends up averaging coupons and other price discounts across all customers, irrespective of the price actually paid. As a result, firms overvalue transactions and undervalue relationships.

This flawed approach has another serious drawback when it comes to determining how much of the superior value generated by long-term customers should be shared with them in the form of increased service or reduced pricing. Many firms today overcharge their best customers because they are unaware of the true margins these customers generate.

PUTTING IT ALL TOGETHER

Gathering and analyzing your own data on all these effects—acquisition cost, base profit, revenue growth, operating costs, referrals, and price premium—will give you quite an accurate picture of the lifecycle profit patterns of your customers. But how do you put this information to work? A lifecycle profit pattern is only as useful as the decisions it helps you make, and we have yet to answer several critical questions. For example, what's the actual value of a new customer in today's dollars? And how big an investment is an increase in customer loyalty actually worth?

Answering these questions accurately is a little trickier than you might suppose, so let's walk through the process one step at a time. First, to find the value of new customers, you have to know the annual profit pattern (or cash-flow pattern, if cash flow differs significantly from profits) that customers typically generate through the years. You also have to know how many years they're likely to stay with your firm.

Figure 2-4 shows customer profits for a typical credit card company, based on all the factors just described—acquisition cost, base profit, revenue growth, operating costs, referrals, and price premium. Obviously, a customer's value increases the longer he or she keeps and uses the card. A customer who stays two years will generate $26 of profit (the $80 acquisition cost is offset by profits in the first two years of $40 and $66). A customer who stays five years will generate $264 in cumulative net profits (−$80 + $40 + $66 + $72 + $79 + $87). By the same kind of arithmetic, ten-year and twenty-year customers will generate net profits of $760 and $2,104.

Figure 2-4 Customer Lifecycle Profit Pattern in the
Credit Card Industry

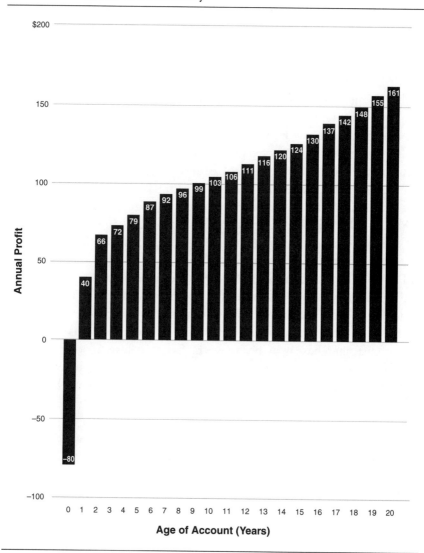

These differences in customer value are enormous, but they are not entirely comparable. For instance, you would be wrong to pay $760 for a customer who will stay ten years, because much of the profit stream will occur in the future, and cash in the future is not worth as much as cash today. You need to discount those future earnings to bring them to their present value. Using a fairly standard discount rate of 15 percent, that $760 in cumulative profit translates to a net present value of $304. (For the purposes of this example, we are assuming that the profit for each year comes in on December 31. To find the net present value of the first year's profit, therefore, divide $40 by 1.15. For the second year, divide $66 by 1.15 squared, or 1.3225. And so forth.) If you are satisfied with a 15 percent annual rate of return, you can pay up to $304 for a customer who will last ten years.

Now that we know how to calculate the value of a customer based on life expectancy, or expected tenure, the next logical question becomes: What is the expected duration of a new customer in your company? The only way to answer the question accurately is to develop retention rates that differentiate among customers by age, source, profession, cohort, and maybe a dozen other criteria. Some companies—life insurers, for example—enjoy the luxury of measurement systems that do all this. Most companies have to estimate.

The simplest way to approximate average customer tenure is by calculating your overall defection rate and inverting the fraction. This is easily done. First, count the number of customers who defect over a period of several months, then annualize this figure and express it as a fraction of the customer base you began with. Say you lose 50 out of 1,000 customers over the course of three months. This works out to 200 customers a year, or one-fifth of all the customers you had at the outset. The second step is to invert, which simply means turning the fraction upside down. One-fifth is inverted to 5 over 1, or 5. Presto: your average customer stays with you five years. (In percentage terms, which is how we usually express these ratios, losing one-fifth of your customers means your defection rate is 20 percent, and your retention rate, consequently, is 80 percent.)

Figure 2-5 summarizes the relationship between annual retention rate and average customer tenure. It shows how small increases in retention can compound into substantial changes in average tenure, especially at retention rates of 80 percent and higher. For example, 90 percent retention means an average tenure of ten years, but 95 percent retention doubles the average to twenty years.

Approximating retention rates in this way is sometimes a useful shortcut. It gives a general idea of how well a company is performing and paints a graphic picture of the relationship between tenure and retention rates. But estimates are by definition rough, and many companies have

Figure 2-5   Relationship Between Customer Retention Rate and
Customer Duration

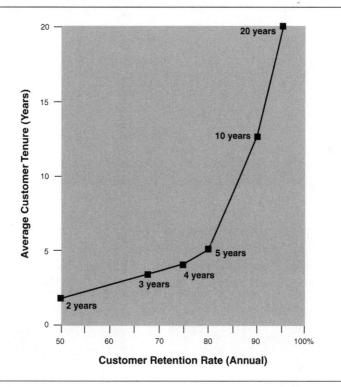

found them so inexact that they cannot use them in their profit accounting systems.

To quantify customer cash flows with accuracy, we must make some
important refinements. First, the method of estimating we describe presumes that defection rates are constant throughout the customer lifecycle.
Such is rarely the case; defection rates run much higher than average in
the early years, and much lower later on. In the first two years of
customer tenure, it is not unusual to see defection rates two to three
times the overall average. Figure 2-6 shows the actual pattern of defection
for a credit card company whose weighted-average defection rate is 10
percent. As you can see, the only customers who defect at precisely a
10 percent rate are those in their fourth year of tenure.

Figure 2-7 shows the difference in cumulative defections between the
actual decreasing-rate pattern and the constant-rate pattern assumed in
the steady-state scenario. Let's assume an entering class of a hundred

Figure 2-6   Actual Versus Constant Defection Patterns

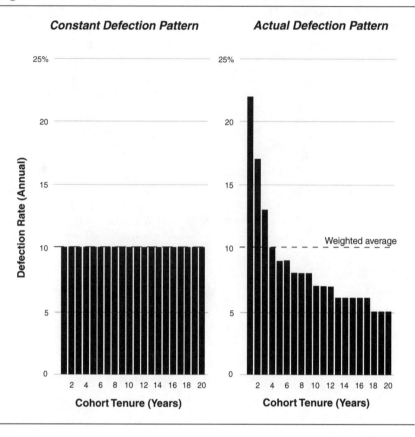

thousand new customers and look at the time it will take for half of them to defect. The actual defection pattern shows the half-life of this customer group to be 4.1 years, while the constant-rate pattern gives a figure of 6.2 years. When we use these numbers to calculate customer net present value, the difference is enormous. Applying the actual and constant rates from Figure 2-7 to the customer profit pattern from Figure 2-4, we find that the constant-rate assumption overestimates the real value of a customer by 40 percent! Because we can't get accurate calculations with averages, we must work with the actual rates for each separate class of customers.

There is one more refinement we must make to calculate the true value of a customer. In fact, we have done it in the last two paragraphs.

Figure 2-7 Cumulative Defections: Actual Versus Constant Patterns

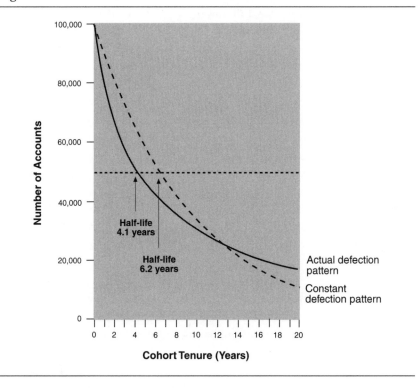

Instead of trying to calculate the value of a single, static, "average" customer at a single moment, we need to think in terms of annual classes of customers moving through time. In the real world, a company acquires a new pool of customers each year. Some of these defect quickly; others may stay for decades. But the investment is made in the entire pool, so to calculate the present value of the average customer, we must study the entire group over time.

Take the scenario in Figure 2-7, in which a hundred thousand new customers enter the inventory at time zero. The credit card company has invested $80 in each customer, or $8 million for the whole class. By the end of the first year, 22 percent of the class has defected, leaving only seventy-eight thousand customers to generate first-year profits and begin to pay back the $8 million invested. By year five, when annual profits start to get really attractive, less than half the incoming class will still be on hand. To calculate the present value of a customer accurately, we must estimate the set of cash flows the entire class will generate as it diminishes over time, then divide by the size of the entering class—in this case, one hundred thousand.

Let's take a concrete example. On page 52, we somewhat simplistically estimated the net present value of a credit card customer who stayed ten years at $304. Our credit card company, with its 90 percent retention rate (ten-year average tenure, assuming a constant rate), might be tempted to use this estimate for decision making. But to do so would be dangerously inaccurate because many customers defect long before the tenth year. In fact, many defect before they've paid back the firm's $80 acquisition investment, and those losses must be borne by remaining customers, not swept under the carpet. In this case, an accurate calculation based on the actual defection pattern shown in Figure 2-7 and the profit pattern shown in Figure 2-4 gives us a net present value of $172 per customer. Our first estimate of $304 overvalued a customer's worth by 76 percent!

These are not theoretical calculations. Our credit card firm might get a proposal from an outside marketing agency offering to generate additional new customers at a fee of $200 each. Assuming each customer is worth $304, the company might take that offer, destroying a great deal of value. So too, auto dealers need to know how much they can really afford to pay to acquire a new customer, and so do life insurers, telecommunications companies, banks, and office equipment manufacturers. In short, businesses need to know what a customer is really worth, and only actual defection rates for particular classes of customers will tell them.

Once you have an accurate picture of the true value of a customer, you're in a position to calculate what it would be worth to increase your customer retention rate—which is the only realistic way of evaluating investments in customer acquisition and customer loyalty. Glance back at Figure 2-1 and you'll see that in the credit card business, a 5-percentage-point increase in customer retention increases the value of a customer by 75 percent. Just exactly how did we perform that calculation? First, we adjusted the cumulative defection curves in Figure 2-7 for a weighted average of 5 percent instead of 10 percent, as shown in the middle of Figure 2-8. By combining the profit pattern from Figure 2-4 (displayed again at the top of Figure 2-8) with this 95-percent retention pattern (bottom of Figure 2-8), we obtain a present value of $300 for each new customer—a 75 percent increase over the $172 we got by assuming 90 percent retention.

Figure 2-8 Calculating Customer Value

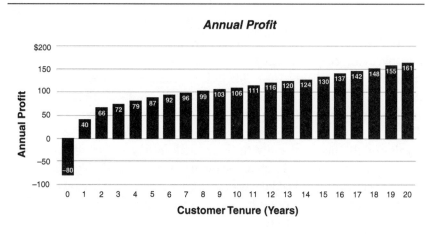

Annual Profit

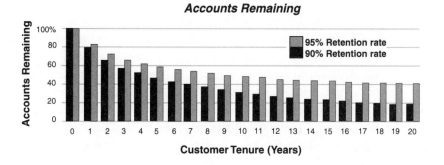

Accounts Remaining

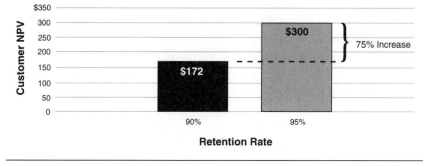

Customer NPV

MAKING RATIONAL DECISIONS

In our experience, once companies understand the potential value of customer retention, they tend to fall into a trap. Eager to produce rapid improvement, they shortcut their analysis of customer cash flow. Understandably but foolishly, they conclude that getting bogged down in the details of a proposition they already accept as fact—that improving customer retention will improve profits—is a waste of time and money. The omission usually comes back to haunt them. The only way to put loyalty at the heart of daily decision making is to take the economic effects of loyalty seriously, measure them rigorously, and link them firmly to reported earnings. The best way to reduce misunderstandings between different parts of the organization, and to surface and resolve them when they do occur, is to make the loyalty numbers so trustworthy that everyone accepts them as a basis for investment and strategy decisions.

Take the case of a large insurance company. Having studied the economics of loyalty at the broadest level, and having compared the company's own retention rates with the competition's, senior management introduced half a dozen new customer retention programs, from service quality enhancement to modified sales commissions and customer recovery units. A year later, however, they found little or no compliance with their initiatives. Middle managers were dragging their feet. Closer examination located the root of the problem in the actuarial staff, a powerful department in most insurance companies. The actuaries disagreed with the financial consequences of increased loyalty as estimated by the accounting department. They believed that greater customer retention had to mean holding onto unprofitable, high-risk customers that the company ought instead to purge. It took a thorough analysis of the claims and cash-flow records of former customers to convince the actuaries that defectors were attractive customers—much more attractive than the average new customer. Even then a few were not convinced but had to be shown precisely how the superior retention rates of their best competitors explained their superior profits.

Retention economics lets companies make rational, dollars-and-cents decisions about the value of increased customer loyalty and tells them accurately, for the first time, which loyalty-enhancing investments will meet their hurdle rates of return. Where retention economics remains an off-line system—an article of faith for some departments, perhaps, but an unknown quantity for others—loyalty will never carry real weight in key investment decisions. Where retention economics has never been tested under fire, even companies that have bought into the concept will quickly revert to old measurement systems in times of profit pressure. Companies that are serious about improving customer loyalty will eventually find that they *must* invest in the systems that measure retention and its economic consequences. The earlier they make this investment, the better.

REVISITING REPORTED EARNINGS

To this point, we have been speaking the language of investment and net present value. But to make loyalty economics a trusted part of management's toolbox, we must perform one final operation. We must translate these numbers back into the kind of reported profits on which so much of today's decision making is based. Outside of the insurance and direct-marketing industries, very few companies have taken this last step. Walking through an example will help to show how it's done and perhaps explain why it hasn't been done before.

Let's stick with the credit card example, and look at what happens to reported earnings over a ten-year period if a firm operates at 95-percent retention as opposed to 90-percent retention. Figure 2-9 shows reported earnings in each of these two scenarios. A real company will first need to unravel its current inventory into tenure classes, or cohorts. It can be a little embarrassing to go to your customers and ask them how long they've been doing business with you, but it can be done. From this starting point, future earnings streams can be estimated on the basis of the long-term earnings and defection patterns we've already seen. In the hypothetical example in Figure 2-9, we assumed that the firm has one million customers, operates at 90-percent retention, acquires customers at a steady rate of a hundred thousand per year, and has an unchanging customer profit pattern (Figure 2-4). The result is a company with an average customer tenure of seven years and earnings of $80 million at the beginning of the period.

In the 90-percent retention scenario, as you can see, earnings grow very slowly to $96 million at the end of ten years. With 95-percent retention, however, earnings grow almost 50 percent faster, to $141 million by the end of the tenth year. If we make some reasonable assumptions about customers' terminal value—the profit stream they will produce during their remaining years with the company—the increase in

Figure 2-9   Profit Growth at 90- Versus 95-Percent Retention Rates

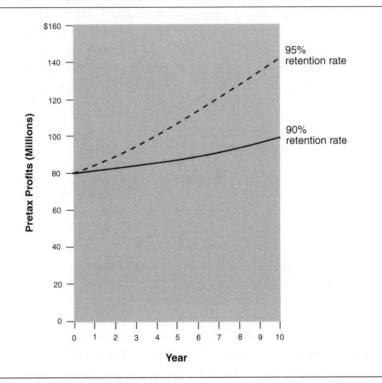

total value for the 95-percent retention case is even higher, approaching 75 percent.

These numbers are not merely impressive; they are also simple and straight forward. And the kind of customer-tracking systems we're talking about are no more complicated than many of the accounting systems companies have in place today. A few businesses—a few whole industries—*have* built accounting systems based on the economies of customer retention. Life insurance companies have tracked their customers this way for decades; so have direct marketers like L. L. Bean and Lands' End. USAA has a near-perfect customer tracking system that other companies might use as a model. The question is why more companies have *not* built them. Part of the answer is that regulators and investors don't require it. Managers have to provide shareholders with information on current profits but no one demands an accounting of any of the factors that loyalty economics builds on.

Another part of the answer undoubtedly has to do with the time frame in which the financial effects of customer loyalty reveal themselves. Customer loyalty yields returns over several years; manager bonuses are determined annually. Understanding a business's loyalty economics can produce some powerful short-term improvements in profit performance, as we will see in Chapter 10. But on the whole, the temptation is great to put off investing in the kind of rigorous measures that enable steady learning and continuous improvement over longer spans of time. Companies that are serious about tapping into the long-term benefits of loyalty must overcome that temptation and build reliable measures. This is how MBNA discovered that a 5-point increase in retention lifts per-customer profit by more than 125 percent. This is how State Farm determined that a 1-point increase in retention will increase its capital surplus by more than $1 billion over time.

PUTTING IT TO WORK FOR YOUR BUSINESS

Knowing how much improved retention will increase earnings at State Farm or MBNA won't do much to help you make better investment decisions in your own business. Figuring out how to invest your own resources more effectively means constructing a model of lifecycle cash flows, defections, and profits for your own particular customers.

Loyalty-based management is not a matter of investing blindly in your customers in the hope that somehow profits will grow. It's a matter of making rational business decisions about which projects to fund and which ones to cancel. In the real world, business decisions involve budgets and priorities. Slogans like "Our customers are our most valuable asset" are not only useless at budget time; they are often wrong. True, the development of systems to measure, analyze, and manage loyalty-based cash flows can often lead companies to make investments that create value for both customers and company. But sometimes the same systems reveal that earlier investments in customer satisfaction based on intuitive judgments or flawed logic have actually destroyed value. Often the quickest way to improve earnings is to stop investing money in such programs.

One credit card company discovered that a proposed multi-million-dollar billing system would chiefly benefit a segment of customers whose long-term value to the company would be insignificant. At another company, a study of lifecycle profits and defections revealed that the firm's largest marketing investment—in the acquisition of young customers just out of high school—represented a net loss. As we will see in Chapter 3, mature companies often find that 20 to 30 percent of their new-customer acquisition investments should be scrapped.

Managers in some industries—banking, for one—roll their eyes at the seeming complexity of a loyalty-based customer measurement system. They are struggling simply to reach a consensus about which customers are profitable or unprofitable at a particular point in time. But consider the alternatives: on the one hand, an admittedly complex system that incorporates customer lifecycle profit calculations, variable defection rates, the customer volume effect, the profit-per-customer effect, and dynamic cohort-flow economics—particularly potent in banking—but that, in the end, produces an accurate picture of customer profitability. On the other hand, a simple, static model that is easy and inexpensive to produce—and incorrect. Is this a difficult choice? And is it a difficult choice in banking, where 20 to 50 percent of the investments in new-customer acquisition are currently directed at target groups with a negative net present value?

Bank managers would never think of buying annuities for their own retirement accounts without understanding their probable lifetime returns and cash-flow patterns. Why not apply the same diligence to managing customers? Potentially, at least, customers *are* annuities: they require an up-front investment, and the long-term streams of revenues and costs they generate are the fundamental building blocks of corporate cash flow.

Intuitively, all of us have always known that customer loyalty was a good thing, in Sunday school terms. But few of us have grasped its direct link to profits. Loyalty economics is a rigorous method of measuring the value of customer retention in the concrete terms of cash flow, and of providing the tools that enable a company to manage the real drivers of cost, growth, and profit.

3

The Right Customers

THE FIRST step in managing a loyalty-based business system is finding and acquiring the right customers: customers who will provide steady cash flows and a profitable return on the firm's investment for years to come, customers whose loyalty can be won and kept. Loyalty-based companies should remember three rules of thumb:

1. Some customers are inherently predictable and loyal, no matter what company they're doing business with. They simply prefer stable, long-term relationships.

2. Some customers are more profitable than others. They spend more money, pay their bills more promptly, and require less service.

3. Some customers will find your products and services more valuable than those of your competitors. No company can be all things to all people. Your particular strengths will simply fit better with certain customers' needs and opportunities.

The more customers you can attract who belong to one or two or even all three of these groups, the better your chances of reaping the rewards that go with superior customer retention. In practice, these rewards tend to spiral upward, building on their own success. Better customers create a cash-flow surplus; part of that surplus goes into the delivery of still greater value; more and more value along critical dimensions makes loyal customers more loyal still. We saw the economic calculus of this spiral in Chapter 2. In this chapter, we will look at ways of identifying all three kinds of loyal customers and winning their business, sometimes through new distribution channels. We will also look at the phenomenon of what's called adverse selection, which is what happens when a company foolishly or inadvertently attracts exactly the disloyal customers it least wants. Finally, we will consider the plight of mature companies in maturing industries, where the need for continuing growth makes thoughtful, cautious customer acquisition look like an unaffordable luxury.

THE LOYALTY COEFFICIENT

All companies look for more profitable customers. Most of them put a lot of thought and labor into pursuing that elusive market segment that will find their offerings irresistible. But few realize that some customers are *inherently* more loyal than others.

To understand the true long-term profitability potential of any group of customers, you have to know something about its predisposition to loyalty. You have to know how much economic force it would take to move these customers from one supplier to another. This notion of the energy and resistance involved in customer movement is a relatively simple idea, but no one has made it a science.

As it happens, physicists *have* made a science of the fact that some things are harder to move than others. An engineer could not possibly choose the right materials for an effective mechanical system without precise knowledge of the force required to move them relative to their weight (it's a lot easier to slide a hundred pounds of ice across a floor than a hundred pounds of granite). Physicists have developed a measure for this purpose, called the friction coefficient. As a tool, the friction coefficient lets scientists and engineers quantify and catalogue the "movability" or "slideability" of different materials and calculate their suitability for various systems applications. Using friction coefficients, auto engineers have incorporated new metals and alloys into the wear surfaces of critical moving parts, and NASA engineers have developed special ceramic-tile surfaces to deal with the intense friction of atmospheric reentry.

The friction coefficient concept is one that business can borrow to describe customers, some of whom are much harder to move than others.

Some will defect to a competitor for a 2 percent discount; others wouldn't switch for 20 percent. The amount of economic force required to move different kinds of customers—what we might call their *loyalty* coefficient—is critical information for someone trying to design a high-performance business system, because such a system won't run on an inventory of unreliable customers. In some businesses, the best way to measure this loyalty coefficient is to analyze the historic switching behavior of different customer segments. In others, especially those in which the future is likely to be quite different from the past, the task is to figure out how high a price discount must be to make customers defect.

No one has given much thought or attention to the problem of measuring and interpreting the loyalty coefficients of various types of customers. Most companies try to understand the current profitability of different customer groups, but this is difficult to do without studying *patterns* of loyalty. In fact, few businesses have tracked customer loyalty closely enough even to supply the data for such an analysis.

One notable exception is the life insurance industry, with its huge quantities of historical data on policyholder persistency (the insurance term for customer retention). A life insurer I'll call Northern recently resurrected one such dusty database, studied it closely for what it revealed about loyalty, and found some striking demographic and social variations. For instance, customers in the Midwest and in rural areas were very loyal, while Northeasterners and city-dwellers were quick to switch. Married people exhibited higher loyalty than singles. Renters were not nearly as loyal as homeowners. Insurers already knew that young people were less loyal than older people and that income levels affected loyalty, but even after adjusting for age and income, Northern found that different segments of the population exhibited average retention rates ranging from a low of 72 percent to a high of 94 percent.

Given the fact that in the life insurance business, five percentage points can move lifetime customer value up or down by 90 percent, these are stunning differences. Northern's conventional methods of evaluating customer inventory and targeting investments in new-customer acquisition suddenly seemed inadequate.

For some time, Northern's leaders had admired and envied a large competitor—let's call it Western—whose far superior growth and profits depended almost entirely on outstanding levels of customer persistency. In looking for the root causes of its own higher defection rate, Northern had commissioned satisfaction surveys and other customer research, which led to a concentration on service quality. But Northern's ability to invest in superior service was limited by its marginal profitability and high costs. Again and again, poor cash flows had forced the company to postpone investments in agency salesforce and improved service.

Northern's new look at its old data gave the company some food for thought. If different customer segments displayed different levels of *inherent* loyalty—and they did—then Northern needed to ask itself a new question: How much of Western's persistency advantage was due simply to the fact that the customers it sought and captured were intrinsically more loyal? In asking this question, Northern glimpsed a whole new approach to its problem. But the company knew too little about loyalty coefficients to get the question answered. All its analyses so far had looked only at the loyalty and defection patterns of its own customers, and that left too much room for distortion. For example, a weaker agency in one state or stiffer competition in another might both show up, falsely, as lower innate loyalty. To get an accurate picture of customer behavior and some indication of its causes, the company would have to study the competition's customers as well as its own.

Northern made the investment. It surveyed thousands of people across the industry and managed to isolate customer variations and distinguish them from dissimilarities in the competitive environment or in the company's own operations in different states. With this new data, Northern was able to compare its own segment mix with Western's and to quantify the differences in retention rates that were due exclusively to customer selection and had no other cause. What the company discovered was that if it could match Western's customer mix, more than half its retention disadvantage would simply disappear.

Perhaps by intuition, perhaps by luck, Western had put its agents in regions with high intrinsic loyalty. Moreover, Western's products appealed to the age and income segments that showed the highest loyalty within those geographic areas. Stronger cash flow from more loyal customers then gave Western the wherewithal to hire better agents and invest millions in information systems and other quality improvements— service advantages that gave Western an edge over its competitors even within very loyal segments. But Western's basic advantage came from getting the right customers to start with.

Northern modified its strategy. Instead of trying to compete on the basis of catch-up service improvements, the company first had to place agents in high-loyalty geographic regions and retune its product lines to fit the needs of high-loyalty customer segments. As Northern came to understand what a big share of its cost problems sprang from low customer retention, it made other changes as well. It canceled a planned layoff that might have saved money but would certainly have impaired service. It also altered agent compensation. Like most other insurers, Northern had always paid big first-year commissions for each new policy an agent wrote. Now the company began to base a part of performance bonuses on 24-month persistency—the percentage of new policies that remained in force for at least two years. To increase their own incomes, agents began learning how to evaluate a prospect's loyalty coefficient. They also began to see that certain kinds of policies brought in customers who were inherently more loyal, so they began to market and advertise those products more actively. Some products were so attractive to the right customers that agents began using them as loss leaders, whereas other products—renter's fire and theft insurance, for example—tended to attract customers with such terrible loyalty coefficients that agents grew reluctant to offer them to new customers at all.

Northern's new grasp of loyalty coefficients had other benefits as well. It opened a whole toolbox of new management techniques. And it allowed the company to analyze and compare regional performance more accurately, since management could now tell the difference between superior customer selection, superior service, and superior value creation in other forms. Like most large companies, Northern sets uniform policies and procedures for all its regional offices. But that doesn't keep different management teams from gradually developing significant differences in approach and execution. Earlier, headquarters had no way of knowing precisely what those differences were, much less how and how much they contributed to customer retention. The use of loyalty coefficients—including the ability to measure customer retention rates within segments but across regions—allowed the company to identify, capture, and disseminate best practice throughout the organization.

LOOKING FOR LOYALTY IN ALL THE RIGHT PLACES

Northern Insurance improved its loyalty rates by studying its customer inventory and then focusing intently on particular segments defined by criteria such as geographic area, age, and income. Other criteria can be equally productive. The credit card industry includes an exceptional company—MBNA—that has understood the importance of segmenting by profession and affinity group in order to get highly loyal customers.

Whether teachers, for example, carry a credit card from Chase or Citibank or One-Horse First National, they tend to stick with it. Accountants, nurses, engineers, and many other professionals show the same innate loyalty, and MBNA has built its acquisition strategy on getting as many of them as it possibly can. As far back as the 1970s, when its competitors were mailing applications indiscriminately to millions of disparate households, MBNA had focused in on the question of getting the *right* customers, not just a lot of them.

MBNA found that the most effective way to reach the customers it wanted was by marketing through affinity groups, like the National Education Association and Georgetown University. The company built a specialized salesforce, customized product offerings to meet specific needs, and created cards that featured each group's name and logo. MBNA also does its own backroom processing. It would cost much less to farm out processing to a large-scale vendor, but by doing its own, MBNA can make each group's package distinctive; customize its pricing and software to the needs of each of the more than two thousand affinity groups it serves; and enhance its ability to hold onto old customers and market effectively to new ones.

Given the success of MBNA's affinity group strategy, one obvious question is why other credit card companies never followed suit. The fact is, many tried, including industry giants like Citicorp. Affinity marketing became such a fad in the late 1980s that *The American Banker* and other industry periodicals gave it front-page treatment as the next important wave in marketing. But most of the companies that launched affinity group campaigns found the results disappointing and eventually pulled out. Few of them knew why they'd failed, but there were any number of reasons.

First of all, MBNA was never gunning for pure volume and market share, as most of the newcomers were. The others saw affinity marketing as just one more business in which national or global scale would decide the eventual winner. So they repeated with groups most of the mistakes they had previously made with individuals. MBNA reasoned differently. With great care and at considerable expense, it targeted groups of such high inherent loyalty that customer cash flow would become a virtual perpetuity, eventually overwhelming the company's larger up-front investment.

A second reason the others didn't succeed was that MBNA's superior customer-selection strategies left the competition nothing but scraps to fight over. MBNA not only picked off the best groups first; it developed an ability to single out the individual members of each group who were most likely to become highly profitable customers—the people who would carry substantial credit balances and still be good credit risks.

Since administrative cost per customer varies only slightly in the credit card industry, profit is principally a function of two other factors. The first is interest-revenues, where MBNA's advantage lay in its ability to find people who would carry higher-than-average balances. The other key driver of credit card profits is the level of bad-loan chargeoffs. Here too, MBNA's customer-selection strategy gave it an economic advantage. While MBNA was using targeted acquisition and careful screening to build customer quality into the system, the competition was using complex credit-scoring schemes designed to screen out bad customers from the thousands of applications mass mailings can generate. MBNA's charge-offs run about 3 percent; its leading competitors have never fallen much below the traditional range of 5.5 to 6 percent. More important yet, because MBNA is not filling a leaky bucket, it doesn't have to bring in as many new customers to achieve a given level of growth. The best risks are the customers a company already knows, and MBNA has a higher percentage of long-term customers than any of its principal competitors.

According to MBNA's 1994 annual report, a typical customer has fourteen years on the job, makes a family income of $59,000, owns a home, and most important of all, has been paying bills promptly for fourteen years. At most companies, that list would describe an outstanding customer. At MBNA, it's *average*. Since the total number of customers is finite, moreover, competition for customers is a zero-sum game. As long as MBNA goes on pulling above-average customers out of the general customer pool, what's left for the competition has to be below average. The bigger MBNA becomes, the more its competitors' customer inventories deteriorate.

While MBNA took a restrained approach to growth in the early years—it was thirty-eighth in total credit balances in the early 1980s—its customer acquisition and retention policies have since raised it to second among all bankcards, with more than $19 billion in balances. More than thirty-eight hundred affinity organizations endorse the company's credit cards, and its customers now include 827,000 teachers, 300,000 engineers, 200,000 attorneys, 325,000 nurses, half the nation's dentists, 43 percent of all U.S. physicians, and 75 percent of medical students. Its customers carry balances that are 67 percent above the national average, use their cards 12 percent more than average, and spend 4 percent more per transaction.

Superior customer acquisition has transformed MBNA's relatively modest size and profitability into physical and financial greatness. Equally important, MBNA's leaders have learned to sustain this value-creating machine by thoughtfully allocating the spoils of loyalty. MBNA gives its employees superior compensation and benefits (including day care and on-site shopping) in handsomely appointed work facilities. Its investors have enjoyed a return on equity of nearly 30 percent, and have watched the value of the company increase by $3 billion over the decade.

CHANGING CHANNELS

MBNA's remarkable success grew in part from its particular approach to customer segmentation, but also from its decision to create a new distribution channel. While competitors like Citicorp, Chase, and Bank-America continued to experiment with incremental refinements to a standard distribution channel (direct-mail solicitation), MBNA gradually built a new channel—its own specially trained salesforce—to deal directly with affinity group administrators. The extra expense was substantial, but it greatly improved the quality of company decision making with regard to the acquisition of new customers. In MBNA's view, these are the most important investment decisions the company makes. And in practice, the new channel paid off handsomely.

Many other companies well attuned to the value of customer retention have taken similar steps, creating new channels uniquely suited to the needs of loyal customers. State Farm could have sold insurance through independent agents the way most other insurers did. Instead, it chose to build a special marketing partnership with its own agents. Initially, the company used a part-time salesforce made up mostly of farmers, but in the 1950s the company began a shift toward full-time agent-partners who sold State Farm products exclusively. Today, the company sees this partnership as the heart and soul of its success. Lexus could have sold cars through existing Toyota dealers but decided instead to invest millions in building a new network of dealers carefully groomed and trained to meet the needs of target customers. In loyalty-based management, the sales channel isn't just as a way of attracting lots of customers; it's a way of attracting lots of the *right* customers.

Diesel Fuel for Diesel Engines

Another company that understands the importance of customer selection, USAA, also created its own brand-new distribution channel. Unlike MBNA, USAA did not choose to concentrate on customers with inherently higher profitability or obvious loyalty. USAA was formed to serve military officers and their families, a group of customers that was an expensive nuisance for the typical auto-insurance company using the traditional distribution channel, local agents. Military officers moved around a lot; every time they moved they had to cancel their old insurance, sign up with a new agent (who had to be paid a new commission), and go through underwriting all over again. Underwriting—the process of evaluating a driver's true level of risk—is expensive and time consuming, and the frequent commissions and underwriting made military officers extremely unprofitable. In fact, the system worked well for no one. Companies were losing money, and officers were finding it harder and harder to get good insurance.

USAA's first innovation was to design a new, nationwide distribution channel that would serve these customers by mail (later by phone) and eliminate the need for agents. When officers moved from one base to another, even overseas, they kept the same policy. USAA's second innovation was to understand its customers in extraordinary depth. For example, the company knew—when no one else did—that military officers would turn out to be unusually loyal, reliable, and honest customers, partly because of the self-selection process that leads people to choose military careers and partly because the military code of conduct takes such a very dim view of dishonesty, disloyalty, and nonpayment of bills. (Customer integrity may also help to explain USAA's later success in diversifying into financial services like credit cards, life insurance, and mutual funds.)

By designing a better system, USAA was able to capture the insurance spending of a group of exceptionally loyal but also exceptionally transient customers, whose frequent moves were obvious but whose loyalty wore camouflage. By studying active and retired military officers and their families, USAA learned a great deal about its customers' particular needs and opportunities, then reinvested the surplus economic value of all this learning and loyalty in superior service and lower prices. Which brings us back to the now familiar spiral, where loyal customers generate superior cash flow, which funds lower prices and better service, which then pushes loyalty still higher. Today, less than 2 percent of USAA auto-insurance customers defect voluntarily each year.

USAA recruits former military officers for most of its executive positions, which helps it stay current and well-informed on customer lifestyles and problems. Because its products and services offer such good value, the military academies present the company as one of the benefits available to those who've chosen a military career. Much of the cash that flows from this mutually beneficial business system also goes to employees. In San Antonio, Texas, where it has its headquarters, USAA is widely considered the employer of choice. Compensation is excellent, benefits extraordinary. Most employees work four-day weeks. The corporate campus is beautiful, recreational facilities are extensive (including a golf driving range), and there is plenty of cash left over to finance rapid growth. USAA is now the largest private employer in San Antonio and the fourth largest company of any type that does business entirely by telephone and mail.

Luxury Cars

MBNA and USAA demonstrate that customer and channel selection are powerful economic drivers in financial services. These strategies are no less powerful in other industries. Take automobiles. Every maker wants its customers to buy the same brand again, but in practice most automakers live with repurchase rates that run from 30 to 40 percent. Lexus is setting new standards in customer loyalty with repurchase rates averaging 63 percent for the 1993 and 1994 model years. The contrast between Lexus and Infiniti is particularly interesting, since both were recently created from the ground up to serve the luxury car market, have established brand-new dealer networks, and have achieved superior repurchase rates. Yet at 42 percent, Infiniti's repurchase rate for the same period is 21 percentage points below Lexus's. Why?

The answer lies in the power of using the loyalty coefficient in customer selection. Assiduously applied, it can produce what is very nearly a different concept of competition. Infiniti's parent, Nissan, heard about Toyota's Lexus program more than a year after its inception and set its sights on beating Toyota to the punch. Though both cars were aimed at the upscale market, Infiniti decided to focus on fashion and high performance rather than on classic good looks and lasting value. Using all its formidable design and time-to-market skills, Nissan produced a car with a fresh, affluent look and stunning performance characteristics and managed to bring it onto the market almost simultaneously with Lexus.

Whereas Infiniti was after the people who drove BMWs and Jaguars, however, Lexus designed its product to appeal to Mercedes and Cadillac owners, who were older, less interested in fashion and high performance, and more attracted to service, reliability, and long-term value. One key reason that Lexus chose this market was that Mercedes and Cadillac drivers were historically the most loyal customers in the industry. Switching them from their current brands might be a formidable task, but if Lexus succeeded, it would build a solid foundation for a loyalty-based business. Furthermore, Lexus believed that Mercedes and Cadillac had opened the door to customer defection by failing to reinvest the spoils of loyalty to create ever-increasing levels of customer value.

Both Lexus and Infiniti succeeded in delivering superior value and in capturing significant numbers of their target customers. Yet Infiniti's success may prove less durable, because its customer base is so full of young buyers looking for trendy styling and hot performance—two dimensions that are hard to stay on top of. Lexus's 21-point repurchase advantage, won in part by targeting customers with a superior loyalty coefficient, is enormous.

Tractors

A parallel but complementary example involves a much less glamorous product, tractors. Again, one company has achieved a really stunning level of loyalty, partly by means of a cautious and unusually intelligent distribution policy. The Lexus story is impressive, but that company is still young and not yet a market leader. Deere & Company, established in 1837, has been selling tractors since 1918, and its venerable success has stood not only the test of time but also the test of cutthroat competition. During the worldwide farm recession in the 1980s, tractor makers in Europe and Japan fought an intense battle for market share—a battle that bankrupted International Harvester, among others. John Deere not only survived but continues to lead the industry, thanks in part to remarkable manufacturing and design improvements and in part to an understanding of the way distribution channels can leverage loyalty.

Perhaps the stiffest competition has come at the smallest end of the product line, consumer-oriented lawn-and-garden tractors sold through lawnmower dealers and garden centers. While Deere has consistently designed and built its tractors for a quality-conscious customer, the company does not control its customer acquisition. Its products are sold by independent dealers who carry competing brands like Toro, Cub Cadet, and Kubota.

As the competition hardened, many manufacturers responded by signing up as many dealers as possible, to maximize market access. Even Deere found itself sliding in that direction when growth became a challenge in the 1980s. But Deere discovered that although willy-nilly dealer accumulation may bring more customers, it doesn't bring the right kind of customer—those who value reliability and service first and foremost. Deere examined the economics of its distribution strategy and came to the conclusion that the company and its core customers were better off choosing dealers who could afford to provide first-class service and support—and who were likely to survive. Repurchase cycles for Deere products are very long, since they're so well made; when the customer is finally ready for a replacement, the dealer should still be in business. When Deere factored in the costs of second-rate dealers—credit, increased logistical complexity, lower customer loyalty—it found that the economics of marginal dealers and their often marginal customers simply didn't make sense. A strategy of targeting the right customers by acquiring and supporting the right dealers has allowed Deere to earn lawn-tractor repurchase loyalty of 77 percent—a prodigious achievement for a product that typically lasts eleven years!

To a company like John Deere, however, eleven years is a blink of the eye compared to the time span it has set its sights on. Deere pays little attention to annual retention rates; it wants *generations* of a family to buy its tractors. Delivering great value over generations requires more than a superior dealer network; it requires an entire business philosophy. Consider the way Deere manages spare parts. Most manufacturers see parts—especially for old equipment—as an opportunity for exceptional profit margins. Customers have so little choice in repairing old machinery that manufacturers usually price at many multiples of cost. Deere takes a very different approach: it makes parts available for decades, and sets margins for all parts at about the same level. From a profit-centered prespective, this may seem irrational—almost as irrational as paying homeowners more than their policies require so they can rebuild their houses to last.

Should All Manufacturers Worry about Loyalty?

Some businesses may be entirely insulated from the frictional costs of disloyal customers. In such cases, selective customer filtering makes no sense at all. But few businesses are *fully* insulated, and some are probably much less insulated than they think they are. Take home appliance manufacturers like General Electric, Whirlpool, and Maytag. Historically, their competitive strategy has been to gain as much market share as possible in order to realize economies of scale, and to sell through independent retailers, most of whom carry all the major brands. On the surface, these two strategies are not so different from the John Deere approach, but there are differences below the surface that produce profoundly different results. Unlike Deere, the appliance manufacturers have done their utmost to get all their products into as many outlets as possible, and to persuade retailers to stock up on inventory so they'll have an incentive to push the brand. (If the concept of an unprofitable customer exists in this industry, it can only be at the retail level, since high fixed manufacturing costs make every incremental sale look good to the manufacturer.)

Of course, the manufacturers' effort to load the system with additional sales outlets and inventory squeezes retail margins. That makes it harder for high-service retailers to compete, since the low-price superstores carry the identical brands. Apparently manufacturers see this as a good thing, however, since lower retail margins mean lower consumer prices, which usually lead to increased unit demand.

The opposite perspective—what we might call the John Deere perspective—is that when retailers suffer, so do manufacturers, at least indirectly. Lower margins for retailers lead to poor sales support and service. Products become commodities; retailers push only the brands that happen to be running price promotions at the moment (which further encourages consumers to look primarily at price). And having every brand in every retail outlet increases everyone's logistical costs. Value diminishes for *all* participants in the system.

For manufacturers in particular, the result is an abysmal repurchase rate (averaging 40 percent in washing machines, for example) and frustration that profit margins are so much lower than those of other branded consumer products. What the manufacturers should probably ask themselves is whether it isn't time to adopt a more selective outlet strategy, like the one John Deere pursues with such success. To evaluate this alternative and others—to know what it might be worth to improve retention rates to 77 percent—they will need to think creatively about loyalty economics and apply the paradigms in Chapter 2 to their own situations.

CAVEAT MERCATOR

So far, we've been talking about strategies to attract the right customers. But sometimes it's even more important to concentrate on filtering out the wrong ones. The principle of *caveat emptor,* or buyer beware, has been with us at least since Roman times. For most businesses today, however, the more relevant principle might be *caveat mercator*—seller beware. Buyers have become pretty good at minding their own interests. Of course, they run some risk every time they make a purchase, but on the whole they learn from their mistakes, and when they get bad value, they rarely come back for seconds. The *emptor*'s brain stops his hand from reaching for the wallet one more time.

Businesses, on the other hand—especially big businesses—can be very sloppy about deciding which customers to seek out and acquire. The mind, hand, and wallet of the *mercator* are not always tied together in a single closed loop. As a result, the brain often fails to learn any lesson from the customers who defected before their net present value climbed out of the minus column. Sometimes the fault lies with an organizational structure that isolates the sales department from the knowledge of good and evil—that is to say, the knowledge of which customers turn into profitable annuities and which don't.

It is simply not possible to build or maintain a healthy business without learning how to get the right customers. In many businesses, the customers most likely to sign on are precisely the worst customers you could possibly find. We call this phenomenon adverse selection. We know it best from the insurance industry, partly because it is so damaging to profits and partly because insurance companies have accounting practices that measure and make it visible. Insurers have developed a rigorous discipline called actuarial science to deal with the probable lifecycle patterns of cash-flow to and from pools of customers. Actuaries must know their customers' defection patterns because they must build them into the economic models they use to set prices. Decades of tracking policy lifecycles have given them a deep appreciation of the unhappy consequences of adverse selection.

Adverse selection takes place because customers have a natural tendency to seek out the best deals they can find, whereas the insurer who offers the best deal is evaluating risk and setting prices on the basis of averages—that is, making the rosiest possible assumptions about the true risks and costs of serving a particular customer. Let's look at an example. Consider a pool of one thousand customers who appear to belong to a similar risk class. An insurer can accurately estimate the true losses the thousand customers will incur over the next year, then set a reasonable price to cover those expected losses. Unfortunately, once the price is set, the customer is free to accept the offer or to pick another insurance company. Those among the thousand who are slightly better-than-average risks will tend to get better offers elsewhere, and will probably take them. So the customers who accept the company's offer will tend to be worse-than-average risks. Since customers know their own situations better than the company can (you know whether or not you often park your car in a high-crime neighborhood; the company is only guessing), and since they will have a range of price offers, they will tend to select the company that is making the worst guess. Incoming classes of customers almost always have bigger losses than underwriters estimate.

Creative Filtering

Insurers have developed ingenious methods to minimize adverse selection. For example, Amica Mutual—a small company based in Rhode Island that perennially wins top service-quality awards—accepts new customers on the basis of referrals from current customers. In other words, Amica uses its own high-quality customer base to filter out poor risks and keep its losses low. To keep the spiral functioning, it then passes on excellent value to the people it insures.

Progressive Insurance, based in a suburb of Cleveland and specializing in higher-risk niches like motorcycle insurance, has found that not all motorcycle drivers are bad risks. Since young people are bad on average, however, Progressive's pricing is less than competitive for young drivers. On the other hand, it actively solicits the business of certain older motorcycle drivers by targeting direct-mail offerings to those with lifestyle profiles that suggest they are better-than-average risks. Progressive also discovered that many of the worst drivers tend to walk into agency offices off the street. Apparently, they shop as impulsively as they drive. To avoid these customers, the company encourages agents to locate their offices in out-of-the-way office buildings, never in retail locations with high traffic.

One auto insurer found that its worst new risks, as well as its least loyal customers, very often found the company's agents through advertisements in the *Yellow Pages*. Needless to say, the company now discourages its agents from placing such ads. Another company discovered that recent arrivals in any town were likely to have higher-than-average risk levels, as well as high rates of defection. When the company began to compensate agents partly on the basis of overall customer profitability, the agents began to avoid newcomers. One potential customer tells the story of walking into an agent's office and having the receptionist ask him how long he'd lived in the town. When he told her he'd flown in the day before, she explained that the agent was very busy, and it would be another week before she could squeeze in an appointment. Meanwhile, through a partially opened door, he could see the agent sitting alone in his office.

Was this a case of prejudice? In a way, yes, but not on the usual grounds. The man was a white Anglo-Saxon with an excellent job. His only failing was newness. In practice, screening out low-loyalty customers rarely has anything in common with the red-lining and discrimination that occur in some industries. It is not a matter of rich versus poor. Loyal and disloyal segments exist across the whole spectrum of incomes, professions, and social backgrounds. One bank was surprised to learn that the wealthy, high-balance customers it had always coveted were in fact less loyal and much less profitable than it had believed. Wealthy customers were sophisticated defectors. They took greatest advantage of average pricing, were likely to prepay mortgages at just the worst times, and made maximum use of the implicit free options that most fixed-rate lending and deposit products offer. Which customers do you think renegotiated their certificates of deposit most aggressively when rates leapt up in the 1980s?

The idea that one key to success is *avoiding* certain groups of customers will strike some businesspeople as counterintuitive or downright preposterous. But look again at MBNA. By selling primarily through selected affinity groups, MBNA not only gets a richer mix of the best customers;

it has far fewer bad customers trying to crash the gates. Credit card companies that do mass mailings or place boxes of applications beside cash registers at Kmart write off a lot more bad debt and lose a lot more customers prematurely. Any business that makes a significant investment in customer acquisition makes an implicit assumption about how long the average customer will stay and about the period required for the company to break even and then earn an adequate return on its investment. The MBNA approach tends to weed out bad risk and bad loyalty at just the right moment—before either one gets through the door.

Courting Disloyal Customers

Mortgage companies provide another good example of adverse selection at work. Credit risk on a mortgage is minimal. For one thing, the loan is secured by a lien on the property, and for another, most loans are underwritten according to standards set by Fannie Mae or some other government agency, which then insures the loan. But mortgage lenders can still lose their shirts. Sales commissions, underwriting costs, and other up-front expenses often make loan origination a losing proposition for the lenders, who need several years to break even and start earning a fair return on their investment. The investors who fund mortgage loans, and the processing companies that buy servicing rights, are betting that no more than a small percentage of borrowers will pay off their loans quickly (mostly by selling the property or refinancing it). If the bettors guess wrong, they can take a beating. Bad loans, disloyalty, and prepayment all run rampant in the mortgage business. Instead of learning from these mistakes, however, the industry seems to seek out new ways of injuring itself, using adverse selection as the weapon.

For example, the industry relied on historic prepayment patterns as the basis for its recent experiment with mortgage products free of points and closing costs. The tradeoff was that the interest rates on these mortgages were slightly above market—an arrangement that could create value for borrowers, because interest is immediately tax deductible whereas points and closing costs are not. And the lender was no worse off provided that the life of the loan met expectations, allowing the higher interest rate to compensate for the higher cost of originating the loan. The trouble was, the customers who jumped at this bait were precisely the ones most likely to refinance their properties the moment rates came down. Or they were people who knew they were going to move or sell next year. Though the new mortgages needed extra-long payoff periods to be profitable, the loan provisions actually *encouraged* prepayment by making the whole transaction cost-free to the customer.

As if this weren't enough, several additional factors now shifted adverse selection into a higher gear. To begin with, brokers and salespeople were (as usual) getting commissions completely unrelated to the long-term economics of the loans. Premature payment of a mortgage didn't hurt the brokers. On the contrary, they earned a *second* commission when they brokered a refinance. On top of that, interest rates in general continued to drop. When the lenders introduced the program, mortgages were at 7 percent. Then they dropped to 6.5 percent. Some brokers advised clients with applications already in process to go ahead and close their loans at the higher rate—which after all cost them nothing but an hour at the closing table—and then to turn around and lock in a new application with another lender, at 6.5 percent. In addition, the brokers advised their clients to pay application fees and closing costs on the *second* loan in order to get slightly lower interest rates. The second set of closing costs was low anyway, of course, because so much of the spadework—appraisals, credit checks, verifications—had been done by the first company, were still valid, and cost nothing to reuse. Mortgage brokers became experts at helping their customers find the best possible deals, which meant that mortgage companies that worked through independent brokers were subjected to the adverse selection of *professionals*—as if amateurs, in the form of customers acting alone, had been too modest a challenge.

This was adverse selection doubled and redoubled. Prepayments reached disastrous levels—in many cases, the first monthly bill for mortgage number one had not yet arrived when the closing took place for mortgage number two—and mortgage companies found themselves eating enormous sums in unrecoverable origination costs. Quickly, they modified or withdrew the new point-free, cost-free mortgages.

Commissions Versus Loyalty

Adverse selection at this lunatic level can occur whenever premature customer defections are allowed to have no effect on salesforce compensation. There is always tension between commission sales and customer loyalty, because a salesforce paid on commission and hell-bent on customer volume generally finds that the easiest prospects to sell are the ones whose loyalty is low. By definition, customers with a high loyalty coefficient are hard to switch away from their current suppliers.

State Farm clears this hurdle by paying equal property/casualty commissions for new and renewing customers, thereby aligning the interests of the company and its agents. But most companies pay salespeople for conquests, not continuity. Even if a company does compensate the salesforce for repeat business, most salespeople aren't planning to hang around long enough to reap the benefits.

Cellular phone companies and paging services are classic examples of the inherent tension between commissions and loyalty. Pager salespeople work on commission, so signing up more and more new customers has always been the route to higher income. As time has passed, however, it has gotten harder and harder to find doctors and contractors who don't already have beepers on their belts. So salesforces began looking elsewhere. Their greatest discovery was lawn services and landscapers. These were ideal customers. They cancelled the service every fall and started fresh every spring, so the salesperson was getting one commission per customer *per year.* A much superior arrangement—except for the phone companies, which subsidize the equipment price in expectation of a long string of fat monthly bills.

The result has been that many companies no longer pay sales commissions on new accounts that last less than 12 months. Not surprisingly, their salespeople are spending much less time pursuing seasonal contractors. Some companies have begun tracking retention rates by salesperson, and the best now compensate on that basis. Giving salespeople an incentive to find customers with high inherent loyalty and to screen out those most likely to defect can produce remarkable results, even without precise guidelines on how to tell the difference. This is especially important for companies that sell equipment—such as copiers, telephone switchboards, even electrical generators—at very low margins, in expectation of an ongoing stream of service, parts, and upgrades.

The salespeople who signed up MBNA's affinity groups in the early years worked for an outside contractor, but MBNA's agreement with this independent salesforce succeeded nevertheless in aligning their interests with the company's. The bargain was simple. The contractor paid all salesforce expenses and did all solicitation mailings. In exchange, MBNA paid the contractor an ongoing share of the profits each affinity group generated. This arrangement gave the salesforce the proper incentive, not just to find groups that were easy to sell, but to sell groups that would produce a steady stream of profitable customer annuities. The members of this salesforce developed a sophisticated understanding of loyalty coefficients and lifecycle profit patterns across the universe of affinity groups, and they made a great deal of money for themselves and MBNA. The final proof of their success is MBNA's superior retention rates, which show clearly that their customers are as pleased as everyone else in this business system.

Coupons and Price Promotion

Adverse selection takes myriad forms, and surprisingly many require and get the active complicity of the company that suffers the consequences. For example, if you or your business decided to do just the opposite of MBNA—that is, to scour the marketplace for the worst imaginable customers with the lowest possible coefficients of loyalty— you could hardly do better than to choose price discounts or mass distributions of coupons. Near the beginning of this chapter we talked about friction, loyalty, and the relative difficulty of moving a customer from one supplier to another. One of our points was that the customers who glide into your arms for a minimal price discount are the same customers who dance away with someone else at the slightest enticement.

Coupons and price discounts find these customers like heat-seeking missiles. Why would you *want* customers who will renounce their loyalties to save a dime, or even a dollar? Traditionally, retailers have gone to a lot of trouble and expense to attract such people, with results that are largely negative, or at the very least, neutral. But even retailers are now trying other strategies—everyday low pricing, for example. In addition, some retailers and consumer product companies have begun using coupons in a new way. Instead of distributing them *en masse* to bring hundreds or thousands of new and probably disloyal customers into the store, these businesses are directing coupons to existing customers in order to broaden their purchases. Staples, the office-supply supermarket chain, has developed a unique system of its own. This startup invested $5 million of expensive money—venture capital, which carries interest rates as high as 35 percent—to convert information entered at the cash register into a database for tracking customer purchase patterns over time. The store can then issue special coupons to customers who are buying in lower volume or variety than other customers like them. For example, if Staples knows that the average real estate brokerage uses a hundred sheets of copy paper for each ruled pad, it's easy to spot the customer who's buying copy paper somewhere else. Instead of printing a coupon in a newspaper ad and eating a discount on every sale, Staples sends a coupon to a few carefully chosen customers—the ones who seem to need it.

In most businesses other than retailing, the costs of acquiring a customer, setting up an account, and checking credit are so high that the economics just won't work unless the customer stays loyal. Yet coupons and price discounts generally have the opposite effect. They foster adverse selection, do little or nothing to inspire loyalty in new customers, and actually discourage it in old ones.

Take the example of premium-rate certificates of deposit. When banks think institutional interest rates are too high, they sometimes decide they can raise money more cheaply by selling CDs at a bonus rate. To attract new customers, they run promotions offering interest rates a quarter to half a percentage point above the going local rate—though still below what they'd have to pay in the debt markets. The trouble is, this hot money rarely lingers beyond the rollover date, partly because the banks pull back on CD pricing as soon as institutional rates improve. Bank officers who think this makes economic sense are usually ignoring the havoc it wreaks as branch employees spend hours opening and closing accounts for low-margin strangers instead of seeing to the needs of loyal customers. And this is not the only cost of on-again, off-again pricing that the banks overlook. They also disregard the fact that attracting hot money will heat up the rest of their customers, too. They are training customers to shop for price while teaching them they cannot trust the bank to deliver consistent value.

Or consider the case of an industrial printing firm that used pricing to generate volume whenever sales fell below bonus threshholds toward the end of a fiscal year. Salespeople were encouraged to offer discounts at such times—but only to new customers, on the theory that discounts to established customers might compromise pricing levels for the year ahead. Of course the old customers resented the practice, and found that service and quality tended to deteriorate at year-end as overworked press operators struggled with unfamiliar job requirements. Needless to add, the new cut-rate customers rarely came back with repeat business unless they were offered the same destructive discounts once again.

Some industries—fast food, for example—have always used price coupons to get new customers to try their products, and to get old customers to come back more often. Chick-fil-A had qualms about the practice, and decided to study the behavior of coupon customers in detail. It discovered that customers who come in with coupons generally spend less, are less likely to give the store repeat business, and are very likely to use coupons during peak traffic hours, when handling coupons slows the lines. The company also discovered that loyal customers who do not have coupons feel short-changed, and that frequent price promotions tend to convince them that your product is not worth its normal price. As a result of its analysis, Chick-fil-A took the unusual—and in its industry, courageous—step of virtually eliminating coupons. It now uses them primarily to introduce new products or packages.

To my knowledge, the only company that has used price promotion to generate new business *and* minimize adverse selection is MCI. Its Friends & Family program offers customers discounts on calls they make to specific telephone numbers, provided the entire group signs up with MCI. If a group of six relatives includes one who is specially concerned about price, he or she may talk the other five into joining. Those five may be less price-sensitive, but they switch to MCI out of loyalty to cousin Harry—which makes them exactly the customers MCI is after; people whose group loyalty multiplies their inherent individual loyalty. Once they're on board at MCI, it becomes very difficult to pry any one of them loose, and capturing the entire group probably takes a discount deeper than even AT&T or Sprint can readily afford. So far, this brilliant program has brought 10 million new customers to MCI, and their defection rates are well below the MCI average for new customers.

GROWTH AND DISLOYALTY

There are dozens of ways for companies to undermine their own future health and welfare by embracing some form of adverse selection. For example, the need for growth can cause companies that have captured the best of their natural customer base to recruit more and more of the less desirable customers who remain. But it's a poor bargain. As customer quality declines, so does the firm's ability to deliver value; which in turn discourages good customers, stifles growth, demotivates employees, weakens the process of value creation, and encourages the salesforce to chase customers who are even less likely to be profitable and steady. In short, the entire spiral turns upside down and drills the company into a hole.

Commercial banks are often good examples of self-inflicted adverse selection. We have found case after case where many new branch customers are actually destroying value for the rest of the business. In one of the largest branch systems in the country, 25 percent of new customers were staying less than 18 months, the breakeven point at which the bank earns back the initial cost of setting up an account. Here, the culprit was the practice of pushing growth with sales commissions instead of *earning* growth by delivering excellent value to the customer. This particular bank had a new-account bonus program for branch managers, and oddly, the branches that earned the biggest bonuses also seemed to have the lowest customer retention rates. On looking closer, management discovered that many big-bonus, high-churn branches were located near colleges or universities, and that to earn the incentive pay for signing up new customers, managers were closing student accounts at the end of every school year and opening new ones in the fall.

When they push growth too hard, bankers run into similar problems in commercial lending. Loan officers whose performance is evaluated on the basis of volume do book more loans. But no matter how hard the credit committee tries to screen out bad risks, adverse selection always rears its head in the form of a surge in loan-loss ratios two or three years later. We've seen banks where new-customer loans account for 30 percent of loan balances—and 70 percent of bad debts.

Insurers are considerably more adept than bankers at managing adverse selection, but despite their cadres of actuaries, even they can make mistakes. One large company held a sales promotion every fall and awarded luxury cruises to the winning salespeople. These competitions were very popular with agents and invariably produced a surge in volume. But when the company took a closer look at its fall customers, it found defection patterns far worse than for any other season of the year. In fact, defections were so high they turned the economics of the fall promotions negative. To cover costs, the company needed to keep an average customer six years; the average promotion customer lasted four and a half.

How can an insurance company get tripped up this way? In this case, the culprit was averages. Now, insurance actuaries know that averages are perilous. A good example of actuary humor is the one about the guy who drowns in a river only two feet deep—on average. Insurers also have a better grasp of customer lifecycle economics than any other industry, and they've learned to view the world through the lens of loyalty. What they haven't done is to turn up the magnification enough to see distinct customer segments distinctly. Or to put that another way, the averages they work with are too broad. Actuaries recognize that policy lapse patterns vary with a customer's age, but they ignore most of the other variables that can drive differences in attrition. For all their insights and their jokes, broad averages are precisely what they use.

Take, for example, the current practice of pricing insurance policies for teachers. Actuaries use actual historic data to estimate the particular lifecycle revenues and cost patterns for teachers, but when it comes to duration, the industry presumes that teachers will defect at the same rate as all other customers. In reality, teachers are far more loyal than the other customers, so their average tenure is much higher. Because the industry fails to calculate specific averages for teachers as a group, it tends to undervalue them. Rigorous analysis of the kind we described in Chapter 2 will show that teachers are worth three to four times as much as an average customer. This kind of discrepancy gives an enormous competitive edge to companies that understand the significance of loyalty coefficients.

If the insurance business still holds unrecognized segments as rich as this one, it's a good bet that even better opportunities lie hidden in the industries that have not yet begun to track loyalty coefficients. Yet it's hard to concentrate on customer quality when gaining quantity is so much easier. Look at the cellular phone business. Everyone in the industry measures retention because they know it's vital to growth and profits, yet the industry continues to live with annual defection rates as high as 40 percent! The cellular companies have made a massive investment in network; now all they can think of is growth. And as long as customers are plentiful, why resist the lure of new sales? Besides, marketers know how to do promotions. They're much less familiar with the tools of loyalty-based management.

LOYALTY IN MONOPOLIES

We see the same phenomenon in cable television. Targeted customer selection seems ludicrous in a monopoly. These companies have invested a lot of cash in licenses and wiring; surely now the point is to generate free cash flow with promotions and discounts, raising prices as swiftly as the laws allow. Yet the fact is monopolies don't last. Cable companies will soon face competition from new players and technologies, and today's unfocused, opportunistic growth strategies do nothing to produce a strong franchise of loyal customers, impressed by the level of value they're receiving. Moreover, regulators are beginning to step back in and cut industry returns.

To see the effects of loyalty-based management on a business like pay television, take the case of Canal Plus, a French firm that has grown to become the world's leading pay-TV company, with $1.9 billion in sales and profits of $125 million in 1994. Customer retention at Canal Plus runs at 97 percent, compared to an average of 80 percent for French cable TV. (Another comparison: HBO in the United States has customer retention rates below 50 percent.) The company now serves six million subscribers in France, Spain, and Germany and has grown at a rate of 30 percent per year. There are two keys to its success. First, Canal Plus understands its customers in depth and offers each core segment a unique value proposition. Second, the company offers superior customer service by building a loyal base of employees (turnover is less than 5 percent). Cable companies that earn these kinds of statistics will find the post-deregulation world a much more prosperous place than cable companies that don't.

In telephone long-distance, the monopoly vanished more than ten years ago. MCI and Sprint have cherry-picked AT&T's customer base, and prices have dropped 35 percent. Luckily, customer usage has increased more than enough to keep cash flows healthy. But all three of these companies—and a dozen others—have learned that customer loyalty can make the difference between success and extinction.

The local side of the telephone business has its trials still ahead of it, and they are likely to be severe. Sometime very soon, technology and deregulation together are going to bring local service monopolies under sustained attack. In hopes of thwarting new competitors, who will try to skim off the best of the customer base, local companies with their wits about them are hard at work analyzing the loyalty coefficients and lifecycle profit patterns of their various customer segments. Prices will probably drop the way they have in long-distance markets, but it is much less likely that local usage will increase to offset the decline. So the cash flows that support the regional operating companies are very much at risk.

The most forward-thinking local phone companies are taking action before the crisis hits. By segmenting their customers, they have discovered that the most valuable 10 percent are worth ten times as much as the least valuable 10 percent. Using feedback from these best customers, they are designing special programs to attract and hold onto them. For example, small businesses are always eager to retain their old phone numbers when they move to new locations. It makes it easier for customers to stay in touch, and prolongs the usefulness of old advertising and promotional material. To earn the ongoing loyalty of this very attractive segment, one local phone company is developing the capacity to offer the same phone number regardless of a company's location. Another local phone company is working to provide its best customers with a full range of value-added services, such as call forwarding, cellular, long distance, and charge card, all combined on one billing statement. This company believes that the key to success in a deregulated future is to earn the loyalty of its best customers. It knows that the time to start building such a capability is now, before the full force of deregulation hits.

Electrical utilities are about to enter a similar free-for-all as their markets are deregulated. This is already happening in the commercial markets, where large customers are building their own generation facilities and wholesalers are offering an array of low-cost packages. Utilities that cannot earn the loyalty of their target customers (or even figure out who their target customers ought to be) will be left in the dust. The fact is, all the monopolies now facing deregulation will have to learn the basics of loyalty-based management. Unless they do, new entrants smart enough to focus superior value propositions on the most attractive customer segments will drive them out of existence.

THE PERILS OF MATURITY

One final but sometimes subtle danger for maturing companies is simply the fact that times have changed. As markets mature, margins and real prices decline. This rule applies in almost every industry, and one result is that customer-acquisition investments that may have made sense in the old days make no sense whatsoever now. In the credit card business, a customer segment with 75-percent retention (and a roughly four-year average life span) was a good investment in 1982. Of course, 90 percent would have been better still, but even so, the 75-percent segments earned more than the usual 15-percent hurdle rate. So bringing them aboard in droves was a fine idea, provided they did not constrain the company's ability to recruit high-loyalty customers as well.

Those days are gone. At current margins, segments with 75-percent retention are no longer good investments. It's true that most credit card companies still don't *realize* that they're investing in customers with a negative net present value, but they are seeing their profit margins erode. What is worse, they are now trapped between a rock and two hard places. To begin with, virtually every creditworthy individual in the nation has five or six credit cards already. And second, stock market analysts want to see more and more new cards issued to support the somewhat exaggerated price-earnings ratios a lot of these "growth" companies possess.

In the third place, these credit card companies are competing with companies like MBNA. They are discovering that the best customer segments are no longer available; the customers they're forced to bring on board generate inferior cash flows and initiate the kind of downward spiral described earlier: smaller margins, higher prices, growing defections, increased costs, accelerating cutbacks and layoffs, lower efficiency, poorer service, still greater churn, still lower profits. It's a spiral that is hard to break out of.

Every maturing company facing slower growth and greater competition needs to learn these lessons. Beware the customer-acquisition strategies that seemed to make sense yesterday. Pay close attention to the value of incoming customers in a marketplace where the best and most loyal are already spoken for. Take a very close look at the net present value of the new customers you're bringing in to replace the old, or to grow. Beware of quantity for its own sake; winning more and more new customers may put you slowly out of business. Across the business spectrum, companies that expect to achieve sustainable high performance must begin studying lifecycle profit and tenure patterns, then use their insights to focus their customer investments.

The strategic advantage now enjoyed by companies like Northwestern Mutual, State Farm, MBNA, and John Deere shows why acquiring the right customers is so critical. As capital ratios decline, their competitors, gasping for breath, trade leftover customers back and forth in the increasingly vain and frantic hope of maintaining growth in a mature market. If companies are to prosper into old age, they must build a foundation of loyal customers. This is true even in newer industries—perhaps especially in newer industries—where many competitors can earn respectable profits for a time, but where sooner or later, there won't be enough good customers to go around. The smart competitors will find ways to get the best ones early. And the smartest of the smart will then shift their growth strategies away from new-customer acquisition and toward building and broadening their relationships with the good customers they've already won.

As industries mature, an initial advantage in customer inventory can give a company a permanent edge. The key to achieving that kind of advantage is to design a customer acquisition strategy that searches out the three customer characteristics described at the beginning of this chapter: inherent loyalty, profitability, and fit. Lock up the customers at the top of those three lists, and you'll have gone far toward securing your company's maturity and old age. Sustainable loyalty-based systems have a lot of moving parts. The first step in getting all of them moving smoothly and efficiently together is to fuel them with high-test customers.

Still, getting the right customers is only the critical first step. Once you have them, and the cash-flow surplus they can provide, you have to reinvest part of that cash in delivering the kind of value that will earn their continued loyalty. So the next step in this virtuous cycle is to use the superior cash flow from superior customers to hire and retain superior employees.

4

The Right Employees

GETTING THE right customers is a critical step in building a loyalty-based business system, but it is only the first critical step. Once a company has loyal customers and the cash-flow surplus they provide, it needs to reinvest a solid share of that cash in hiring and retaining superior employees. If you wonder what getting and keeping the right employees has to do with getting and keeping the right customers, the answer is everything. Employees who are not loyal are unlikely to build an inventory of customers who are.

There are some very practical reasons why this is true. For one thing, it takes time to build solid personal relationships with customers. For another, loyal employees have greater opportunities to learn and to increase their efficiency. For a third, the money these employees save their employers in reduced recruiting and training costs can be invested somewhere else—for example, in measures that will increase customer satisfaction. Finally, the same business philosophy and operational policies that earn employees' loyalty and boost their morale are likely to work for customers. In this chapter and the next, we will see examples of these effects (and others). We will look at loyalty leaders in industries as varied as advertising and fast food to see how the best companies build employee loyalty and use it to improve customer retention.

DESTROYING EMPLOYEE LOYALTY

Most managers would *prefer* to have loyal employees—just as they would prefer to have loyal customers—but few are willing to spend the money and make the effort to earn that loyalty. On the contrary, a lot of companies today pursue policies that discourage or even destroy employee loyalty. Many observers have begun to wonder if we're not witnessing the death of corporate loyalty altogether. Cynics will tell you it never existed anyway; but as Oscar Wilde observed, a cynic is a person "who knows the price of everything and the value of nothing." Knowing what your employees cost but not what they're worth is worse than deeply cynical; it is deeply countercompetitive. Peter Drucker puts it this way:

> *All organizations now say routinely, "People are our greatest asset." Yet few practice what they preach, let alone truly believe it. Most still believe, though perhaps not consciously, what nineteenth-century employers believed: people need us more than we need them. But, in fact, organizations have to market membership as much as they market products and services—and perhaps more. They have to attract people, hold people, recognize and reward people, motivate people, and serve and satisfy people.*[1]

The managers of loyalty-based companies have internalized that last sentence. Once they have built the foundation for a cash-flow surplus by acquiring a base of loyal customers, their first investment priority is to allocate some of that surplus to recruit and retain the best possible employees. And the best employees, like the best customers, are those who get swept up in a kind of value-and-loyalty spiral. Specifically, the best employees are those with the talent and motivation to raise their own productivity (and consequently their own incomes) swiftly enough to fuel their motivation further still, producing even greater improvements in service and productivity and therefore a growing surplus of value for company and customers.

Yet the general trend in business today doesn't seem to involve a search for ways to keep employees longer and help them earn more money. It often seems the goal is quite the opposite: finding ways to pay employees less, or actually get rid of them, especially those with the greatest experience and the highest compensation. Not a day goes by without some newspaper story about new early-retirement schemes and fresh layoffs.

The victims of these layoffs can have a tough time regaining their balance. They also carry away an important lesson: never, ever to give that kind of blind dedication and loyalty to any company again. But the survivors have a tough time as well. *The Wall Street Journal* reports that most Fortune 500 corporations are suffering the effects of what's called the layoff survivor syndrome, in which mistrust and anxiety replace feelings of loyalty and security. Survivors have to cope not only with their natural anxiety about future rounds of cuts, they also have to take on the added workload of those who were laid off. And for this increased workload, they see little in the way of increased compensation. Across the United States, the median weekly income of full-time workers, adjusted for inflation, has not risen since the late 1970s.

The view that loyalty is a thing of the past is gaining ground, even among noncynics. More and more, the conventional wisdom is that employees must take full responsibility for their own careers and that the key to success is watching out for number one. The *Boston Globe* ran a series of articles on the subject, titled "Broken Promises: Work in the 90s," which concluded that the workplace is composed of

> *employees who are scared and bitter, working increasingly for only one thing—a paycheck. More and more, says Audrey Freedman, an economist and president of Manpower Plus in New York, the relationship between workers and employers is exploitative on both sides. "Employees are saying, 'All right, you use me, I'll use you.'"*[2]

Some executives are concluding that the corporations of the future—in the postcapitalist society—will need to be more like nomadic tribes, pitching their tents anywhere on a moment's notice, and less like plodding agriculturalists, rooted to one place and one core competence. This may seem a reasonable response to the increasing disorder and confusion of the business world. And the picture it paints of dynamic flexibility and adventurous energy may be very attractive. But consider how little progress nomadic tribes have made compared to the great civilizations with their enduring institutions, their sciences and cities, their ability to cope with change from a stable base.

A lot of academics seem attracted to a dog-eat-dog philosophy, perhaps because of their own experiences on the road to tenure. (Teamwork and loyalty aren't exactly hallmarks of most university departments.) Some academic futurists insist that the workforce of the future will move to the opposite extreme from Robert White's Organization Man. No one will have a career path within one company. Flexibility will matter more than loyalty. Employees will jump from one assignment to the next independent of corporate bonds.

Many of today's best and brightest seem to have taken this professorial advice to heart. On average, Harvard MBAs change employers three to four times in their first ten years out of school. Some executive recruiters advise that a change of job every three to four years is an absolute necessity for the kind of resume that will appeal to a modern corporation. Long, uninterrupted stints with a single company signal narrow experience and lack of ambition.

Under these circumstances, it probably makes sense for employees at every level to spend a part of each workday figuring out how to maximize their own careers, searching for safety nets or better opportunities elsewhere. At the current rate, after all, nearly everyone will be laid off at some point in the course of his or her career. But while some businesses have no choice—some have to lay people off or go under—many of today's layoffs are being taken by profitable companies.

Not so long ago, for example, the *New York Times* ran an article headlined "A Profitable Xerox Plans to Cut Staff by 10,000." Why was Xerox taking this step? The answer is predictable: "Despite being consistently profitable, the Xerox Corporation said yesterday that it would cut . . . nearly 10% of its work force, over the next three years to improve productivity. Xerox thus becomes the latest big company to try to improve the efficiency of its operations by dismissing large numbers of people."[3] There followed a long list of major companies that had announced staff cuts of more than 5 percent during the three months prior to the article: Philip Morris (8 percent), Woolworth (9 percent), Martin Marietta (12 percent), US West (14 percent), AT&T (15 percent), RJR Nabisco (9 percent), Eli Lilly (12 percent), Warner Lambert (16 percent), American Cyanamid (9 percent), USAir (5 percent), Computervision (40 percent), Upjohn (8 percent), Anheuser-Busch (10 percent), Chemical Waste (23 percent).

Now, what is this all about? Productivity always matters, but why does it suddenly matter so much more than it used to? One possibility is that the unsettling volume of recent CEO firings has forced top executives into making virile gestures in hopes of demonstrating their mettle and resolve. While most CEOs hate the idea of layoffs—they know perfectly well that no business leader ever achieved greatness by firing people—they feel trapped. The institutional investors who drive the stock market are showing less and less patience with mediocre earnings, and executives have to please those investors if they want to keep their jobs. Xerox's stock surged 7 percent on the day its layoffs were announced. This kind of news exhilarates short-term investors. But in its next Sunday Business section, the *Times* asked Xerox the important question: "In a company that prides itself on worker harmony, will those remaining stay loyal?"[4]

After all, a layoff rarely exhilarates employees. What it does do is stifle creativity, discourage risk-taking, and destroy loyalty. The fear that goes with a layoff soaks up energy and draws people's attention to their own safety and careers, away from the success of the enterprise. There is growing evidence that over the long term, firms that resort to frequent or massive layoffs significantly underperform the market.

The Economist reported recently on a study by the American Management Association which concluded that fewer than half of the firms that have downsized in the past five years have subsequently increased their profits, and that only a third have reported higher productivity. Another study, reported in *The Wall Street Journal*, found that downsizing companies outperform the S&P 500 only slightly during the six months following news of a restructuring, then lag badly, netting a negative 24 percent by the end of three years. This really should come as no surprise. Companies forced to jettison their human assets *should* be worth less—in the same way that a ship that jettisons part of its cargo will be worth less when it finally arrives in port.

In late 1993, John Case of *Inc.* magazine wrote an article for the *Boston Globe* called "The Question We All Wonder About: 'For Whom Do You Work?' " in which he concluded that

> *in today's new economy, we work for ourselves . . . because companies have taught us a lesson, which is we can no longer afford to work for them. . . . They can't even guarantee we'll have a job a year, or two years, or five years from now. Career moves used to be the province of the ambitious, the upwardly mobile. Now, anybody who isn't pondering his or her career options is living the life of an ostrich, head planted firmly in the sand. . . . As for loyalty—well, loyalty these days means not looking for your next job on company time. If I'm blindly loyal to an organization that won't be—can't be—loyal to me, then I'm a fool.*[5]

Loyalty is indeed a two-way street, and companies that dump people when earnings are down (much less when earnings are *up*) are sowing the seeds of their own failure. Every company falls on hard times now and then, and it's the loyal devotion of key employees that pulls most of them through. By showing people that the company won't stick by them in adversity, a firm can almost guarantee that the next time it's in trouble, its most talented employees will jump ship just when they're needed most.

PRICING EMPLOYEE LOYALTY

The reason managers underinvest in loyalty is probably that, like Oscar Wilde's cynics, they know its cost but not its value. Laying people off saves money; that seems clear. But the ongoing cash-flow consequences of diminished loyalty are not so obvious. Human resource departments have tried to quantify the price of employee turnover by tracking the costs of recruiting, training, even of the productivity lost when new and inexperienced workers replace older hands. More creative analysts have tried to add in the cost of the poorer service that results from employee turnover. But these numbers have failed to convince managers, because they aren't tied to accounting numbers or cash flows.

The true cash-flow consequences of employee turnover far exceed most managers' intuitive estimates. In fact, the turnover tax on corporate earnings, although invisible in most accounting systems, is larger than any state or federal tax. At one trucking company, one of our consulting teams carefully quantified the economic penalties of excessive employee churn and found that the client could increase profits 50 percent by cutting driver turnover in half. In a stock brokerage, we found that a ten percentage point improvement in broker retention (from 80 percent to 90 percent) would increase a broker's value by 155 percent! The economics of agent retention in the insurance business are similar. The key to quantifying the cash-flow consequences of employee turnover in all these industries is essentially the same: to recognize that employee retention is not only critical for cost efficiency but an important factor in revenue growth as well, because of its direct link to customer acquisition and retention.

The first hard evidence we saw of this linkage was in the auto service business. In the course of consulting work at one leading national chain, we discovered that the service outlets with the highest customer retention also had the best employee retention. We then surveyed competitors by type and found that local garages had the best employee retention, followed by regional chains, national chains, and auto dealers, in that order. Customer retention across these four classes of competitors followed exactly the same pattern.

When we interviewed customers to find why they were especially loyal to local garages, we found an interesting contradiction. On the one hand, people believed that mechanics at chain outlets and auto dealers had better training and more sophisticated equipment. On the other, they put more faith in the local mechanic's judgment and believed he'd give them better service. In a word, people simply felt more comfortable doing repeat business with the same individual, regardless of technical finesse. They stayed with the local mechanic because they knew him, and because he knew their cars. At the larger outlets, customers rarely saw the same mechanic twice. Though chains and auto dealers have invested heavily in modern facilities, computer diagnostics, and brand advertising, they have not been willing to do what it takes to earn the loyalty of their mechanics. They seem resigned to high levels of employee turnover.

We discovered that employee loyalty affected new-customer volume as well as retention. We asked how people came to choose a particular garage. Predictably, satisfied customers were the number-one source of referrals. But we were unprepared for the second most common source: referrals from garage employees themselves, who as insiders know how much value their shops provide. If an operation gives the kind of value that makes employees proud, they will naturally recommend it to friends and relatives. The real surprise is that their opinion has more impact on new-customer volume than advertising and promotion put together.

The case for a high-loyalty strategy becomes even stronger when we examine the productivity advantages. When one chain ranked its stores on both loyalty and productivity, it found that the top third in employee retention was also the top third in productivity, with 22-percent-higher sales per employee than the bottom third. Even the fast food business, with its prodigious employee churn, shows the effects of relative employee loyalty. When one chain analyzed turnover store by store, it found significant variation, from well under 100 percent per year to more than 300 percent. And it found something else as well. Stores with "low" employee turnover (100 percent on average) had profit margins more than 50 percent higher than stores with high employee turnover (averaging 150 percent).

In the brokerage industry, our consulting firm interviewed hundreds of customer defectors and found that more than half had switched firms because their brokers had switched. Among the most profitable defecting customers, some 70 percent left for this reason. Broker disloyalty is a real problem in the industry; competitors regularly get into bidding wars to recruit each other's best people. A brokerage executive complained in *The Wall Street Journal* that 30 percent of the brokers in the industry had switched firms more than three times. One brokerage tracked customer retention rates for groups of customers with different rates of broker turnover. It found that four-year customer retention rates declined from 75 percent for customers who kept the same broker to 61 percent for customers who had worked with two different brokers, all the way down to 53 percent for those who had had three or more brokers.

To find out how all this affects the economics of the industry, we did a close comparison of customer retention, broker retention, and profitability at the major national brokerage houses. As expected, the most profitable firm, A. G. Edwards, also had the highest retention rates. It also had a higher "share of wallet"—the percentage of each customer's total assets entrusted to a brokerage—which further extends its economic advantage and increases its brokers' productivity and income. Another firm studied the relationship between broker turnover and share of wallet and found that customers who'd suffered an involuntary change of broker invested less of their total assets with the company—by 20 to 30 percent—than those who'd kept the same broker.

Of course, in brokering as in any other business, the idea is not just to hold onto brokers, it's to hold onto the *right* brokers. The potential for lawsuits and regulatory problems means that retaining an incompetent broker can be even more costly than losing a capable one. In our survey of defecting clients, we discovered that the second most common reason for changing firms—right after deciding to follow a good broker to a new company—was the desire to get away from a poor broker.

Obviously, brokerage houses need to focus a lot of energy on hiring the right people and keeping them. But actual practice is not impressive. Year in and year out, the typical firm loses 15 to 20 percent of its brokers.

CATEGORIZING DEFECTORS

Sometimes it's difficult to decide whether or not a departing employee is genuinely disloyal. Fast food restaurants hire teenagers who can be expected to leave when they graduate from high school. Consulting firms hire MBAs who stay for three or four years to gather valuable experience and cross-industry perspectives, then graduate into other lines of work. Many of those who leave have had a positive experience and recommend their former companies to friends and relatives as great places to work. In consulting, some even hire their old employers to consult for them as they progress up the corporate career ladder.

If such people don't qualify as disloyal in the strict sense of the word, how about those who go to work for a direct competitor, or who leave the industry but have nothing good to say about their former employers? Or take a knottier problem: employees who stay for decades but whose diminishing productivity makes them a burden to the rest of the firm. Is the employee who leaves for a 5 percent pay raise disloyal? What about a 50 or 200 percent raise? What about a 50 percent raise when the employee's departure will bankrupt the company and destroy the careers of hundreds of other employees?

Employee loyalty can only be evaluated in the context of specific personal situations and the realistic career paths available. The best firms don't simply track defection rates; they categorize departures and then track defection rates by category. MBNA, for instance, tries very hard to be an excellent place to work, so when an employee who's performing well quits, the company does an exit interview to find out why. The questions depend on the circumstances. People who leave because their spouses have been transferred to the west coast are not lumped in with people who are going down the street to work for a competitor. In MBNA's view, a move to the competition is the most serious kind of defection, since the employee in question clearly likes the industry and the general job description. But it's a serious problem even when people leave for an entirely different kind of work. When people don't like their jobs, recruiting, training, and career path management may all need improvement.

Each category of defection yields its own implications and teaches its own lessons. Sometimes the recruiting department can learn from a departure; sometimes the training department. Sometimes the feedback is relevant to a specific boss, who needs to improve certain management skills. When good, productive employees begin to flow out the door because their future careers strike them as limited, top management needs that feedback to modify the system in ways that permit promising individuals to learn and grow.

THE ECONOMIC MODEL

In the course of studying a range of industries over more than ten years, Bain has developed a generic model of the seven economic effects associated with employee loyalty (see Figure 4-1). Not all industries will show all seven, and the effects will vary in relative importance from one industry to another. A quick run-through will help you decide which matter most to your company.

1. *Recruiting Investment.* Most of the costs of hiring are obvious: recruiting fees, interviewing costs, relocation expenses, and so on. Don't forget, however, that if you have to hire three trainees

Figure 4-1   Why Long-Term Employees Create Value

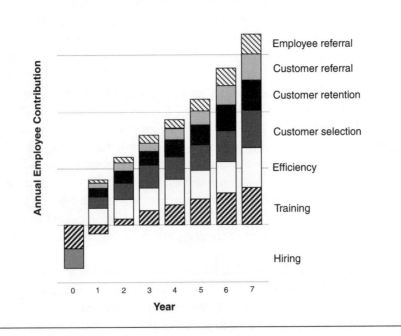

to wind up with one long-term productive employee—and that's common in brokering, life insurance, and several other industries—the true investment per employee triples.

2. *Training.* Giving new hires a foundation for productive work often involves formal classroom training as well as on-the-job training. Wages paid during the training period yield little or no contribution to the firm. While good companies continue to invest in training, even for their most experienced people, the expense is more than offset by the free training senior employees give their junior colleagues. For long-term, loyal employees, in other words, training ceases to be a cost and becomes a net benefit.

3. *Efficiency.* On the simplest level, employees learn to work more efficiently as they gain experience on the job. Their increasing efficiency means they require less supervision, which brings additional efficiencies. On top of these gains, however, it's important to remember that efficiency is the product of how intelligently people work times how hard they work. As a general rule, employees who stay with the company because they're proud of the value they create for customers and pleased with the value they create for themselves are more motivated and work harder.

4. *Customer Selection.* Experienced salespeople and marketers are much better at finding and recruiting the best customers. In the life insurance business, for example, new business persistency is much better for experienced agents than for trainees. In many cases, policies written by new agents have such low persistency, they represent a net loss for the company.

5. *Customer Retention.* As we saw in banking, brokering, and auto service, long-term employees create higher customer loyalty. Even in manufacturing, however, where employees rarely meet customers, long-term employees can produce better products, better value for the consumer, and better customer retention.

6. *Customer Referral.* Loyal employees are sometimes a major source of customer referrals, as we saw in the case of local garages.

7. *Employee Referral.* Long-term, loyal employees often generate the best flow of high-caliber job applicants. This not only raises

the average quality of new hires, it also cuts recruiting costs. Companies with the highest levels of employee retention consistently hire the vast majority of their recruits through employee referrals.

This model of employee loyalty bears some striking similarities to the model of customer loyalty laid out in Chapter 2. Since the two sets of effects are mutually reinforcing, the economic advantages of loyalty are often more powerful than intuition might suggest. In fact, they're so closely connected that for analytical purposes, it's often difficult to keep them separate. Yet we must make the distinction if we're to make intelligent investment decisions and allocate value to customers and employees in a manner that sustains the business. The key is to develop a clear understanding of cause and effect.

Simply getting your employees to stay with the company longer won't necessarily produce superior economics. A lot of firms are loaded with dead wood. For example, several of the Baby Bells are struggling with the problem of employees whose productivity stopped growing years ago. The old promise of lifetime employment attracted people who, in the new competitive environment, no longer earn their salaries. Cutting *their* defection rates will not create value. Nor is the problem confined to old-timers; in any company, some new hires turn out to lack the skills or motivation they need. Holding onto them destroys value.

Many companies seem to be trapped in a blind alley. Individual productivity is insufficient to keep the company competitive, yet managers can't tell which employees are underperforming, because they can't track individual productivity and contribution to profit. In other cases, the company can track the first but not the second, sometimes because a team, often a very large team, is the relevant driver of output. For instance, a bank can measure how many transactions a teller processes in one day, or even how many errors each teller makes, but it can capture overall customer retention, say, or referrals, only at the branch level. Sometimes banks can't even do that, since few of them have reliable customer measurement systems, or even branch profitability systems. Such banks—that is, *most* banks—simply ignore the economics of customer and employee retention, even though these often overwhelm the economics of conventionally measured productivity.

Consider the teller who slows down the line a little to get to know a customer, then manages to save that customer when she comes in to transfer 90 percent of her balances to a mutual fund. The teller gets the customer to talk with the branch manager, who can explain the advantages of the bank's own family of funds. Contrast this teller with another, however pleasant, who moves the line along briskly and simply processes the customer's withdrawal. Which one has the higher productivity?

Banks aren't alone in their inability, or at least their failure, to measure employee contributions effectively. Yet some businesses have found ways to track teams and individuals in a manner that makes the economic effects of employee loyalty both visible and comprehensible. Perhaps because the sales function is inherently easy to measure; perhaps because brokerage firms have been more thoughtful about their profitability systems, we can explore the cash-flow consequences of broker loyalty in some detail. Since individual brokers keep individual books of business, we can track all but one of the economic effects of our seven-point model individually. (The employee referral effect shows up only at the branch level.)

Figure 4-2 summarizes the profit contribution of the average broker as he or she gains experience. The up-front cost of hiring a trainee exceeds $50,000. (Counting fixed costs and capital costs, the total outlay involved in bringing a new broker to the point of profitability exceeds $100,000.) By the second year, the new brokers will earn about $25,000 as a contribution toward their own fixed costs. They won't earn any real profit for the firm until their third year.

Figure 4-2 shows quite clearly that keeping good people longer can have a substantial economic impact on the firm. As brokers gain experience, they learn to target customers more effectively, and their customer retention and share of wallet increase. As more and more new customers come to them by referral, they spend less time prospecting. By the fifth year, the average broker's productivity has risen to more than $200,000 in gross commissions. That is very profitable for the firm, which earns $52,000 in annual profit contribution, and for the broker, who nets 35 to 40 percent of gross.

If there's still any doubt about the value of keeping good brokers longer, we can dispel it with one final number. To see it, we need more than the lifecycle profit pattern shown at the top of Figure 4-2. We also need the broker attrition pattern (middle of Figure 4-2), which shows that given 80 percent retention (a figure typical of most firms today), more than 50 percent of new hires have left by the end of the third year—just as they're beginning to earn a profit for the company. This

Figure 4-2   Calculating Broker Value

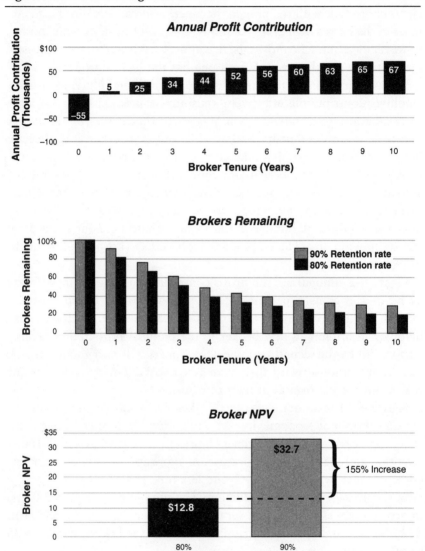

means that the real investment needed to produce a profitable broker is more than the $100,000 mentioned earlier. The firm will actually have to hire and train *three* new brokers to get one who survives long enough to make an acceptable return. So the true investment in each long-term broker asset is closer to $300,000. Which helps to explain why an increase in broker retention from 80 to 90 percent will improve the value of the average new broker by 155 percent.

Calculating the value of employee retention in your business may not be quite as easy as it seems, however. You'll probably have to create new measurement systems and then learn to analyze the results. But there is little doubt about what you'll find: the amounts you now invest in hiring and training will impress you. The profits you fail to realize because of inexperienced employees—their substandard productivity, deficient customer targeting, poor customer retention, and inferior share of wallet—will startle you. And the potential effect on profits of an increase in employee loyalty will just possibly shock you into action.

Those who are still skeptical need to look at the relationship between broker retention and profitability at the principal national brokerage houses. The firm with the highest broker retention, A. G. Edwards, also happens to top the list in profitability. Edwards' average return on equity over the decade exceeds 18 percent, more than twice the industry average. Its broker turnover rate, at 8 percent, is about half the industry average. Once again, the macroeconomics of competition seem to corroborate the microeconomics of retention.

But exactly how does A. G. Edwards do it?

EARNING LOYALTY

Really *earning* employee loyalty—not just backing into it by luck or circumstance—is more than a matter of having the right loyalty tools. The right tools—measurements, practices, policies—are all very important, as the case of A. G. Edwards shows. But A. G. Edwards also shows how important it is to begin with the right mind set, to *think* in terms of loyalty and value creation before developing strategies and tactics.

To start with, A. G. Edwards seeks out a different breed of broker than its competitors. Instead of looking for the Supermen and Wonder Women of sales, the firm screens for individuals who share its philosophy: that the broker's role is to act as an agent for the customer. The firm's

CEO, Ben Edwards III, puts it this way: "We want someone with character who shares our values and who will fit into our culture. We're looking for a long-term, happy marriage."[6]

Another aspect of A. G. Edwards' thinking that improves employee selection is the firm's attitude toward growth. The company has no arbitrary goals or budgets that pressure managers to dip deeper into the talent or character pool than makes them comfortable. Most other firms set hiring goals, then evaluate recruiters on whether the goals have been met. Not surprisingly, recruiters stretch their quality standards, which are not inherently easy to measure, in order to meet their volume standards, which are. A. G. Edwards hires at a relatively steady pace, and has maintained a stable force of brokers through market ups and downs—as opposed to its competitors, who in the boom years hire far more trainees than they can possibly train and assimilate, then cut back drastically and hire almost no one in the bust years.

Ben Edwards also shuns the industry practice of using up-front bonuses to lure brokers from the competition. "It would tend to attract the wrong kind of people," he says, "and it would be unfair to our loyal employees. The message would be that the best way to make a lot of money is to jump around from firm to firm."[7]

Another link in A. G. Edwards's high-retention system is its policy of seldom rotating branch managers. When managers come along who are really good at building new branches, the company encourages them and, since new-branch profits are low, pays them according to a modified compensation system. The vast majority of branch managers stick where they are, their compensation dependent on how well they build the profits of their own branches. From 90 to 95 percent of promotions come from within the company, which further reinforces the loyalty culture. The nine-man executive committee has an average tenure of more than twenty-five years, and all members have a significant financial stake in the firm.

Treating people fairly is a hallmark of the A. G. Edwards system. After apologizing for how corny it sounds, Ben Edwards describes the most important element of the firm's management approach as "following the golden rule—treating people the way you would like to be treated."[8] Fairness extends to executive compensation. Like other loyalty leaders, Edwards pays its senior executives less than most of its competitors. Ben Edwards himself has averaged less than $1 million per year over the past several years, which he estimates is probably one-third to one-fifth what his counterparts get at other firms.

A. G. Edwards works very hard to hire the right kind of trainees, people who will maintain or improve the character and integrity of the firm. It works equally hard to help them achieve a level of productivity that meets their income aspirations, and to earn their ongoing loyalty. So when defections occur, management tries hard to understand why a successful, productive broker might leave. The firm performs exit interviews regularly to search for the root causes of dissatisfaction.

Of course, character and loyalty aren't the only criteria for brokers; trainees must also have the skills to become economically productive. However, Edwards has engineered its system so that brokers don't have to sell as much volume as they do at other houses to make a profit for the firm. For one thing, the company has smaller branches, with eight to ten brokers (compared to an industry average of twenty to thirty). Branch managers act as player-coaches, handling some customers themselves. In addition, space costs are lower per person. Based in St. Louis, the firm is the only major brokerage house to avoid Manhattan overheads by locating its headquarters outside New York City. For that matter, the firm has historically concentrated on geographical areas that reinforce the loyalty culture, particularly smaller markets and suburban locations. A representative sample of new branch openings includes South Hills, Pennsylvania; Lima, Ohio; Tifton, Georgia; Branson, Missouri; Boynton Beach, Florida; and Morgantown, West Virginia.

A. G. Edwards does no national advertising, which not only saves money, it also reinforces the message that the best source of growth is referrals. The firm also uses a single-tier compensation system, which eases the pressure on candidates who are slow to build up to acceptable sales volumes. Competitors pay reduced commission rates to low-volume producers to weed out the laggards, but that practice encourages new brokers to push products even harder, sometimes in ways that are not in the customer's best interest.

The company passes on some of its efficiencies directly to customers. *Smart Money,* the personal finance magazine of *The Wall Street Journal,* recently ranked brokerage firms on price. To no one's surprise, A. G. Edwards won top honors. "If we charge the customer a little south of the average and pay the broker a little north of the average," says Ben Edwards, "we can make up the difference by being more efficient."[9]

A. G. Edwards also wins the *Smart Money* award for best ongoing broker training. The firm gives training such high priority that Ben Edwards often leads the seminars himself. But where training at many other firms includes instruction on how to pitch the products that are most profitable to the firm, Edwards concentrates instead on how to serve the customer more effectively.

A. G. Edwards is unique in the industry in its refusal to manufacture its own investment products, because of the potential for a conflict of interest. Other firms can't resist the fat margins they earn on in-house mutual funds, so some of them pay brokers bigger commissions to push a house fund, even when an outside fund might be a better choice for the customer. Worse yet, when an investment banking department gets stuck with inventory it can't sell (stalled initial public offerings, dubious partnerships) the temptation is to increase commission rates to pressure brokers into unloading the investments on unsuspecting customers. When brokers see their firms placing short-term corporate earnings above the best interests of the customer, they can hardly help concluding that it's all right to put their own interests above the customer's. This kind of conflict is rare at A. G. Edwards.

When Ben Edwards writes at the end of an annual report, "We are committed to doing the best job we can for our faithful clients,"[10] it's more than lip service. His company enjoys the lowest level of arbitration awards in the industry—less than half that of the next-best-performing firm, Merrill Lynch. What Edwards does not point out is that the combination of good, dependable income, low-pressure selling environment, and a policy of putting customers first has also produced happier brokers. Broker turnover is less than half the industry average. By engineering a loyalty-based business system that achieves 92-percent broker retention in an industry where 80 to 85 percent is typical, Edwards has made winners of its customers and employees—and of its investors too. Remember, return on equity has averaged more than 18 percent over the past decade.

CHICK-FIL-A

Another company that's done a remarkable job of earning employee loyalty is Chick-fil-A, the chain of quick-service, shopping-mall restaurants we discussed in Chapter 1. As we'll see, there are striking similarities between the basic business philosophies at Chick-fil-A and A. G. Edwards, despite the obvious gulf between the industries. Both companies begin with some form of the Golden Rule. Chick-fil-A has translated it into a system that aligns the interests of outlet operators with those of the company, and gives the customer ultimate power over both.

The results are impressive. In an industry where annual turnover in store managers runs between 30 and 40 percent, Chick-fil-A loses only 4 to 6 percent of its operators every year, almost none of them from the top two-thirds in performance. The economic benefits of this superior loyalty have allowed the company to open six hundred stores over forty-nine years without using any outside capital. Chick-fil-A's loyalty-based system has funded not only impressive growth but superior compensation for the store managers themselves. Fast-food managers in general make $30,000 to $35,000 per year. The average Chick-fil-A manager makes about $45,000, and the top 10 percent make better than $100,000—a salary almost unheard of in the industry.

Obviously, superior compensation plays a role in earning superior operator loyalty. But how can Chick-fil-A *afford* to pay 30 to 50 percent more than its competitors in the price-sensitive world of fast food? At the heart of Chick-fil-A's success is the partnership deal it strikes with managers. New operators post just $5,000 in earnest money (very modest given the cost of a new restaurant—at least $250,000—and the fact that the company refunds the money if and when the manager leaves). They are guaranteed a base income of $24,000, and they get 50 percent of store profits, after paying 15 percent of revenues for company-provided services. This is Chick-fil-A's way of aligning its managers' interests with the company's. Both operators and headquarters have a big incentive to help each other succeed. Unlike most competing chains, where every additional dollar of salary for managers means a dollar less for the company, Chick-fil-A will do everything in its power to help its operators earn more.

Another striking contrast with competing restaurant chains is Chick-fil-A's concept of what makes a career. Most chains transfer managers from one location to another, gradually increasing their responsibilities and compensation. People progress from small to medium-sized to big stores, then to turnaround situations or to new markets. The person who succeeds at all these challenges may then move up to a regional staff position, and the superstars are eventually called to corporate head-quarters. Chick-fil-A thinks this approach is backwards. The company would never think of rotating operators among different stores and destroying the relationships they've developed with employees and customers. That could cut into everyone's profits.

Few operators seem to mind the lack of any prospect of a job at corporate headquarters. They're in the restaurant business, not the administration business. Most of them probably don't want to move their families to Atlanta anyway, especially when they can earn more than $100,000 a year right where they are. Instead, Chick-fil-A does its best to give local growth opportunities to talented, ambitious operators who've managed their stores well. Despite a strong, historic belief in the one operator, one store principle, the company now gives its best store managers the chance to run additional outlets, catering and party services, pushcarts, and school lunch programs that build on their knowledge of the local market. The company has also begun to license operators at college campuses, hospitals, and other institutions, and it pays its best operators to train managers for these new sites.

Chick-fil-A's growth is determined by the availability of first-rate management candidates and by the company's ability to generate cash, not by the number of new outlets it would take to maximize the current stock price. This strategy allows Chick-fil-A to be very particular about the people it chooses to run its stores. Recruitment of store managers combines good common sense, high ideals, and a lot of time and effort getting to know the candidates, most of whom come as referrals from present managers or staff members. Prior experience in the food business is not a requirement, or even a consideration. Instead, the company looks for applicants with character, drive, and a liking for people. Truett Cathy, the company's founder, puts it this way: "We don't select or even seriously consider an operator unless we want the individual to be with us until one of us dies or retires." The final decision on whether to hire a candidate often comes down to a single question in the interviewer's mind—"Would I like my son or daughter to work for this person?"

Crew turnover is also lower at Chick-fil-A than at other chains (about 120 percent per year versus 200 to 300 percent for the industry as a whole). This is partly because the company tries hard to find managers young people will want to work for, and partly because a store manager who expects to stay put is naturally more careful in hiring and managing staff. But company policies help here as well: any crew member who stays for at least two years and averages twenty hours per week or more is eligible for a $1,000 scholarship. The company awarded more than a thousand scholarships in 1993.

If all this sounds like a Golden Rule approach to business, that's exactly what it is. Truett Cathy is so earnest a Christian that all Chick-fil-A stores are closed on Sundays, which makes their financial success all the more impressive. The competition is open seven days a week. (While the six-day strategy has clear religious underpinnings, it also helps the firm to attract a group of talented operators who don't want to work seven days a week.) The core value at the heart of Chick-fil-A's partnership agreement with its managers, and of its treatment of crews and customers, is the same ancient saw, no less true for being a truism, that Ben Edwards cites and that lies at the heart of all loyalty-based systems. As Cathy puts it, "treat the other fellow the same way you'd like him to treat you."

Loyalty-based systems pay off in many ways. One striking advantage of Chick-fil-A's well-aligned partner relationships is that the firm requires very little overhead to manage and control its chain of stores. The entire field staff consists of twenty-five people. And by giving its operators a meaningful livelihood rather than just a career stepping-stone, Chick-fil-A has constructed a cash-flow engine that has funded steady growth for twenty-five years. Annual revenues now exceed $400 million; growth rates over the past ten years have been in the range of 10 to 15 percent; and in the entire history of the firm, there have been no down years.

I asked Truett's son Dan what the key element of Chick-fil-A's strategy has been, and he said, "It's not the recipe for the sandwich, or the food quality, or the mall concept, or the training. These are all important, but the key is our operators, their capabilities, and our relationships with them. Over time, our system will change and evolve so that it can meet the full potential of our best operators."[11]

Every Chick-fil-A store has a plaque engraved with this principle: "Associate yourselves only with those people you can be proud of— whether they work for you or you work for them."

STATE FARM

On average, only 20 to 40 percent of new insurance agents stay with their companies at least four years. At State Farm, more than 80 percent stay four years or more. State Farm's secret recipe for this kind of loyalty is very like the recipe at Chick-fil-A, despite the vast difference in product lines. At both companies, the loyalty system has four principal ingredients: careful recruiting; career paths designed for maximum productivity growth; a concept of partnership that aligns the company's interests with the employees; and once again, a dedication to something very like the Golden Rule.

Just as the first step in earning high customer loyalty is to search out the right kind of customer, so the first step in gaining agent loyalty is careful recruiting. As *Fortune* magazine put it, "New State Farm agents are hired with the care one might give to choosing a spouse—which in a business sense is not too far from what's happening."[12] Unlike an employee who can be fired at will, agents once appointed typically stay with the company for life, unless they choose to quit or break the law. Given that the average agent has been with State Farm fifteen to twenty years, the spouse analogy may actually understate reality.

Despite State Farm's sterling track record, the company plans to go one step further. In the future, agent candidates will have to spend two or three years in an employee position before becoming eligible to be agents. New agents will know their business better, and the company will know its agent-partners better; the process will be more like selecting partners in a law firm than hiring salespeople. The career path for agents at State Farm is unlike career paths at most other large insurers. Most State Farm agents want to keep their jobs for the rest of their careers—and most want to stay in their original territories. A few eventually decide to go into management, but that usually means a cut in pay and a substantial reduction in potential future income. So the people who transfer to management are those who actually like administration and are probably good at it. What is even more surprising, the administrator who rises to become president of the company will make only a fraction of what top agents earn.

Though other insurance companies are experimenting with nonagent forms of distribution—telemarketing, direct mail, marketing through bank branches—State Farm is loyal to its agent-partners. Since direct mail is the low-cost way to do business with some customers, State Farm has developed a direct-mail capability at its home office. But it offers the service to agents, to use as they see fit; headquarters never sends mail to an agent's customers unless the agent requests it (and by the way, pays for it). The company has also invested heavily in computer systems to improve agent productivity and has established eleven hundred local claims-processing centers to provide—and enable agents to provide—better customer service.

State Farm agents are independent contractors who invest cash in their own businesses. Where most insurance companies pay for and manage their agents' offices, employees, and support systems, then deduct an allowance for those expenses from the agents' commissions, State Farm pays its agents a gross commission and allows the agents to decide how to spend the money—on offices, on staff, or on themselves. A typical agency will employ two to four people, all of them on the agent's payroll, and each agency pays its own rent and expenses. In other words, the commission structure at State Farm creates incentives very like those at Chick-fil-A and supports a similar alignment of interests, encouraging the company and the agents to work for one another's success. Because State Farm agents are spending their own money to run a local business, they make spending and investment decisions thoughtfully, like partners. In return, State Farm distributes its products only through its agents and involves them in all decisions that affect them or their customers. It's this partnership approach that has made the marriage work. The fifteen to twenty years the average State Farm agent has been with the company compare well with a six-to nine-year average for the industry as a whole.

In 1993, the newspaper in State Farm's hometown published an interview with the newly appointed agency vice president, Chuck Wright, the man responsible for relations with the company's eighteen thousand agents. The article summed up the company's philosophy this way:

> *Customer and employee loyalty is not a new-fangled idea for State Farm Insurance Companies. . . . It has been a part of the company's way of doing business since 1922, [Wright] said. "We have thrived on long term retention of our employees, our agents, and we have tried to be loyal and caring with our customer base."*[13]

George Mecherle, the company's founder, said something similar as far back as the 1930s:

> *The tiny seed planted in the year 1922, which has been nurtured by the sunlight of agency devotion and sustained by the life-giving waters of policyholder persistency, has grown in root and branch— spreading a mantle of service and protection throughout the nation—until today the ripened fruit of its many branches is falling as a benediction into the lives, homes, and hearts of our people.*[14]

Mecherle's phrasing may be florid, but his sense of service and moral obligation is as striking as Truett Cathy's. Ed Rust, Sr., who later took over leadership of the company, had this to say about the basic values on which Mecherle founded State Farm: "Never have I known him to take a position in regard to company affairs without first applying the proposition to himself to make sure that, if he were the insured, he was being treated fairly."[15]

No matter where in the United States we may be, when the name State Farm comes up in a presentation about loyalty-based business systems, a State Farm customer will almost always approach us afterward with a story. A man in Minnesota had had a typical experience. His house caught fire in the middle of the night several years earlier, and his State Farm agent was one of the first to arrive on the scene. The fire chief had called the agent when the alarm came in, and he arrived only minutes behind the fire trucks—and ahead of the next-door neighbors. "Like a good neighbor, State Farm is there" is more than just an advertising gimmick. It's an ideal that agents and employees work hard to live up to, one that customers notice and remember. It is also one of the reasons employees and agents are so loyal. It gives them pride and satisfaction to devote their careers to a company whose fundamental purpose is being a good neighbor.

Another man told us that he had once lived just outside Bloomington, Illinois, down the street from State Farm's CEO, Ed Rust, Jr. At 5 o'clock one morning during his first Bloomington blizzard, he heard a roar outside the house. Throwing a coat on over his pajamas, he ran out to find Ed Rust on a front-loader, clearing the snow from his driveway. It turned out that Rust plowed snow regularly for *all* his neighbors.

One of the most important decisions in engineering a high-loyalty system is the choice of a senior executive. As a Unitarian minister once wrote, "We are all preaching an unspoken sermon with our lives." The way corporate executives live their lives has a lot to do with the level of loyalty they can expect to earn from their employees. State Farm's essentially moral approach to business earns high customer and employee loyalty and gives new meaning to the phrase *Golden Rule.* Agents see their jobs as gold mines—and with more than $20 billion in retained earnings, the company has been dubbed "the Fort Knox of the insurance business."[16]

LEO BURNETT

Employee partnership based on loyalty and the Golden Rule seems to be very profitable in brokering, fast food, and insurance. But can it work in even more competitive and chaotic industries, like the dog-eat-dog world of advertising? Leo Burnett, the agency with the lowest turnover and the highest productivity in the business, seems to show that it can.

Phil Schaff has observed and worked at Leo Burnett for thirty-three years—fifteen of them as one of its top executives. He was one of the company's early employees, joining shortly after he got out of the Navy at the end of the Second World War, he succeeded its founder, Leo Burnett, as CEO. Asked to describe Burnett's strategy for attracting the best employees, Schaff began his answer by telling how he himself came to join the firm. When Schaff got out of the Navy in 1946, he knew he wanted to go into advertising. He talked to everyone he could, especially the customers of different advertising agencies. What he kept hearing was, "You should join up with Leo Burnett. They have an outstanding product, and they're people of outstanding integrity and character." That's what he was looking for, so he went for an interview.

Phil Schaff retired in 1980, but Burnett attracts employees the same way today—by delivering the highest-quality product and service to its customers, and by carefully directing its recruiting efforts toward people with character and integrity as well as talent. Why? Because as Schaff says, "to do an outstanding job for the client, you've got to attract the right people."[17] The firm interviews recruits at least five times before hiring, and its advertising professionals do the interviews, not the human resources staff. Since new hires take several years to reveal themselves as good or bad investments, Schaff insisted that interviewers put their comments in writing so he could look back later and see which of them were the best judges of talent and character. Eventually, those with superior track records got to do most of the interviewing.

According to Schaff, the number one draw in attracting the right kind of recruits is still the character and integrity of the people at the top. What recruits are looking for, he insists, is character—the integrity, honesty, and trustworthiness of the CEO and his closest associates. Schaff believes that the second thing a company must do to attract good people is to maintain high quality standards for its products and services. If a company consistently acts in its customers' best interests and delivers only products of the highest caliber, recruits with integrity will know it's the kind of place they want to work.

Continuing to put the customer's interest first also turns out to be the smart way of *keeping* the best employees. That, after all, is why they joined. If the firm suddenly reversed course and started shortchanging customers in order to boost quarterly earnings, those carefully selected employees would reverse course and defect. As a private firm, Leo Burnett has consistently been able to put the customer first. Schaff refers to the firm's private ownership (it is owned by its employees) as its secret weapon, because it allows the company to treat its employees with great respect. In the firm's entire history, it has had to endure only one downsizing: in 1993, when it laid off about two hundred fifty people, or about 4 percent of its workforce.

Another way that Burnett holds onto its best people is with exemplary policies on promotion, pay, and benefits. This too goes back to the behavior of senior managers. Do they give raises and promotions on the basis of performance, or do they surround themselves with friends and cronies? Do they pay themselves enormous salaries, while refusing to cover health-care benefits for the mailroom clerks? Schaff says, "I always felt that if you dropped the payroll book on the floor, and somebody made copies and sent them all around the office, people might not like everything they saw, but in the final analysis they might grudgingly admit that they were reasonably and fairly paid in relation to other people." The Burnett system aims always for superior compensation based on superior productivity. While Burnett's most senior executives earn less than many of their counterparts, pay and benefits for the rest of the firm are well above the industry average. Burnett shares profits with all its employees; and the typical payout ranges from 15 percent of total compensation, for employees on the lower pay scales, to more than 100 percent for the most senior managers.

There is no single reason why Leo Burnett has the best employee retention in the industry. The company has engineered an entire system on the belief that the only way to deliver the best value to customers is to hire and keep the best employees. And the only way to make such a system work is to promote leaders who will run it in such a way that people can be both productive and proud of their association with the firm. This philosophy has enabled Leo Burnett to grow global revenues to more than $600 million without ever seeking outside capital.

Though companies like Leo Burnett can do a great deal to make their employees want to stay, no company can guarantee employment. Only the customer can do that—and customers will keep buying only as long as they receive superior value. Therefore, employees must know how much value they are creating, if not individually, then at least as members of relatively small teams. Chick-fil-A has found a way to let them know; so have State Farm, A. G. Edwards, and Leo Burnett. In Chapter 5, we'll see how these companies develop partnerships with employees, and with them engineer the continuous growth of value and productivity.

5

Productivity

PRODUCTIVITY IS a dismal term for a fascinating topic. Though the word sounds bland and technical, the phenomenon of productivity is central to our national and personal well-being, the role it plays in business success is absolutely primal, and its literal meaning—"the pace of creation"—is little short of majestic.

In a business, productivity usually refers to the rate of employee value creation, and *growth* in productivity is essential to a healthy company and a healthy society. Productivity growth is a prime source of sustainable cost advantage and the only source of sustainable compensation growth for employees (and thus a vital factor in determining their standard of living). Recognizing the critical importance of productivity, U.S. companies have invested countless billions of dollars in productivity-enhancing technologies, from mainframes to PCs to information networks, and from copiers to faxes to cellular phones. They have also reengineered processes and laid off millions of workers.

And yet something is awry. If the logic behind all this technology improvement and job elimination were sound, U.S. productivity would have skyrocketed. But productivity growth in the United States has lagged that of the world's other major economies, as Figure 5-1 shows. Since 1960, U.S. productivity has inched ahead at little better than a glacial pace, with the service sector showing the weakest performance. Granted, there is some question about the accuracy and reliability of government

Figure 5-1   Cumulative Growth in Real GDP per Employee, 1960–1992

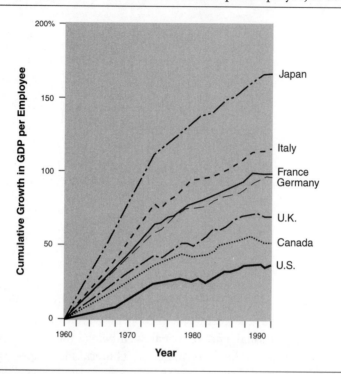

Source: Department of Labor, Bureau of Statistics, *International Comparison of Manufacturing Productivity and Unit Labor Cost Trends, 1993* (Washington, D.C., 1993).

productivity statistics; but whether U.S. productivity is crawling or merely creeping upward is academic. The magnitude of recent investments in technology should have sent it into orbit.

There are some exceptions to this dreary record. In contrast to the U.S. economy as a whole, loyalty leaders have managed to achieve exceptional levels of productivity, and it is superior productivity that has sustained their ability to grow employee compensation, customer value, and profits. Not surprisingly, these companies take an unconventional approach to productivity issues. USAA, for example, has invested heavily in technology; it is currently investing at a rate of 7 percent of revenues. But instead of replacing people with machines, the company's consistent goal has been to enrich each job and improve every employee's ability to serve the customer effectively. USAA also invests aggressively in training and education; in 1994 it spent nearly 3 percent of revenues on about a million hours of training. (Probably the most telling demonstration of USAA's productivity credentials is the fact that the company has increased its assets one hundred times with only a fivefold increase in workforce.)

Neither one of these huge investments would pay off in superior productivity, of course, if it weren't for one more investment USAA makes. The company invests in employment and compensation policies that make employees *want* to stay with the company, apply their knowledge, and use their tools to create superior value for customers. In 1970, USAA's employee turnover exceeded 40 percent—not unusual for a telephone sales company—and productivity was mediocre. Today, annual turnover has declined to 6 percent, which means that average employee tenure has increased from a little over two years to more than sixteen.

Taken together, USAA's investments mean that when customers call in for service, they deal with an experienced employee who knows the business, knows the company, and knows how to make maximum use of the available technology. It means that sales and service reps resolve 90 percent of customer requests and problems on the first try, no follow-up required. That means one of the highest productivity levels in the industry.

Conventional approaches to improving productivity take quite a different tack. They often utilize big investments in automation, but the thrust of those investments is to displace employees, not empower them. The resulting layoffs, coupled with compensation policies meant to minimize compensation growth (and therefore compensation cost), often lead to reduced employee loyalty and soaring turnover. In contrast, loyalty leaders believe that the only way to reduce costs effectively is to make it possible for employees to earn *more*. However counterintuitive this may sound, it is hardly a new argument. Several generations ago, Henry Ford put it this way: "Cutting wages does not reduce costs—it increases them. The only way to get a low-cost product is to pay a high price for a high grade of human service. . . ."[1]

DEFINING LOW COST IN A SERVICE ECONOMY

What was true for Henry Ford is even truer in a service economy, where employee talent plays a much more immediate role in creating customer value. Customers will buy more, and at higher prices, only when they see quality and service increase. So to increase revenue per employee—in practice, the best definition of business productivity—companies are increasingly dependent on the loyalty of first-rate people. (Of course, some businesses have high material and/or capital costs, and for these, gross margin or value added per employee are better measures of productivity than revenue. We will simplify the discussion here by focusing on revenue per employee but the logic holds no matter which measure is used.)

One common barrier to better loyalty and higher productivity is the fact that a lot of business executives, and virtually all accounting departments, treat income and outlays as if they occurred in separate worlds. The truth is, revenues and costs are inextricably linked, and decisions that focus on one or the other—as opposed to both—often misfire. What links them so closely is the fact that, today, employees either control or represent the lion's share of costs and at the same time—in an economy where even manufacturing can often be seen as a form of service—how well they serve customers is directly responsible for the lion's share of revenues. In short, businesses need to stop thinking about revenues and costs as two separate or separable cash flows. In today's service economy, for the first time, employees tie the two together by exercising a decisive influence on both.

In the old manufacturing economy, it was possible to manage production separately from sales. In a factory, widgets per machine was the right measure of productivity, and by concentrating on that ratio, manufacturers could lower their costs. In today's service economy, not the machine but the employee drives costs, and what gets processed is customers, not widgets. In the course of this processing, employees must balance two beneficial outcomes. They can minimize the time they invest in each customer and hold down costs per transaction; or they can spend more time and give customers greater value, which may lead to higher revenues. Raising productivity in this situation is a matter of making intelligent tradeoffs. Employees must understand the economics of their job functions, and they must know a great deal about customer preferences and needs. Only these two skills in tandem will allow employees to maximize the value they create in every customer interaction.

Take a simple example from banking. Tellers can choose to move their lines along quickly, or they can take extra time when customers—especially high-balance customers who are vulnerable to the competition—need individual help or information. Most banks have tried to reduce costs by emphasizing transaction volume per teller. The inevitable result has been a deterioration in service quality and reduced revenue growth.

Transaction volume per person is just one of the many partial productivity ratios companies have developed in an effort to manage productivity more effectively. Loyalty leaders don't ignore these measures, but they put far more emphasis on the complete measure of productivity: *revenue* per person. A good example from retailing, an industry in which many companies concentrate on sales per square foot, is Nordstrom's, where the principal performance yardstick is revenue per salesclerk. The company prints this number on every salesclerk's paystub, and the rank-order performance of all clerks is prominently posted on the employee bulletin board. As a result, employees work to serve customers in ways that will earn them repeat business. Overselling is effectively discouraged by netting customer returns against each salesclerk's revenue total.

To make a productivity ratio work, the numerator of the ratio has to capture the *value* of output, not simply its volume. That is why revenue is the best numerator—because we want to capture productivity and value from the customer's perspective, not the engineer's. We want employees to maximize the value they create for customers, whether they do it by lowering costs or by increasing the worth of the company's offering. Only when revenue per employee increases, is it possible to increase compensation and/or profit. Take the example of a pizza chain that was hugely pleased because its productivity had increased by 25 percent, as measured by the volume of pizza served per employee. Unfortunately, the quality of the pizza had not kept pace with the quality of competing brands, so the chain had to cut its prices, and the revenue realized per pizza declined by 28 percent. It's pretty hard to take that kind of productivity increase to the bank.

Of course it's important to track the volume of pizza, but volume is just one component of the productivity algorithm. It would be much better to get employees to focus on revenue by encouraging them to think about such things as menu variety, quality and taste of the product, and efficiency of staffing. The right objective is not lower cost per unit but lower cost as a percentage of revenues.

As this example demonstrates, with employees in effective control of both revenues and costs, the old definitions of productivity grow not just obsolete, but downright obstructive. Companies that fail to recognize these new facts of life will also fail to appreciate the critical importance of their employees to the company's success. The fact is, with employees in de facto control of both revenues and costs, companies must alter their employee policies to produce or enhance two effects: employee learning and the alignment of employee and business interests.

LEARNING CURVES IN A SERVICE ECONOMY

One of the greatest problems with the old approach to productivity, which focused primarily on costs, is that manufacturing, at least in the nineteenth century, saw workers as easily replaceable. For the most part, experience and learning were captured in the architecture of the machine and the process design of the factory. Today, in services and in the service functions within manufacturing, the learning curve is individual, has a profound effect on both revenues and costs, and is longer and steeper by far than it was in the age of manufacturing. It grows out of the cumulative decision-making experience an employee builds over time through relationships with customers, vendors, and fellow employees.

The concept of learning curves was formalized and studied over the course of this century in industries ranging from military airframes to automobiles to semiconductors. Engineers noticed that the time and money required to build each unit declined predictably as production volume grew. In fact, the cost per unit dropped by 20 to 30 percent with each doubling of cumulative volume. (That is, the fourth unit cost 20 to 30 percent less than the second, the eighth unit, 20 to 30 percent less than the fourth, and so on.)

These discoveries became part of the manufacturing toolbox and eventually came to play a role in corporate strategy as well. Unhappily, the whole notion of the learning curve as a basic business principle lost much of its luster—too much, probably—because some companies over-extended and misapplied the concept by focusing almost *entirely* on cost and market share, to the exclusion of learning in other forms.

Eventually, these companies were ambushed by competitors who improved customer value through performance and quality innovations instead of cost and price reductions. This is what happened to Henry Ford's Model T, which was available at wonderfully low cost but in only one model and one color. When General Motors offered customers greater variety, it stole Ford's market leadership. In sum, single-minded concentration on cost reduction has led companies to render themselves less flexible and innovative by substituting capital improvements for people, who after all are the actual source of all creativity.

Measuring and managing costs independently of value took its toll in the tire industry as well. Several manufacturers made early decisions against radial technology; they stuck with bias-ply because of its superior unit cost. Those manufacturers failed to appreciate the new tires' extra benefits to customers—superior durability, better gas mileage, and greater safety. But customers saw the advantages clearly and paid the higher prices happily. The early adopters of radial technology— Goodyear, Michelin, and Bridgestone—are industry leaders today, while most of the others have faded into the background. The lesson, once again, is that meaningful productivity measures must incorporate the value of output, not just its cost or volume.

Personal computers provide another example. They've enabled workers to do far more calculations per hour than they ever could with a hand-held calculator. But if many of these additional calculations are superfluous—if the extra output has little value—there is little if any real gain in productivity. If productivity ratios are to capture at least the minimum value delivered to the customer, they must always include sales revenue as their numerator. Customers will never pay more for anything than the value it creates for them. (In practice, they often wind up paying less, sometimes a good deal less, than the product or service is ultimately worth to them. This excess value—economists call it the consumer surplus—is why productivity ratios based on revenue tend to understate the full amount of value created.)

Historically, the misuse of learning curves has been to look at cost instead of value; to presume that learning potential is entirely a function of the number of units produced; and to fix on increased market share as the only route to lowering costs. In many service-driven companies— including some manufacturers—the relevant driver of learning potential is not a company's worldwide market share or cumulative production volume. Rather, it is how long individual employees have interacted with specific customers, vendors, and fellow employees in their specific niches in the company's business system. Companies don't learn; individuals do, and their learning takes time.

So for service or knowledge-based businesses, it is more relevant to measure individual learning than to look at the so-called company learning curve. Figure 5-2 shows the average individual productivity (and learning) curves for several industries. (We have indexed revenue per

Figure 5-2 Employee Tenure Versus Productivity

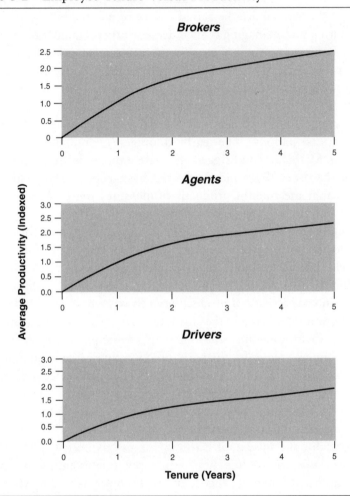

Source: Bain analysis.
Note: Productivity is defined as revenue per person and indexed to year 1 (1 = 1.0).

person so that 1.0 represents productivity in the first year of employment.) In each case, productivity (as measured by annual revenue per person) grows substantially as the individual gains experience. This is true of stockbrokers, truck drivers, insurance agents, and many, many others. The length and steepness of the curve varies significantly with the nature of the job—and even more with the individual employee's share in the benefits of a productivity increase—but for the vast majority of jobs, the learning curve is steep for at least the first several years.

Vertical and Horizontal Learning

There are only two ways to improve the learning curve. You can steepen the curve, or you can prolong the climb by increasing employee loyalty. Steepening the curve is chiefly a matter of "vertical" interventions like process redesign or automation. (In banking, for example, automated teller stations let each employee do much more work, so the number of branch employees can be reduced.) Vertical interventions are important opportunities, and companies need to pursue them. In essence, by enabling people to be more productive than their years of experience would normally allow, such interventions create precocious employees. But vertical investments accomplish little unless they're combined with a second strategy of horizontal investment to increase loyalty so employees will stay and climb higher on their learning curves.

Many companies are more intent on building precociousness than on building loyalty, ignoring or forgetting the fact that without loyalty, their investments in precociousness won't pay off. A company's productivity is simply the average of all its employees' individual productivity. When you make vertical investments to lift the productivity curve, your bottom line will show no gain unless your employees stick around long enough to learn and then apply their learning. Loyalty must remain constant or improve. Yet many kinds of vertical intervention—automation coupled with layoffs, for example—tend to decrease loyalty and reduce average employee tenure, causing productivity to slip back down the learning curve.

The personal productivity of the individuals in a company is the product of how hard they work times how smart they work. To some extent, it's possible to use fear and insecurity to drive people to work harder. But the plain truth is that talented people work hardest when they're proud of what they do, when their jobs are interesting and meaningful, and when they and their team members are recognized for their contributions and share in the benefits. How smart a person works depends very much on training, but the fact is, the vast majority of training comes on the job. If employees are not loyal to a business long enough to learn and use their learning, they and their company will never achieve superior productivity.

Sustaining a Productivity Advantage

Will Rogers said, "Even if you are on the right track, you'll still get run over if you're just sitting there." You may not feel you're sitting still, especially when you know how far you've come from where you were. But in business, motion is relative. What really matters in the race for superior productivity is not making improvements, but making them faster than the competition. Since the numerator of the productivity ratio (revenue) includes price, and since in most industries real prices drop as competitors learn to deliver the product or service more effectively (that is, with fewer people), effectiveness must increase faster than prices decline if productivity is to improve. The challenge is most obvious in high-growth businesses like personal computers, where experience doubles every few years and where prices may drop 30 to 40 percent over the course of a year. For example, Dell Computer's flagship 386 personal computer dropped from $4,965 at the end of 1991 to $2,394 by mid-1993. (The same thing happens in more mature industries, but it's less visible due to slower increases in experience.)

This is one reason why curve-steepening investments alone often fail to produce the projected productivity improvement. They're just too easy for competitors to copy. An insurance company spends millions on a state-of-the-art software system, supposedly an exclusive, then discovers that its competitors have built similar systems—either because software engineers float from one company to another, or because the critical insight was inevitable, and several designers had it at about the same time.

Even process redesign is fairly easy to duplicate. National Car Rental introduced its Emerald Isle express service on St. Patrick's Day in 1987. Customers could go from their flight straight to National's parking lot, pick out a car they liked, and drive it away simply by showing their IDs and driver's licenses to the guard on their way out. This was reengineering at its best; it increased value to the customer and eliminated a number of process steps. The only trouble was, less than a year later, Hertz introduced its own #1 Service, which matched the key elements of National's express service.

Conversely, improvements in employee loyalty and duration are much harder to match, for a human resource system is built on intangibles, subjective inducements, and circumstances peculiar to one company: hiring strategies, career paths, training, compensation, and measurement. Properly coordinated, these intangibles can be the source of a sustainable productivity advantage that competitors will strive in vain to duplicate. State Farm, for example, has enjoyed its agent tenure advantage for decades.

Loyalty leaders base their competitive strategies on these more permanent advantages. They recognize that the only way to reach and sustain superior productivity is to share its benefits, which encourages employees not merely to stick around but also to apply their knowledge and drive productivity higher still. State Farm is a good example of this approach. Figure 5-3—the learning curve for the personal property and casualty industry—shows how dramatic the results can be. We see that average individual productivity grows rapidly at every company as agents gain experience, and that average agent tenure is between six and seven years. We also see that State Farm's average agent tenure is more than double the industry average. If State Farm's agent learning curve were identical to the industry learning curve, we might expect the productivity of the average agent at State Farm to be about 25 percent higher than at most other companies. Their actual productivity is higher still—40 percent above the industry average—which may indicate that State Farm has built in some vertical advantage. But the bulk of State Farm's productivity

Figure 5-3 The Loyalty Surplus

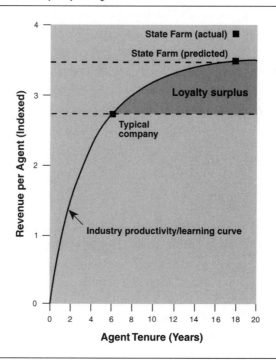

advantage is horizontal, or tenure-based. Agents with eighteen years tenure are almost as productive at competing firms as they are at State Farm. The competition just doesn't have as many of them.

The key to State Farm's advantage, as well as to its agent-retention strategy is the shaded area in Figure 5-3, which we call the loyalty surplus. It consists of the excess productivity created by agents who stay longer than they do at a typical competing company. State Farm shares this loyalty surplus with its agents, but it does so through a level commission structure that allows agents who build up a large book of business to realize the profits only as they stay and serve those customers over a period of years. The higher the level of revenue an agent achieves, the more he or she will want to stay at State Farm and share in the loyalty surplus. State Farm apportions another part of the loyalty surplus to its customers in the form of lower prices. A third portion flows to the company's own balance sheet, to finance growth and protect against future catastrophes.

This formula is essentially the same one used by Chick-fil-A, Leo Burnett, A. G. Edwards, and other loyalty leaders. By sharing the spoils of loyalty with their employees, they have built a tenure-based productivity advantage. In many cases, their average employee duration is 50 to 100 percent better than the competition's. In such companies, learning persists and grows. In companies where employees perpetually leave in mid-career, learning is forever falling back to nil.

Cost-Cutting Versus the Productivity of Employee and Customer Retention

Few industries are struggling harder than the life insurance industry to reduce costs and improve profits. Insurance companies have been among the most enthusiastic converts to the reengineering gospel—it's a rare article or book on the subject that doesn't include an insurance example—and experts predict that over the next few years, the industry will cut its workforce 15 percent or more. *The Wall Street Journal* surveyed seventeen large companies and found that most were planning or already implementing layoffs. "Many insurance companies say they are aiming ultimately for leaner, less costly staffs that also will give faster, surer service to customers," the *Journal* reported. "But for now, the main goal is simply to reduce costs and improve profitability in an industry where many companies have severe financial problems."[2]

As the *Journal* went on to report, however, a lot of observers are unimpressed by the early results. "Insurance costs aren't declining as insurers cut employees, says a spokeswoman for Citizens Action, a group of 38 state organizations that work on insurance issues. 'It's a lose-lose situation,' for workers and insurance buyers alike, she says."[3] In fact, "lose-lose" stops short of the reality; lose-lose-lose is closer to the truth. For if customers and employees come out behind, there's no way the company can come out ahead for very long.

Yet insurers do need to cut costs and raise revenues. So the question is: Have any life insurance companies achieved superior levels of productivity in this difficult environment without shooting themselves in the foot? And if so, how have they done it? Figure 5-4, which examines home-office cost efficiency for the life insurance business, reveals that the firm with the lowest costs is Northwestern Mutual. Not coincidentally, Northwestern Mutual has not laid anyone off. On the contrary, Northwestern Mutual was the only company in *The Wall Street Journal* survey that was slowly but steadily creating more jobs. (Although State Farm

Figure 5-4 The Relationship Between Cost and Customer Retention in the Life Insurance Industry

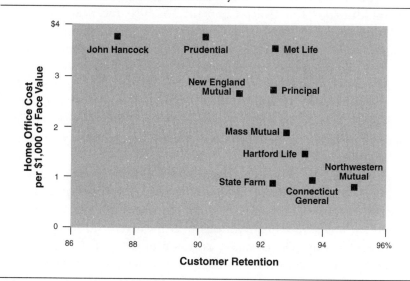

Source: A. M. Best, *1994 Best's Insurance Reports—Life/Health.*

Note: Top ten life insurers, ranked by 1993 ordinary life premiums: five-year average ordinary life expense per $1,000 of face value and five-year average retention rates.

is also creating jobs, and ranks among the top six companies in terms of new life insurance policies written, industry surveys often ignore it because of its historic emphasis on auto and home insurance.)

Northwestern Mutual isn't just the best company in terms of productivity; it also happens to have the highest customer retention rate among the major insurers, as Figure 5-4 shows. This is no coincidence, of course. In reality, customer retention seems to *explain* the productivity differences among these companies—partly because customer retention and agent retention go hand in hand, yielding higher productivity as a covariant, partly because customer retention requires fewer employees to handle start-up activities like underwriting from scratch, establishing files, answering questions, and solving new-customer problems.

Although reengineering and other cost-reduction tactics can be worthwhile in their own right, life insurers should always ask themselves if the change they're making will contribute to the delivery of superior value to customers. If it does not—for example, if cost reductions are contemplated purely to increase profit margins—then there will be no increase in customer retention. And Figure 5-4 makes it hard to believe that such cost reductions will be real or sustainable.

In the life insurance industry, the only way to create a lasting improvement in productivity is to engineer out the friction of defections. Northwestern Mutual, "The Quiet Company," is also the near-frictionless company, with policy persistency rates exceeding 95 percent. Since actual customer defections are lower than policy lapse rates, Northwestern Mutual probably suffers true customer defections of no more than 2 to 3 percent. By minimizing the costs of churn, the company has been able to maintain a ratio of one employee at headquarters for every two agents in the field and still deliver outstanding customer service and field support. Furthermore, Northwestern Mutual has better agent loyalty than any of its competitors.

As it happens, Northwestern, the master of loyalty, is also famous for its careful cost management. Where other insurance companies throw fancy conventions at famous resorts and foot the travel bill, Northwestern Mutual holds all its conventions in Milwaukee and makes agents pay their own way. The company is proud of the fact that it recently switched from paper to cloth napkins in its cafeterias, saving $30,000 a year, and that it saved another $18,000 annually with a new system for replacing toilet paper. Yet all of Northwestern's savings would not sustain superior productivity if they weren't reinvested in the delivery of superior value to customers and agents, earning their loyalty in the process. James D. Ericson, Northwestern's CEO, is constantly reminding his company "that this is a business of long-term relationships and loyalty."[4] To which we will only add, "and learning."

ALIGNMENT—SPENDING MONEY AS IF IT WERE YOUR OWN

We've looked briefly at a number of the mechanisms linking employee retention, learning, and productivity. We've also seen how loyalty leaders like Northwestern Mutual and State Farm use these links to raise efficiency and profits. Here's another example: high-loyalty business systems create the conditions that motivate employees to handle expenses—including the biggest expense, their *time*—as if they were spending their own money.

In their book *Free to Choose*, Milton and Rose Friedman describe a useful framework for thinking about the relative efficiency of spending money different ways. Figure 5-5 illustrates their four spending assumptions, spending your own money on yourself or someone else, and spending someone else's money on yourself or someone else. The most efficient case is the one where you spend your own money on yourself. The family

Figure 5-5 Resource Allocation Matrix (Friedman Matrix)

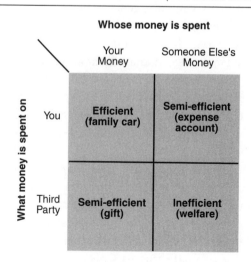

car is a good example: you know what you can afford, and you buy a car you like. The two partially efficient cases are when you spend someone else's money on yourself (the expense account lunch—you may spend too much, but you get the food you want) and when you spend your own money on someone else (a gift—you spend a prudent amount, but probably don't buy exactly what the other person was hoping for).

Both these cases have some inefficiency built into them, but either one is better than the fourth case—someone else spending your money for the benefit of a third party. The Friedmans' example is welfare: Congress spending taxpayers' money on poor people. The government spends an unreasonable sum of money, but the poor don't get what they think they need. Though the Friedmans used this construct to underline the atrocious inefficiency of our current welfare policy—a failure from almost anyone's perspective—it applies equally well to private businesses, which regularly set up purchasing, salary, and investment structures that have Department A spending the company's profits for the benefit of Department B.

What the loyalty leaders have done is to construct business systems in which a high proportion of purchases are treated like the family car. That is, outlays are controlled by the person or team that will benefit from the expenditure, and the money comes out of their own budgets. For instance, State Farm's agents are paid a gross commission, out of which they must pay all their own office and staff expenses. (Most other insurance companies control office expenses from headquarters.) Northwestern Mutual's general agents control office and payroll expenses at the local level, because the money comes out of their own pockets. The conventional logic sounds credible enough: let the agents use their time to sell insurance; management and real estate professionals can find the premises, negotiate leases, hire staff, and operate local offices. The trouble is the potential benefits of professional management and sophisticated control systems are overwhelmed by the effect of moving expense dollars out of the most efficient cell in the matrix and into the least efficient.

Like most of the big insurance companies, most fast food chains figure they can manage individual outlets better than local operators. Store managers are considered upper-level employees; on average, they earn about $35,000, of which 10 percent may consist of incentive bonuses for meeting budgets or getting decent customer-satisfaction or mystery-shopper scores. But compare this to Chick-fil-A's policy of delegating local management to the local store operator, who is not an employee but a profit-sharing partner. Which operator will work harder to find a way to decrease costs by $10,000 per year?

Store managers at Pizza Hut, for example, might earn a bonus as big as $1,500 for beating their budgets by $10,000. Since the turnover rate for store managers runs about 40 percent, the average operator probably expects to be at the store for only another year or two. That means the total bonus for discovering, planning, and implementing an efficiency worth $10,000 a year comes to roughly $3,000—$1,500 per year for two years. In fact, the manager's expected bonus stream would be even lower, because Pizza Hut would ratchet down the target in subsequent years to reflect the $10,000 cost reduction. The only way to earn additional bonus money would be to find additional savings. No wonder turnover is so high.

At Chick-fil-A, on the other hand, store operators get to keep half the store's profit. Given annual turnover of about 5 percent, the incentive to save $10,000 a year comes to $5,000 times the ten to twenty years the manager will operate the store—which is to say, $50,000 to $100,000, or more than twenty times the $3,000 in bonuses at Pizza Hut. Figure 5-6 emphasizes this point visually, and it is worth emphasizing. We will come back to it in Chapter 10, when we talk about the challenges of change management in two different types of business systems.

This number helps to explain how Chick-fil-A can run such an efficient operation with so few controls. Management doesn't have to worry that operators will ignore relatively small (but long-lasting) cost savings, or that they will make shortsighted cuts like skimping on portions or letting quality deteriorate. To the store manager, this month's profit is of little consequence compared to profits over the next ten or twenty years. As cost managers, Chick-fil-A operators are thus ten to twenty times more highly motivated than their counterparts at Pizza Hut. The same goes for revenue, an area where Chick-fil-A's store operators have an equal long-term stake and are equally creative. Consider these three examples from Chick-fil-A's own promotional materials.

> *Doug Jacobson, Operator of the Chick-fil-A restaurant . . . at Buckingham Square in Aurora, a Denver suburb, is successfully working with a local school district to provide students with appetizing lunch alternatives.*
>
> *Doug spent two years talking with school district members before receiving approval to provide Chick-fil-A products for school lunches. While waiting . . . Jacobson decided to try a different*

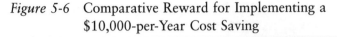

Figure 5-6   Comparative Reward for Implementing a
$10,000-per-Year Cost Saving

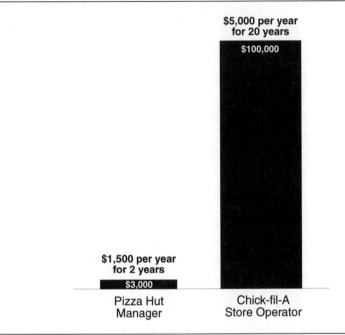

angle by adopting a local high school near his mall restaurant. He worked with their activity coordinator to cater special events . . . such as football games, band performances and senior days.

Jacobson finally received approval from the school district to provide . . . daily lunches to four high schools and lunch once a week to six middle schools and six private schools.

Jacobson [now] provides between 350 [and] 800 lunches a day, averaging 2,400 to 2,800 weekly.

The result of Jacobson's involvement in school catering has been a substantial increase in sales at his mall business.

Tim Burchfield, Operator . . . of the Chick-fil-A located in The Mall in Johnson City, Tennessee, uses an aggressive catering business to add sales and increase profits beyond his mall baseline.

Burchfield caters a variety of events such as business meetings, working lunches, employee parties, training seminars . . . for groups ranging from one to 1,200 people. . . .

"We . . . enhance the satisfaction of our clients [by] serving . . . on linen table cloths and upgrading Chick-fil-A hero sandwiches with gourmet pasta and desserts. . . ."

Recently, Burchfield has found another niche to pursue in the catering market—inflight food service for corporate jets belonging to the executives of some of the nation's top companies.

"Once you build client loyalty to your product, you create a catering 'domino effect.' Each catering job provides you with another audience to build awareness. . . ."

Chuck King, Operator . . . of the Chick-fil-A at Longview Mall in Longview, Texas, has set up a [satellite] lunch location [in a nearby business district] that operates Monday through Friday from 10:30 a.m. to 2:30 p.m.

A spinoff of his delivery service, King built the . . . unit to keep up with his customers' demands for Chick-fil-A deliveries.

"The satellite location provides a lunch option within walking distance of most downtown businesses," said King. "Customers like it because they are able to spend more time eating lunch and less time traveling to and from a restaurant."

King serves a limited menu to more than 150 customers a day. [He also uses] the satellite site for catering requests.[5]

Now, Pizza Hut executives might argue that Chick-fil-A pays these operators far too much for their actual accomplishments. A few creative people at headquarters could probably come up with all these marketing ideas and more. And when one store operator does have a brainstorm, why give equally lavish rewards to every operator who borrows it? Transfer innovation from the center. Nothing these operators have done or could do warrants half the profits forever. Does it really make sense to pay someone more than $100,000 to manage a fast food outlet?

But the counterarguments are stronger. For one thing, reducing costs and growing revenues is a process of discovery unique to each location and its particular environment. For another, it's hard to picture a $35,000-per-year functionary with the energy and drive to implement some of these schemes, let alone the imagination to think them up. For a third, the kinds of programs just described require community relationships that only ambitious, long-term operators have the motivation, time, and opportunity to develop. Finally, innovation often involves risk. The reward system at Chick-fil-A provides enough upside incentive to encourage risk-taking.

By contrast, in the big chains ambitious restaurant managers can't reach the top income echelons—$100,000 and above—by staying in one place. A successful career means getting out of restaurant management and into a regional staff position. Sadly, this approach means that the best store operators move farther and farther away from customers and front-line employees, carrying overhead expenses deeper and deeper into the Friedmans' welfare cell. It becomes harder to put an accurate value on the contributions these managers make to productivity growth. Worst of all, high turnover in store operators means that the company begins to slide back down its own learning curve, counteracting the value of many of the vertical investments the company made to grow productivity and profits.

MISALIGNMENT: THE BUREAUCRATIC MODEL

As State Farm and Chick-fil-A demonstrate, one successful approach to sustained value creation is built on relatively autonomous individuals and small teams sharing the benefits of their own productivity growth. The principal reason is that sharing value—especially sharing it as radically as Chick-fil-A—is a strikingly effective way of aligning the interests, goals, and motivations of the company and its employees. Of course, there is a competing approach, in which individual and team contributions to revenue, growth, and productivity are *not* shared or even measured, perhaps because their measurement is nearly impossible. The best example of this approach is banking.

Banks have had a powerful influence on the whole philosophy of human resource development. Banking was one of the first business bureaucracies, and bankers have always had a predilection for complex systems and confused accountability. To this day, banks have failed to settle on a definitive way of measuring profits by product line. Risk-based capital allocation, arcane accounting conventions (for example, loan-loss reserving), community reinvestment requirements, long risk tails resulting from current credit and pricing decisions, complex asset-liability matching and mismatching (which requires sophisticated option pricing models)—all have combined to make product-line profitability something of a riddle, and the true contribution of an individual employee an almost unqualified enigma. (Insurance economics are equally complex, by the way, but State Farm and others have nevertheless managed to untangle their profit and productivity systems.)

It's not productivity measures that drive a banker's career but the quest for promotion, combined of course with enough skill to sidestep or even prevent life-threatening disasters like Penn Square. In the absence of productivity measures, bankers searched for other ways to compensate their employees, and finally a Philadelphia bank executive named Edward N. Hay came up with a solution: a point system that rated a wide range of jobs on their difficulty and importance. The factors Hay took into account were things like the number of personal reports, the size of the expense budget, and the level of revenue responsibility borne by an employee. For decades Hay's scale has helped executives to determine how much to pay the head of the trust department as opposed to a commercial loan officer. The system is still widely used—in 1943, Hay founded a consulting firm and introduced it to a wide variety of industries—and has strongly influenced compensation philosophies for large, bureaucratic businesses everywhere. At every turn and in countless ways, it works hard *against* all the principles of loyalty-based management. Above all, it turns the principle of alignment nearly on its head by rewarding people for creating and maintaining many of the most counterproductive aspects of bureaucracy.

The idea of paying people for the importance of their jobs—instead of for the productivity of their teams—means that the only way to get ahead and earn more money is to get promoted. The terminal position in a bureaucratic organization is the chief executive, and most career paths point in that direction. It's an absurd system. Only one person at a time can hold the job, so 99.99 percent of the rest will necessarily fail to achieve their ambition. The counterproductive behavior this creates in the form of politics and personal disappointment is enormous.

In branch banking, for example, a good career start is to manage a small branch. Do a good job there, and in two to three years you'll move up to a medium-sized branch, then a large one, then a job or two in regional management before you move to the central office. The race to career success is the race to work at headquarters, the place where an individual's real contribution to productivity, growth, and profit is—by no coincidence—most difficult to track. The most successful, most highly compensated people in a bureaucracy rush headlong toward the least efficient cell in the resource allocation matrix.

Not surprisingly, bureaucracies eventually get into trouble in the competitive marketplace. Banks have suffered serious setbacks as the government peeled back regulations and less bureaucratic competitors stole their customers. While it is true that archaic regulations do hinder banks in their fight against stockbrokers, mutual funds, and insurance agents, the great enemy is still bureaucracy. Over the past twenty years, banks' share of their own customers' financial assets has dropped almost in half, from 40 to just over 20 percent today.

Customers have been defecting because the value banks offer is inferior. Indeed, the exodus got so bad that the banks had to cut their prices, which put pressure on profits, which led the banks to cut costs. Squeezing branch compensation accelerated turnover among branch managers, and that led inevitably to a decline in personal service. Less committed managers hire tellers less carefully, invest less effort in developing their employees, and of course, never get to know their customers well enough to provide superior advice.

Meanwhile, look at the competitive comparison. The average life insurance agent stays with his or her customers more than five years; the average stockbroker, almost ten. The poor bank manager stays at the same branch only three to four years. Even if the agent, broker, and branch manager were equally capable, this wouldn't be a fair fight. But as branch compensation has slipped farther and farther behind, banks haven't been able to attract as many good candidates. And the best of those they do attract escape to headquarters as quickly as they can.

So where Chick-fil-A and State Farm can rely on the inventive drive of their operator-agent partners to manage local productivity and profit, banks have salaried careerists whose main incentive is the prospect of promotion. Finding creative solutions to local branch problems cannot loom large on their horizon. Most banks have no systems for measuring branch or customer profitability, so the banks and their branch managers don't know which decisions are winners and which aren't. Local challenges are addressed at headquarters, but finding a solution that's right for all five hundred branches is next to impossible.

Despite all the bureaucratic counterincentives banks have introduced to keep branch managers from earning customer loyalty, evidence of the link between stable branch managers and customer retention shines through. Where our consulting teams have examined branch bank systems, they have consistently found that branches run by the same branch manager for more than seven years enjoy customer defection rates 5 to

10 percent lower than average. This alone should create plenty of loyalty surplus to share with branch managers, using partnership formulas like the ones at State Farm or Chick-fil-A. In one large branch system, we calculated that the surplus approached $1 million in present value per branch—more than enough to double or triple loyal and productive branch managers' incomes and still have plenty left over for customers and investors.

Customer complaints about poor service have led many banks to increase top-down controls and invest in mystery-shopper programs and satisfaction surveys. But the extra controls wouldn't be necessary if branch managers knew that customer revenues were the only way to earn a good living. The downward spiral that banks now seem to be trapped in has convinced many bankers that the branch system is a dinosaur and will always cost too much to operate. But the truth is, cost alone is not the problem. The problem is productivity.

How can there be no need for the personal service branch banks can offer when most of us can't make heads or tails of the IRAs, 401K, annuities, adjustable-rate mortgages, designer bonds, home equity lines, and the seemingly infinite variety of mutual funds that confront us in the new world of financial "services"? The average stockbroker makes more than $100,000. The average branch-bank manager makes $40,000. Squeezing more cost out of the branch system will eventually kill it.

The State Farms and Chick-fil-A's of the world have demonstrated the solution, and the formula bears no resemblance to the one bankers are pursuing. The answer is not to abandon branches or apply more pressure to costs; the answer is to build a network of value-aligning partnerships and then help your partners to find and exploit local opportunities to increase their productivity. A very small percentage of the partners at State Farm and Chick-fil-A aspire to a job at headquarters. For many, it would mean a cut in pay. The goal for the vast majority is not to be CEO but to run their own local units, achieve the highest possible level of productivity, and make a lot of money. Does that sound dreary? Even when you can turn a mall location into an executive-jet catering service? Monotony shows up in high turnover rates and low productivity. The partners at State Farm and Chick-fil-A are obviously not bored.

Of course banks are not the only businesses that need to break their bureaucratic chains. A lot of big companies suffer the same symptoms. A good way to know if your own company is a bureaucracy is to ask yourself this question: If your employees want more money or greater resources, to whom do they turn? To their immediate superiors? To you? Or do they turn to the ultimate source of all cash flow, the customer?

Some organizations are hard to break up into profit centers. For instance, almost twelve thousand of USAA's sixteen thousand employees are housed in a single massive building in San Antonio. It would be impractical to assign each customer to a specific phone representative. But USAA has found that it *is* possible to group its telephone reps into small teams of eight to twelve people, each with its own player-coach, who work and are measured together. This team structure is one of the key devices USAA has used to avoid bureaucracy and grow productivity.

THE ENEMIES OF PRODUCTIVITY

There is no one secret to superior productivity. Loyalty, motivation, learning, value-sharing, alignment of interests—these are all essential elements, and we have seen how they fit together in a productivity system. The first step is to recognize that costs and revenue are linked, and that it is employees who link them. Cutting costs at the expense of the only people in the business who are in a good position to increase revenue is a fool's solution to the productivity problem, because the proper goal is not low cost per unit but low cost as a percentage of revenues.

The second step is to grasp and confront the implications of the first step, namely, that to magnify employee loyalty and increase productivity, companies must do all they can to promote individual employee learning and the alignment of employee and company interests. One of the best ways of doing so is to make it possible for employees to increase their pay. In other words, the best way to cut costs (as a percentage of revenues) is very often to increase compensation opportunities, counterintuitive as that may sound.

In moving from this general theory to the specifics of company policies and practices, one excellent piece of advice is to look at what loyalty leaders do and then do the same, or as close to the same as you possibly can. Sometimes, too, the easiest way to get started is to look at the whole problem from the opposite perspective—not "What are they doing right?" but "What am I doing wrong?" Any number of the loyalty leaders began addressing and correcting their productivity problems in exactly this way.

Let's walk through some of the worst enemies of productivity, so you can think about ways to remove them from your business.

Fragmented Productivity Measures

Every business has measures. Most have too many. But a lot of companies fail to give employees any way of measuring their own contributions to the creation of value either for customers or the company.

Even when companies do measure productivity, they rarely track the learning curve for employees and teams as they gain experience over time. These businesses are simply unaware of what it might be worth to them to increase the loyalty and tenure of their employees. Banks, restaurants, and chain stores rotate staff from one location to another as a way of transferring best practice, but they fail to recognize the cost in productivity when employees slide back down the learning curve. Paying tellers low wages looks like a good, cheap solution to the productivity problem—until you start measuring the learning and productivity penalties for a high rate of turnover among tellers and customers.

While it makes sense to break down productivity measures into dimensions a specific department can focus on, companies must also tie these specifics to the broadest measures—revenue and profit per employee. Take the claims adjustment department of an insurance company. Most adjusters have no idea how their own productivity combines with other dimensions of the business to create value and profit. For example, claims adjusters are measured on the average size of the claims they approve—in insurance circles, this is called average severity—and claims adjusters are not usually promoted for having poor severity, that is, for being too generous. But when adjusters underpay, they risk alienating customers, who then defect and take their premiums elsewhere. Most adjusters will try to straddle this fence, but in a pinch—say, the end of a month front-loaded with several big claims—almost any adjuster will tend to be stingy.

The solution is to measure the retention rate for the customers who deal with each adjuster. Combining individual severity rates with individual retention rates yields a number that reflects the real revenue and profit impact on the company—a number to base a realistic bonus on. Teaching adjusters the value of increases in retention rate for various customer segments encourages them to make cash-rational decisions about how generous they ought to be on a given claim.

Mismatching Compensation and Productivity

Most people become more and more productive as they acquire experience in a job or business. The steepest learning curves tend to be in businesses where individuals (or the teams they belong to) get to share in the tangible benefits of learning. Chick-fil-A splits net profits fifty-fifty with its independent operators. A. G. Edwards pays branch managers on the basis of individual branch profits. State Farm pays level commission rates that are aligned with the company's own long-term economics: agents must build a good book of customers and then realize the benefits of their labors over time. But many businesses decline to share the gains, and so fail to develop their employees' full productivity potential.

The amount of profit employees contribute lies in the gap between their productivity curves and their compensation curves. In loyalty-based companies, compensation is a function of productivity, and the two grow or shrink in parallel. As a result, individuals are always seeking out ways to increase their productivity. In other companies, compensation is driven by the importance of the job or by tenure. The result is that employees don't know whether they are actually contributing to the bottom line at their current salary levels, so their learning is directed less at productivity than at promotion.

The U.S. Post Office is a classic example. Supervisors assign routes to mail carriers on the basis of what they believe is a reasonable workload for an average employee. With experience, however, mail carriers learn to do the job in less and less time. After several years, a smart carrier can finish a route that once took eight hours in six. But rather than let the carrier add to his route and earn more money, or go home early, or work a second job, the Post Office demands its eight hours. In fact, if carriers consistently finish early, their superiors may expand the size of their routes *without* increasing their pay. The only way to make more money is to get a promotion.

The result, of course, is that the best carriers find other ways to fill their days. Some sit in their cars and read. Some take half a dozen coffee breaks. The Post Office struggles to increase productivity, investing heavily in sorting equipment and electronic zip code readers. But productivity won't improve until employees begin sharing in the value they create.

By now you can imagine the solution: turn all local post offices into profit-sharing partnerships. Productivity, compensation, and service would all skyrocket. For that matter, given the value locked up in the present system, the government could probably get investors to buy post office franchises for enough money to take a bite out of the national debt.

Maybe the Post Office doesn't seem like a serious example, but it has a lot in common with most Fortune 500 companies, including bureaucracy, a unionized workforce, and a steadfast refusal to compensate people on the basis of their measurable contributions to productivity. Too many executives seem to believe that value-based pay is entirely a matter of compensation—of giving away profits, paying more. But in addition to the fact that value-based pay greatly enlarges the pie to be divided, it also eliminates unproductive employees. At a brokerage, for example, brokers receive between a third and half of all the revenues they generate. One of the reasons their productivity curve is so steep is that brokers who can't earn enough commissions to meet their living expenses voluntarily leave the business.

A well-conceived profit-sharing arrangement is a self-cleansing system. Chick-fil-A loses only 4 to 6 percent of its store operators per year, but those who leave are usually those whose productivity won't earn them enough income to live on. Without this cleansing, Chick-fil-A's system could not deliver the kind of superior productivity it does.

Hiring the Wrong People

Two kinds of hiring mistakes destroy potential productivity. The first is hiring candidates who can't raise their productivity fast enough to stay ahead of their compensation. The second is hiring people, however capable, who won't stay with the business long enough to earn back what it cost to bring them on board.

Few businesses are able to focus their hiring on the candidate pools that deliver the most productive and loyal employees, because few businesses have analyzed employee defections closely enough to predict the probable tenure of employees from different sources. We helped one brokerage do this analysis and found that first-year turnover varied from a low of 30 percent for candidates referred by other employees, to 45 percent for college recruits, to 55 percent for candidates responding to newspaper ads, to a high of 67 percent for brokers recruited from the competition. When the firm examined its cash-flow economics carefully, it found that first-year turnover above 50 percent destroyed value for the company. Surprisingly, more than half its new hires were coming from sources with turnover rates below breakeven. More surprising still, even after reviewing this information with branch managers and emphasizing the importance of retention, the company found that most new hires continued to come from the least loyal candidate pools. The basic underlying reason was that bonus cycles were too short.

Short Bonus Cycles

Brokering is the kind of industry where value-destroying behavior ought to be hard to find; after all, everyone's bonus is based on productivity. Yet problems can arise whenever today's decisions affect tomorrow's profit, but the people and teams who make them won't be around long enough to reap what they have sown.

The trouble is, most firms transfer their branch managers too frequently. Since many branch costs are driven by an investment cycle far longer than the average branch manager's tenure, the firm must base the manager's annual bonus on something other than long-term profit. You can't penalize today's manager because last year's manager paid a big up-front recruiting bonus to a broker who defected prematurely. And it doesn't seem fair to burden one manager's profit and loss statement with the whole cost of a recruit's training, when it will take several years for the recruit to start contributing profit—to a different manager's P&L. So bonus formulas tend to get stripped down to pure commission, and that encourages branch managers to do just one thing: make sure that every desk is equipped with a commission-generating broker. Cautious, selective recruiting might be better for the firm, but the only way it's better for branch managers is if they stay at one branch long enough to reap the benefit of their investment. At most firms, no one expects them to stay that long.

Crazy Career Paths

Another productivity monster is the career path that encourages employees to skip the position that drives value creation for the business. In a bank, this position is branch manager; in insurance, it's the local agent; in restaurants, it's the operator. If the primary route to prestige and higher compensation is to move past the terminal line position to a staff job whose impact on value and profit cannot be precisely defined, then customer loyalty, productivity, profit, and overall business longevity must all suffer.

Needless to add, you can't put compensation for the value-driving job into a bureaucratic box. If the salespeople in a sales-driven company find their territories subdivided after a great year, they won't want to be salespeople any more; they'll want to be sales managers. Chick-fil-A, remember, works hard to see that its top operators make more than $100,000. State Farm wants its agents to earn more than their managers.

Companies that compensate on the basis of job "importance" rather than profit contribution distort individual incentive. A position is by definition more important when it superintends more people. While employing fewer people might do more for profit, the point system pushes in the opposite direction—toward increasing costs instead of cutting them.

Inadequate Training

Effective training is critical to superior productivity. But many businesses give it far too little money and attention. Unfortunately, this behavior is perfectly logical. It's silly to invest aggressively in training if your employees defect after two or three years and apply their superior productivity to your competitor's bottom line. A heavy investment in training is not a rational strategy unless you combine it with some strategy for retaining trainees.

Of course, the best training comes on the job, where newcomers learn from older hands. Many firms depend on experienced employees to do much or all of their training for them, and a lot of veterans have become good and willing coaches. But the truth is, the most experienced brokers are not going to spend huge amounts of time training rookies when they could be earning commissions. Chick-fil-A *pays* its experienced operators to train new ones, so it gets their goodwill as well as better training. Chick-fil-A also encourages operators to hire their own assistants and train them, which creates another group of new operator candidates. In return, Chick-fil-A takes training efforts into account in awarding new satellite locations.

Mary Kay, the cosmetics company, has one of the best incentives for getting its people to recruit good candidates and train them well. It pays a small commission to the recruiter on every sale the recruit makes over her lifetime with the company. What's more, the monthly commission check shows veterans which of their recruiting investments are paying off and which could use a little help, encouragement, or extra training.

Ignoring the Difficulty of the Job

For ten years, a leading route-sales business had watched its driver defection rates climb. As more and more women joined the workforce, route operators found fewer customers at home and it grew harder and harder for them to earn a respectable income. The only way to maintain productivity was to work longer hours. Over time, the operators' average real incomes began to fall. Inflation hid part of the decline, but over the course of a decade, the average route operator's income dropped from the eightieth to the thirtieth percentile for workers of comparable skills and training.

The results were twofold. First, without knowing it, the company was attracting less capable employees. Second, fewer and fewer route operators were managing to raise their productivity to an acceptable level, so more and more of them were leaving. But higher turnover affected costs, putting upward pressure on prices, which diminished the relative value of the company's products and made the job even harder to do. The firm invested aggressively in productivity-enhancing tools like automated stocking systems and hand-held computers, but not even technology could bring productivity back up to historic levels.

The moral of the story: watch the average income per hour for your key employees. Unless it's stable or increasing (in real dollars), you are almost certainly attracting lower-caliber applicants, which will damage productivity and weaken the business system. As we will see in Chapter 9, the real solution to an apparent productivity problem may be that the fundamental value proposition the firm is offering customers needs retooling.

Layoffs

Most companies think layoffs are a great way to raise productivity. It's true, of course, that the ratio of revenue to people will go up if you throw some of those people out on the street. But in most cases, the relief is momentary. The truth is, layoffs *lower* productivity; in some cases they decimate it. Granted, some situations require layoffs for the sake of survival, and some require the short-term accounting gains that a layoff brings. But the ultimate price of a layoff is always high.

Take the case of Frank B. Hall, the insurance brokerage (now merged into the Rollins Hudig Hall Group). As Figure 1-2 (in Chapter 1) shows, in 1987 the company was dramatically underperforming its competitors in profitability and customer retention. That year, a group of investors acquired Frank B. Hall, hoping to bring its profitability up to industry averages. But instead of addressing the root cause of the firm's problem, poor customer retention (84 percent, the weakest rate among large national firms), the investors attacked high costs. They immediately laid off 10 percent of the workforce, to get costs back in line. Just the opposite occurred, however. Costs as a percentage of revenues worsened throughout 1988 and 1989. Profit per employee declined from $1,400 in 1986 to a *loss* of $3,300 per employee in 1987, $4,000 in 1988, and $6,900 in 1989. Management may have felt that some employees looked dead from the shoulders up, but clearly their customers felt otherwise; the customer defection rate increased almost as soon as the layoff occurred. Asked to comment on the firm's troubles, one Frank B. Hall executive responded with a fine piece of understatement: "Lost business has exceeded new business for the past couple of years, which has been a problem."

Figure 1-2 shows that the only insurance brokerages to achieve high profitability have also earned high levels of customer loyalty. For some reason, the management at Frank B. Hall thought it could ignore this underlying economic principle. Instead of looking for cost reductions, it should have looked for ways to remedy its excessive defection rate by increasing value to customers. Excessive defections are almost certainly a root cause of high costs, while cost reductions alone will do little or nothing to reduce defections. Managers should be skeptical of any cost reduction scheme that doesn't include a credible strategy for the enhancement of customer retention—which means a credible strategy for improving customer value, since value drives every customer's decision to stay or defect. It's hard to see how a layoff by itself could increase customer value. What layoffs *can* do is raise the level of uncertainty among employees and customers alike. In the case of Frank B. Hall, uncertainty at every level weakened customer retention, and the effect on profits was immediate.

In manufacturing, a layoff won't necessarily affect value to the customer as quickly as it did at Frank B. Hall, and layoffs have indeed become commonplace in the industrial sector, where they often increase short-term earnings. But in services, which now account for 70 percent of the nation's jobs, a layoff can affect customer retention so quickly that even short-term earnings suffer.

Low Growth

Productivity growth and revenue growth go hand in hand. Without plenty of new job opportunities to set their sights on, employees are not likely to identify cost reductions that threaten current job definitions. Moreover, costs have a way of creeping up in every organization, despite everyone's best efforts. The only way to keep the productivity ratio healthy is by growing revenue at a rate that's even healthier. Companies with only modest growth are unable to attract the best recruits and less likely to hold onto their best employees.

Chick-fil-A has steadily reduced its administrative costs as a percentage of sales, and its turnover rate at headquarters is less than 3 percent. These trends won't continue unless the company continues to grow and provide opportunities for all its exceptional people. The company has a target of $1 billion in sales revenue by the year 2000—not to impress Wall Street, but to give itself room to continue increasing productivity and share more and more of the benefits.

Inefficient Organizational Structure

Loyalty leaders seem to have one simple principle with regard to structure. They organize as much value-adding activity as possible into small teams, whose productivity and profitability can be measured. These teams are the basic molecules that make up the company. At State Farm, three-quarters of all employees work for local agents. The field staff is split into twenty-eight separate regions, each of which does its own pricing and manages its own budgets. Each region reports directly to the office of the president in Bloomington. State Farm believes this fragmentation into small teams is what has allowed the company to grow so large that it now serves 20 to 25 percent of the nation's households with a workforce of more than 150,000 people (most of whom work for State Farm agencies, not for State Farm).

Chick-fil-A is built on the same structural principle. The basic unit is the restaurant, run by the company's operator-partner. With only two hundred employees at corporate headquarters—counting field management—the company's six hundred locations produced total revenues of $400 million in 1994. The insistence on a lean central office is a winner in Friedman terms—it's very hard for someone at headquarters to spend a restaurant's money as effectively as the restaurant does itself.

The Friedmans' matrix is a good way to test how efficient your organizational structure allows you to be. Figure out what percentage of company expenses falls into each of the four cells. A typical commercial bank will find that 70 percent of its costs fall into the least inefficient cell. Very few companies will find themselves in the opposite situation, with 70 percent of their expenditures being made the way a family buys a car. Loyalty leaders can have 80 to 90 percent of their expenditures in this most efficient cell.

INTERNATIONAL COMPETITIVENESS

We know that loyalty has powerful implications for the productivity and competitiveness of specific companies, but how does it affect the productivity and competitiveness of nations? Measurements of productivity across national borders are notoriously unreliable. But if we simply examine the macroeconomic equivalent of sales per employee, GDP per employee (see Figure 5-1), we see that growth in U.S. productivity has lagged for more than thirty years—which is why the real incomes of American workers have not grown. Given the remarkable advances in automation, telecommunications, and information technology over the same period, this statistic is somewhat bewildering.

Surprisingly, the explanation may have something to do with the extreme flexibility of American workers. We have always seen this quality as a strength, and in the era of mass production it undoubtedly was one. An adaptable, itinerant workforce meant that we could always bring labor to our industrial needs wherever and whatever they might be. It is so common for Americans to move to a new town, a new job, or a new line of work, all more or less at the drop of a hat, that it amounts to a cultural bias; we see job-hopping as normal, even desirable. But this flexibility has a price: decreased loyalty. And the price goes steadily up as industry moves away from mass production, where learning was captured in factory and process design, and toward services, where learning builds on decision-making experience at the local level. In other words, it is just possible that in an age when competitiveness rests on problem-solving capacities, the versatility and mobility of the American worker has become a liability.

A recent study by the Organization for Economic Cooperation and Development found that the median length of employment for U.S. workers is three years, compared to about eight years in Japan and Germany. Investment in formal training is also much lower in the United States—which is not surprising if the average employee doesn't stay on board long enough to repay the investment. Indeed, if the average job in the United States has a learning curve anything like the learning curves for insurance agents, brokers, and truck drivers, that three-year average tenure may constitute an enormous drag on the potential productivity of U.S. companies. Even if the steepest increase in productivity takes place in the first two years of a job, there is still a significant problem. In the United States, 40 percent of employees stay with an employer two years or less, compared to 20 percent in Japan and 23 percent in Germany.

Another way to think about these differences is to look at retention rates. In Japan, with a 94-percent rate of employee retention, 50 percent of men in their mid-twenties will still work for the same employer ten years from now. In the United States, where the annual retention rate runs at 84 percent, fewer than 20 percent of men in their mid-twenties will still work for their current employer in ten years. In a world that is growing rapidly more competitive and more complex, it's hard to imagine that we won't have to provide employees with more training and teach them how to use more sophisticated tools if we're to stay in the game at all. But better training is hardly feasible in a system that encourages frequent defection. What we now hail as flexibility—companies with no investment in their employees, employees with nothing invested in their companies—is in all too many cases a debilitating weakness.

Japan and Germany have their problems too, of course. Japan's lifetime employment policies have come under pressure recently, and there are some visible disadvantages to inflexible capacity and compensation driven by seniority. Honda, Fujitsu, and other Japanese companies have begun to introduce performance incentives—a painful but necessary change. By itself, longer employee tenure does not guarantee superior productivity—look at the Post Office and some of the telephone companies. But with the right system of tools and incentives, the productivity advantages of greater tenure *can* be substantial. Look at State Farm.

While no country has an ideal system, Figure 5-7 raises some difficult questions. What is the optimal length of time for an employee to stay with a firm? What are the learning curves for typical jobs, and what might they be if the enemies of productivity growth were removed? Can we improve our national productivity and income growth without improving loyalty? In a recent interview in *Fortune,* Wolfgang Schmitt, CEO of Rubbermaid, offered this interesting point of view (intermixed with some observations by the interviewer):

Figure 5-7 Potential Employee Productivity as a Function of Tenure

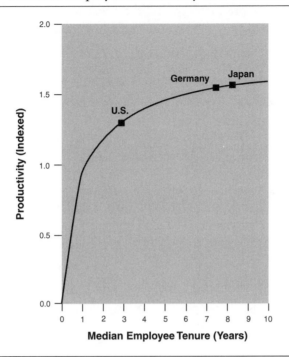

Sources: Median employee tenure, OECD *Employment Outlook,* 1993; typical learning curve, Bain & Company estimate.

"For the U.S. to compete really well in the world, we have to put more thought content into our products. That's what we're really good at."

What we're really bad at is handling people. When times get tough, we throw them away. Rubbermaid's prodigious profit growth has slowed to a mere 11% rise in the third quarter, and Schmitt is under some pressure from Wall Street to cut costs and lift earnings. He intends to do it by increasing productivity, not by reducing people. "Sure, we could take out a lot of our people. But we'd give up our future. One, we'd demotivate the ones who remained. Two, they surely wouldn't have the loyalty they now have. Three, if there were any good people left, they wouldn't be here long. They'd be looking around. And uncertainty reduces risk taking."[6]

Clearly, loyalty leaders and Wall Street take very different views of employee loyalty, productivity, and their link to profits. Just how they differ and what that difference can mean will be the subject of Chapter 6.

6

The Right Investors

So far, our discussion has centered primarily on improving the loyalty of customers and employees. Now it's time to take aim at the third business constituency: investors. In many respects, we've saved the biggest problem for last, since for many companies investor turnover represents an even greater and more intractable problem than customer and employee turnover. The average public company in the United States now suffers investor churn of more than 50 percent per year—more than double the turnover typical of customers and employees.

There's a good deal of irony here. Most management teams have put far more emphasis on delivering value to shareholders than to customers or employees, yet they've failed to improve investor loyalty. On the contrary, it's among investors that the decline in loyalty has been most precipitous. In 1960, an average share on the New York Stock Exchange changed hands every seven years. Today that average has fallen to less than two years. Convert these figures to an attrition rate of the kind we've been using for customers and employees, and you'll find that average annual investor defections have mushroomed from 14 to 52 percent over the last thirty-five years. Corporate owners have become far more transient than employees or customers.

In fact, this is more than ironic; it verges on baffling. Profit-based measurement systems have always been oriented toward investors. Though the streams of value delivered to customers and employees have remained intangible and difficult to quantify, managers can easily calculate value to investors by adding up dividends and appreciation in share price. So not only have managers given top priority to delivering shareholder value; they are also very good at measuring the value they deliver.

Yet here, paradoxically, lies one of the root causes of the decline in investor loyalty. Executives consistently strive to measure and manage the flow of value delivered *to* investors, but by and large they fail to measure and manage its mirror image, the flow of value *from* investors to the company. As a result, they also fail to make any attempt to find the right investors to begin with, the way they do (or ought to do) with customers and employees. To calculate this flow of value to the company, managers must be able to estimate the benefits received, net of the costs incurred, from various types of investors. Benefits include the stability of the cash investors provide as well as the value of their advice, their expertise, and even their constructive questions and demands, which can help managers to build a more successful company. Costs include the unconstructive demands, asset exploitation, managerial distractions, and systems instability that certain kinds of investors generate. By failing to recognize these costs and benefits, managers undervalue the worth and loyalty of the right investors.

Of course, most managers would *prefer* to have loyal investors, just as they would prefer to have loyal customers and loyal employees. But few have put the necessary effort into building a loyal investor base. As we will see later in this chapter, managers can't achieve investor loyalty simply by delivering more and more value to all their investors, no more than they can earn customer loyalty by delivering more and more value to all their customers. In Chapter 3, we saw how a company that continues to invest more and more value in unprofitable customers weakens its ability to provide superior value to its *best* customers. In Chapters 4 and 5, we showed how continuing to compensate unproductive employees eventually cripples a company's ability to deliver superior value to its best employees. In this chapter, we will see how catering to the needs of high-cost investors eventually impairs a firm's capacity to deliver value to the investors who cost the least and give the most benefit.

THE WRONG INVESTORS AND WHAT THEY COST

Let's take a quick look at who they are and where they came from, these high-cost investors who soak up more value from your business than they help to create. The biggest culprits are the short-term, trader-oriented investors who pressure managers to take expedient actions to boost short-term reported earnings. Surprisingly, few of them are aware of the enormous value destruction they are guilty of. They don't understand that their brand of capital has a tremendously high cost to the companies whose stock they buy and sell. Neither do the companies. As we've pointed out, management teams don't even measure the flow of value from investors, much less how it varies from one investor segment to another. To them, one share of stock looks like another. But the worst news is that we as a nation don't recognize the cost of massive short-term investing, so high-cost investors are steadily increasing their share of public capital markets and raising the rate of value destruction. Loyal investors are dwindling in number, and as a result, public companies are becoming more and more difficult to manage.

To understand how this came about—and to offer some corrective proposals—we need to review some recent history. Over the past three decades, public capital markets in the United States have become increasingly reliant on institutional investors, such as pension funds, mutual funds, and the professional investment managers who act as agents and advisors to individuals. According to a recent report cosponsored by the Harvard Business School and the Council on Competitiveness, institutional holdings grew from 8 percent of total equity in 1950 to almost 60 percent in 1990. Furthermore, as institutional ownership has grown, the character of the stock market has changed. Many investors no longer treat a stock as an instrument of ownership in a corporation but only as a derivative of economic factors, risks, and potentials. Interest rate volatility, leverage, commodity cycles, exposure to Beta risk—all have more to do with the decision to buy or sell a stock than the health of the underlying business assets. The volatile interaction of these factors causes perceptions of short-term performance to change so rapidly that many institutional managers rely on computers to keep up. It is common for institutional investors to churn their holdings at rates of 100 to 200 percent per year; some large investors approach a rate of 400 percent.

Now, it is perfectly reasonable to wonder what difference, if any, all this makes. Active trading in a stock does provide excellent liquidity, which should lower a firm's cost of capital. But there are countervailing costs that often overwhelm the liquidity advantage. One such cost is the increase in share price volatility that this excessive churning creates. We often read in the newspaper that a company's stock has plunged 25 to 50 percent in one day because quarterly earnings came in below expectations. It is hard to fathom how the intrinsic value of a business could change so radically on the basis of one quarterly report, but the market behaves as if it did.

Needless to say, it is difficult to manage a company for the long term when short-term volatility whipsaws market value, and with it the company's cost of capital. Any company that depends on the stock market to fund major investments subjects itself to enormous uncertainty. An executive with large stock options cannot help but be distracted at the sight of his or her net worth gyrating wildly on the market's perception of short-term results. The inevitable consequence is that management begins to concentrate more heavily on the short term, which can and does lead to underinvestment in many areas, particularly long-term customer and employee assets.

Another problem is that when short-term owners are in a position to influence management, they tend to make demands that generate destructive profits. For example, the exploitation of a company's balance sheet will often boost reported profits temporarily, exceeding analysts' expectations and driving the share price up—temporarily. Because the tools of exploitation—layoffs, pay cuts, price increases, advertising cutbacks, and cuts in R&D, technology, and training—are at times the right responses to changes in competitive conditions or in the marketplace, it isn't always easy to tell whether a business is being exploited or revitalized. Short-term investors don't care.

We've seen in dozens of ways that investors can prosper in the long run only by earning the loyalty of the right customers and employees. Underinvesting in the human assets of a business should be in no one's interest. But while long-term investors benefit from the delivery of superior value to customers and employees, it is quite possible for short-term investors to benefit at the *expense* of a business system's long-term participants. In such cases, the cost of investor churn is enormous.

Yet another cost comes in the form of increased turnover in the ranks of top management. At most companies, the expected tenure of senior executives is dropping, sometimes as a result of investor impatience with managers who don't meet short-term goals. In other cases, managers themselves see no reason to stick with a business through its inevitable ups and downs, given the lack of loyalty from current owners. In either case, the end result of premature executive departures is poor continuity, limited planning and investment horizons, and a slide back down the productivity and learning curves. Managers who see little chance that they will still be with a company three or four years hence are less likely to invest in the future than to concentrate on highly measurable short-term accomplishments that will embellish their resumes.

William Lynch, the current CEO of Leo Burnett, is dismayed by this executive instability, which is dissipating the knowledge base in many of America's top companies. Excessive management turnover not only destroys value for the company; it hurts others as well. Like any other advertising agency, Leo Burnett has a hard time maintaining effective long-term relationships with clients whose marketing executives bounce from company to company. The result is that customer retention rates have declined for the entire U.S. advertising industry, dragging down profit margins with them. Executive churn radiates through the entire network of suppliers and vendors, diminishing loyalty, lowering productivity, and destroying value for the whole system.

VALUE DESTRUCTION AND THE MARKET ANALYST

Many managers find it nearly impossible to pursue long-term value-creating strategies without the support of loyal, knowledgeable investors. As we have seen, there can be no healthy long-term partnership when the controlling partner attends only to quarterly results and, in doing so, impedes management's ability to manage for the long term and to deliver superior value to core customers, employees, and other investors.

And yet, how can short-term investors be responsible for all these problems? By definition, they don't hold onto their shares long enough to exert any direct influence on management. They probably never even meet the managers. Their computers take them in and out of many a stock before they know what business the company is in.

This is where stock market analysts come into the picture. Analysts know a great deal about specific industries and companies. They do meet managers. And because brokerages hire them to cater primarily to speculative traders (from whom brokerages earn the bulk of their commissions), their views on corporate strategy and management performance are a critical driver of portfolio turnover.

These analysts include a great many bright, insightful people who understand business and know very well that the long term is important. But their best customers are interested in short-term results, and their employers are interested in short-term trading, so they concentrate on short-term earnings and the layoffs and restructurings that drive them. The consequence is that managers too become obsessed with short-term results. After all, the analysts' evaluation of a company's performance can significantly alter a manager's career path. In this way, analysts exert a tremendous influence on how management teams think about their businesses, and on the tradeoffs they make between the short and long term.

To get a rough idea of how much value investor disloyalty is destroying in your company, ask yourself these questions: How much energy does senior management focus on short-term as opposed to long-term strategies? How much time and energy go into the management of earnings, so that stock market analysts will make positive remarks in their reports? How much time do senior managers spend building resumes and safety nets instead of attacking critical long-term problems? Finally, how much more would your company be worth over the next five years if your owners behaved like long-term partners?

The answers to these questions can help you calculate how much your current investor mix is raising your cost of capital. Furthermore, if you reckon that a set of loyal owners would increase your company's long-term earnings trajectory by, say, 5 percent per year, then you should load that opportunity cost back onto the shoulders of the high-churn investors to find the real cost of their capital. Doing this analysis will shed new light on the actual price of short-term capital and give you a new appreciation of the value of low-cost, loyal capital. Fortunately, there is hope. A number of companies, having done the analysis and found the cost of disloyal capital even higher than they imagined, have decided that their investor mix has to change. They've stopped moaning about the problem and begun to fix it. They *have* to fix it if they are to build companies that can deliver consistent long-term value to customers, employees, and investors. If you want that kind of company, you'll have to solve the problem too—and there are practical steps you can take to address it.

PICKING INVESTORS WITH CARE

Just as there are customers and employees who are right for your business, there are investors who are right. These are the investors who bring value beyond their cash. They understand the business; they're guided by the right long-term measures; their investment timeline fits your value-creation cycle. Ideally, they understand that their own long-run benefit depends on the delivery of superior value to customers and employees. They endorse the philosophy of loyalty. They behave like partners.

There is no public company in the world lucky enough to have its shares entirely in the hands of perfect investors. But there are practical alternatives that managers can pursue to decrease their cost of capital. The most dramatic of these is to take the company private, but there are less radical alternatives. The loyalty leaders we've looked at in preceding chapters suggest a range of possibilities.

To begin with, it is no coincidence that so few of the loyalty leaders described in this book are public companies. Some are privately owned— Johnson & Higgins, Leo Burnett, Chick-fil-A—and some are owned by their customers—State Farm, Northwestern Mutual, USAA. Most believe they would find it very difficult to pursue their loyalty-based strategies as public companies.

Nevertheless, some loyalty leaders have managed to prosper as publicly owned corporations. MBNA and A. G. Edwards are both traded on the New York Stock Exchange; Lexus is a division of Toyota, a public company. But these publicly owned loyalty leaders tend to have one or several core owners with a pronounced vested interest in the company's long-term success. Along with his associates, MBNA's chairman, Alfred Lerner, controls 15 to 20 percent of MBNA's stock. When he and his associates believe that other investors are undervaluing the company, they buy shares and stabilize the price. More, perhaps, than any other single factor, this stability in ownership and share price has allowed the company to concentrate on long-term results. At Toyota, the Toyoda family has played a similar leadership role, enabling management to take a long-term perspective.

Ownership at A. G. Edwards is relatively widespread. But the founding family's influence still makes itself felt through Ben Edwards III, even though he controls less than 2 percent of the shares, and insiders as a group control less than 5 percent. The key to pursuing a consistent loyalty-based strategy even without a strong core stockholder is to communicate the company's philosophy to shareholders and get them to buy in. Ben Edwards has succeeded at this task, though he does have the advantage of history. The company has pursued its loyalty-based vision for so many decades, its investors are now largely self-selected—people with confidence in the business philosophy and in management's ability to implement it.

One way or another, each of the loyalty leaders in this book has built a foundation of stable ownership that has freed management to attend to long-term value creation. It *is* possible to overcome or sidestep the disadvantages of public ownership. There are four principal ways of doing it:

1. Educating current investors.
2. Shifting the investor mix toward institutions that avoid investment churn.
3. Attracting the right kind of core owner.
4. Going private.

None of these methods is as easy as it sounds, but a loyal investor base is worth a good deal of extra effort.

Educating Investors

The first approach is to educate investors about the role that customer and employee loyalty play in creating long-term value for shareholders. Lay out for them the principles of loyalty-based economics and explain how they operate in your business. Prove to them with facts and analysis that the companies in your industry with the highest loyalty also earn the highest profits.

Once investors believe that loyalty is a rational goal that leads to higher profit, they will want to see measures of loyalty that can be used to gauge your progress. You must find measures that are rigorous and trustworthy, demonstrate their relevance, and then show how they relate to more familiar measures like accounting-based profit and cash flow. Many investors realize that short-term profit gives an inadequate picture of a business's health and future prospects. But few management teams have ever offered them a satisfactory alternative. It's one thing to wax eloquent about the importance of loyalty and the need for a long-term perspective and another to deliver practical definitions and auditable measures of loyalty. This is especially true if the emphasis on loyalty represents a new direction for the company. Ben Edwards can say "Trust me" to his investors, and they will rely on his record of superior earnings. He's earned the right to continue to hire new brokers right through an industry downswing, with analysts calling for layoffs. But without his track record, you must make a very persuasive case for loyalty.

Unfortunately, arguments about delivering value to multiple constituencies do not have an excellent history. Investors have heard it all before and have every reason to be skeptical. During the 1950s and 1960s, the top managers of many public companies saw themselves as trustees, responsible to a wide variety of stakeholders beyond shareowners. Ralph Cordiner, CEO of General Electric, was a leading spokesman for this camp. He claimed it was management's responsibility to manage "in the best-balanced interests of shareholders, customers, employees, suppliers, and plant community cities."[1] But Cordiner and his peers failed to develop a way to measure the amount of value owed or delivered to each of those constituencies, so in the end they were accountable to no one.

While most management teams of the day did their best to act responsibly, the absence of well-defined measures and clear goals reduced discipline to near zero. As a result, performance languished, and when the system encountered foreign competition—which by the early 1960s had recovered from the devastation of World War II—it began to collapse. From then on, the "best-balanced interests of stakeholders" became a joke, both in investment circles and at business schools. The very concept was derided as an excuse for ineffective, self-serving, unaccountable management. The device the market used most effectively to seize control from undisciplined management teams was the hostile takeover, which flourished through the 1970s and 1980s. More recently, boards of directors have taken matters into their own hands, firing CEOs when necessary.

These well-publicized victories by hostile raiders and boards caused executives with a stakeholder bent to reconsider. Thoroughly modern management teams began to espouse a new philosophy, called "maximizing shareholder value." Indeed, as the market reasserted its control and ousted entrenched and underperforming management teams, maximizing shareholder value took on an almost moralistic ring.

So if you want to distance yourself from the discredited management teams of earlier generations, you must offer a compelling economic argument backed up by precise measures. Even that may not be enough if your company has no history of loyalty-based management. Your investors may be polar opposites to the ownership groups that loyalty leaders like A. G. Edwards have attracted over time. If so, it may not be possible to overcome their resistance and change their minds. In such a case, you'll need to consider a second alternative, which you can pursue in tandem with investor education: altering your investor mix by means of target marketing.

Targeting Low-Churn Institutions

We saw in Chapter 3 that customers have inherently different loyalty coefficients. So do investors. While the average institutional investor may churn its portfolio at a rate of 60 percent per year, it is possible to find institutions that prefer to buy and hold. By searching out these loyal investors and persuading them to invest in your stock, you can steadily enrich your investor mix.

One corporation that has taken this approach is Nike, the athletic shoe company. Nike managers decided they could not achieve their objectives without a core of stable long-term investors. But instead of just complaining about the outrageous short-term speculative behavior of institutional investors, they took their own advice to "Just do it." In 1989, Nike's management team developed a program to attract investors who would buy and hold Nike stock. The company began marketing its stock the same way it markets its shoes: it segmented investors and tailored its marketing approach to the shareholders it wanted.

To follow this segmentation strategy, you must first divide investors into groups based on their portfolio turnover rates. Figure 6-1 shows the 1993 portfolio turnover rates for the seven hundred U.S. investment managers with more than $100 million under management. The turnover rates among these major managers ranged from less than 5 percent to almost 400 percent per year. Average turnover for the group as a whole was 62 percent.

As the figure shows, 39 institutions churned less than 10 percent of their portfolios in 1993. Another 178 churned between 10 and 25 percent. Some of these weren't actively trying to beat the market but were simply indexing. Others *were* trying to outperform the market and were actively seeking positions in companies they believed would generate superior long-term results. A fair number of the 357 institutions showing churn rates between 25 and 50 percent may also have been investing for the long term, because while they traded one group of stocks very actively, they invested in and held another group. Their high rate of trading disguises their core of stable holdings. If your company can qualify as a core holding, then those investors, too, could lower your cost of capital.

Still, the best place to start is probably with institutions that show a real preference for long-term investments. One name that leaps from the list of the ten largest institutions with the lowest portfolio turnover

Figure 6-1 Portfolio Turnover Rates and Average Holding Periods of the Top 700 Institutional Money Managers

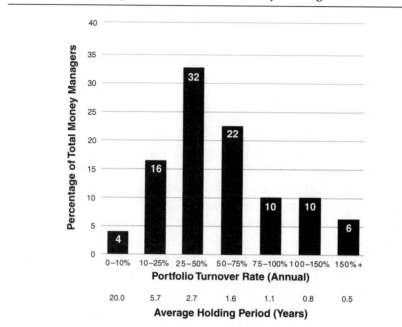

Source: CDA/Spectrum, "13(f) Turnover Report," 1994.
Note: Includes all money managers with more than $100 million in equity assets under management in 1993.

rates is—predictably—State Farm. The Good Neighbor holds more than $18 billion in equities and turns them over at the neighborly rate of only 3.4 percent per year. And no, it is not simply indexing. It seems that the company's philosophy of long-term loyalty and partnership extends all the way to its strategy for investing in public stocks. By sticking with its investments, State Farm has been able to outperform the S&P 500 over the long term, which places its performance solidly in the top quartile of all investment managers.

What gives State Farm the capacity to manage a low-churn portfolio is the highly predictable cash flow it draws from its high rate of customer retention. What gives it the will is partly the fact that low-churn investing minimizes transaction fees and taxes and partly—indeed mostly—the fact that it believes this is the right way to do business. State Farm understands the great economic advantage its own loyalty-based system creates and is convinced that the same approach will work as well in other industries. It therefore seeks to invest in companies whose management teams approach their businesses in the same spirit—companies with a long, continuous culture of building and investing for the long term.

Kurt Moser, State Farm's vice-president for investments, sums it up this way: "We tend to think a long time before we make an investment in a company—and we think an equally long time before we sell. We suspect Wall Street feels we are too stodgy—they think we've lost touch with reality and don't understand about modern theories of money management—but this approach seems to work for us. Our analytical work stresses direct contact with the company. We strive to know the company's management team as well as we can. We talk to them and to their vendors, customers, and competitors. This is how we identify companies with a long-term viewpoint."[2]

Moser notes that few management teams show State Farm their measures of customer or employee loyalty. But he is very interested in getting to know companies that understand the power of loyalty and have built the measurement systems to manage it. Such companies would certainly get an audience with State Farm's investment committee.

State Farm sometimes feels like the Lone Ranger in today's high-churn investment world, and for that matter its approach is growing less and less common. But while there are few investors as steadfast as State Farm, there are more than two hundred institutional investment managers with churn rates below 25 percent. Once you have identified the investor groups with the highest loyalty coefficients—that is, the highest stability and the lowest cost of capital—you need to find the subset most likely to be interested in investing in a company like yours.

The way Nike did this was to analyze the earnings growth and cash-flow patterns it could realistically deliver, sort through the universe of public companies to find those with similar results, and then identify the investors who owned significant positions in those firms. By marketing itself to those investors, Nike was able to shift almost 30 percent of its shares into their hands.

Attracting a Core Owner

The third approach, which pushes the second one step further, is to find an institutional or individual investor who will buy a controlling position in your company. The company remains public, but getting the right kind of investor to buy into your vision of long-term value creation can free you from a lot of counterproductive short-term pressures and help make the vision come true. Needless to say, the things to look for are business philosophy, integrity, and a track record of long-term, stable holdings.

Perhaps the archetype is Warren Buffett, the legendary investor-genius from Omaha. For three decades, Buffett has demonstrated a predilection for long-term partnerships. Portfolio turnover at Berkshire Hathaway, his company, runs at about 8.2 percent, and investment returns have been phenomenal. A purchase of $10,000 of Berkshire Hathaway stock in 1965 would have increased in value to $5,356,940 by 1995. Over the same thirty-year period, Berkshire Hathaway's book value grew at a rate of better than 23 percent annually. Buffett's own stake in the company is now worth more than $10 billion.

Buffett has taken positions in only about two dozen companies over the past two decades, but he buys a significant stake and brings more to his investments than the stability of his money. While he invests only in companies with strong management teams and stays out of their way when they don't need him—in his words, he doesn't try to teach 400 hitters how to hit—he often does provide valuable advice and assistance. Most frequently, he helps to structure the compensation of top management so that their incentives are aligned with the interests of long-term investors.

Buffett's views on value creation are clearly oriented toward the long term. In Berkshire Hathaway's annual report, Buffett emphasizes that he simply doesn't care about the short-term stock price. "What a company's stock sells for today, tomorrow, next week, or next year doesn't matter. What counts is how the company does over a five- or ten-year period."[3] When asked how long he prefers to retain an investment, he often says that his favorite holding period is "forever."

Buffet treats his own investors, the shareholders of Berkshire Hathaway, the way he himself would like to be treated as a stockholder. He spends no time managing the company's reported earnings. In his 1989 annual report he wrote, "We simply don't care what earnings we report quarterly."[4] He refuses to engage in what he regards as window dressing—stock splits and all the other activities investment bankers recommend to make stocks look more attractive. In his annual report for 1992, he wrote:

Overall, we believe our owner-related policies—including the no-split policy—have helped us to assemble a body of shareholders that is the best associated with any widely-held American corporation. Our shareholders think and behave like rational long-term owners and view the business much as [my partner] Charlie and I do. Consequently, our stock consistently trades in a price range that is sensibly related to intrinsic value.

Additionally, we believe that our shares turn over far less actively than do the shares of any other widely-held company. The frictional costs of trading—which act as a major "tax" on the owners of many companies—are virtually nonexistent at Berkshire. . . . [T]here is no way that our shareholder group would be upgraded by the new shareholders enticed by a split. Instead we believe that modest degradation would occur.[5]

Of course, half the businesses in the country would like to attract an investment by Warren Buffett, but Buffett is very selective. He is interested only in companies with a high return on equity, a strong customer franchise, modest capital investment needs, and a simple, comprehensible business. Most important, the market price must be well below Buffett's estimate of the company's intrinsic value, which he bases on a calculation of the discounted cash flows the company will generate. Despite these hurdles, there is already a long line of potentially acceptable companies knocking at Buffett's door.

But even if Buffett isn't a realistic alternative, you don't have to give up. Happily, he isn't the only investor with a business philosophy that hinges on loyalty, patience, far-sighted value creation, and alignment of interests. Another man who pursues this kind of investment strategy is Paul Desmarais, chairman of Power Corporation of Montreal. Desmarais has amassed a personal fortune of more than $1 billion by investing selectively in just a few companies and sticking with them.

Desmarais buys and sells companies only rarely. To sell, he must believe that the price he is offered exceeds the value he could achieve by holding onto the company and continuing to improve it. To buy, he looks for high-grade assets that he can improve well enough to more than offset the purchase premium most acquisitions involve. Although such companies are hard to find, Desmarais and his CEOs are interested in acquiring more. His business managers can therefore seek out good strategic acquisitions without becoming hostage to the whims of the stock market. They know Desmarais will provide the capital for an acquisition whenever it makes good long-term economic sense. They also know he will buy more shares in any of his companies that the market undervalues.

Representatives of Power Corporation or its affiliates sit on the boards of the companies in Desmarais's portfolio and make sure that management concentrates on the right problems and potentials. Desmarais is very loyal to his management teams, believing that capable, trustworthy business managers are hard to find.

Another such investor is Alfred Lerner, MBNA's largest shareholder. Lerner takes major positions in only a few companies. Besides being a skillful investor, he advises the management teams of the companies he buys into. At MBNA, Lerner played a key role in shaping the company's initial public offering, in creating an efficient capital structure, and in designing management compensation so as to maximize both performance and loyalty. The stability Lerner brought to the company enabled it to continue the aggressive loyalty-based growth strategy that has catapulted the firm to the number-two position among bankcard issuers, based on credit balances outstanding.

As we've noted earlier, MBNA sets great store by customer and employee loyalty. Pick up almost any annual report and you'll find some variation of what is in effect the company's motto: "Success is getting the right customers . . . and keeping them." But success in getting and keeping the right customers is partly a matter of getting and keeping the right investors—people like Alfred Lerner. And from the investor's point of view, success means getting and keeping the right management team, constructing the right partnership with them, and contributing to the probability of their success whenever possible by offering advice, counsel, and expertise—or occasionally by simply asking the right questions.

Another approach managers might consider is to look for loyal investors—individuals or institutions—overseas. In countries like Germany and Japan, investors are much more likely to stick with their investments for the long term. In Japan, the average share of stock in a public company is held for seven years, compared to less than two years in the United States.

Toyota, for example, is a publicly traded stock in Japan, but the company has nevertheless been able to run its business according to the philosophy of "Customer first, dealer second, company third." The Lexus success story could never have happened without a patient owner. Dave Illingworth, the first general manager of Lexus (and now group vice president of Toyota, U.S.), believes that Toyota's loyalty-based corporate philosophy gave his team an enormous advantage over American competitors. An example he points to is the support he received from corporate headquarters when Lexus recalled its LS 400 just three months after the car's introduction. The company and its owners stood firmly behind the decision to do what was right for the customer, even though it severely penalized the division's contribution to quarterly earnings. As a result of their support, Lexus was able to reduce the inconvenience of the recall by offering customers free pickup and delivery of their automobiles. Service departments washed the cars and filled them up with gas before returning them.

Illingworth believes that giving high priority to short-term results will end up destroying value not only for the customer and employees, but in the end, for the company itself. In his words, "The more you focus on the bottom line, the harder it is to hit."[6] Imagine how U.S. stock market analysts would respond to a manager with that point of view. Luckily, Toyota's owners aren't listening to the analysts.

Large institutional investors in countries like Japan are used to taking significant ownership positions in companies and then playing an advisory role. Rather than dump shares when they're disappointed in performance or strategic direction, they deal directly with management. In many cases, their holdings are so substantial, they have no real alternative; selling the stock would lower the value of their shares. German banks and insurance companies take a similar role when they buy a company's stock. This kind of close relationship with investors makes some American managers cringe, but the advantages are real. George Siemens described the advantage of the German system this way: "If one can't sell, one must care."[7]

There are worse things in business than a caring partner, especially if your company is in a state of turbulence or transition. At such times, the added stability of loyal investors can make an enormous difference. But of course, it's at just such moments that many institutions find it more convenient to sell than to dig in and help management with its long-term challenges and opportunities.

Going Private

The final approach, taking the company private, liberates managers from the volatility of public markets, the carping of securities analysts, and the short-term thinking of transient investors. This course of action is an ideal solution for some companies and their customers and employees. But there can be substantial risks—two in particular. The first is that most companies must take on additional debt in order to buy back their stock, and not all businesses have the right cash flow to do so safely, especially in times of turmoil. The second and greater risk is the choice of a leveraged-buyout firm to act as your partner. Unfortunately, going private rarely means complete independence. What you'll almost certainly have to do instead is to create a far more intimate partnership than you have ever experienced before. There are plenty of bad LBO partners—asset strippers, financial engineers, corporate breakup artists—who won't help you create value but will simply reallocate your value into their own pockets. Luckily, there is also another kind of private investment firm, and these companies, as partners, are every bit as attractive as Warren Buffett. They're asset builders, and they recognize the value of long-term stability and loyalty. Rather than engineering a financial restructuring, they prefer to become long-term partners in the development of value-creating strategies that leave everyone—customers and employees as well as investors—better off. Experts estimate that the average holding period for private equity investments is four to six years—two to three times longer than the average for public markets.

One successful example of such a private investment group is Bain Capital, founded in 1984 by several former management consultants. According to Mitt Romney, the group's managing partner, the strategy is "to buy companies only when we believe we can help build the business asset and increase its value. We search for growth opportunities, new markets, new outlets, new channels, or merger candidates that would strengthen a franchise. Slashing costs is not our business. We see people as the key asset we're acquiring."[8]

Investment loyalty plays a central role in Bain Capital's value-creation strategy, and it has paid handsome dividends. Since its founding, the firm has invested in eighty companies with cumulative sales of approximately $8 billion. While no LBO firm can succeed in every one of its deals, the group's asset-building strategy has been successful in all but a handful of cases. Returns from its investments have averaged better than 90 percent per year over the past decade.

Bain Capital is structured so that the general partners can earn superior incomes only if the limited partners—their investors—earn superior returns. Unlike pension fund managers, whose pay depends primarily on the size of the asset pool they control, the general partners are compensated primarily on the basis of a carried interest in the money they invest. Specifically, they get 20 percent of the value they create for their investors. Limited partners commit funds for five to ten years, which means general partners can focus on the long-term success of their investments, instead of concentrating on quarterly performance so investors will reward them with more funds. The stability of this structure allows Bain Capital to search out situations where it can create significant value over a period of years. In practice, the partners can pass along this stability to management teams whose plans call for value-creating strategies too bold, too complex, too slow, or too contrarian for public investors.

Corporate Software

One recent example is the acquisition of Corporate Software, Inc., in 1994. Corporate Software was a public company, the leading global supplier of microcomputer software and related support services to businesses. Corporate marketed more than three thousand products from vendors like Microsoft, Lotus, Novell, Borland, WordPerfect, and others. For seven years it traded on the NASDAQ exchange. By 1993, however, the business was in trouble. Corporations were discovering they could purchase software directly from manufacturers and download it over telephone lines—which meant they could bypass distributors like Corporate.

Corporate's managers, who did not intend to stand idly by and watch the company go under, wanted to shift the firm's emphasis from selling shrink-wrapped software to providing software advice and technical support, which they considered a much more dynamic and potentially lucrative field. But the shift in strategy seemed impossible to finance. It would require an aggressive investment and hundreds of new employees: the company wanted to increase its technical support staff from thirty to one thousand over a four-year period. The stock market was convinced that Corporate's business would decline, and the stock price reflected a negative assessment of the firm's future.

The only apparent solution was to take the company private. The *Boston Globe* reported that the management team's aggressive growth strategy was sure to hammer earnings in the short run; the company needed to be shielded from the daily earnings pressures of Wall Street. Morton Rosenthal, the company's chief executive, told the *Globe,* "We felt that being private would give us more flexibility and a more long-term view of doing business as opposed to focusing on quarterly results."[9] An analyst commented that without Wall Street's constant scrutiny, the management team would find it much easier to trade short-term rewards for the long-term gains of switching to the support end of the business. And Mark Nunnelly, one of the general partners at Bain Capital, had this to say about the potential fit between a company like Corporate and a private investor like Bain Capital: "When you are facing a transition from a reseller of software to a value-added support services firm, there could be some significant earnings blips. I believe a private investor is both well situated and capable of understanding those risks."[10] The deal was struck.

The cost of taking the company private was $95 million, and over the next five years, Bain Capital's plan was to pump another $10 million to $15 million into additional staff and new computers. As with all the group's other investments, the fortunes of Corporate's management would rise or fall along with Bain Capital's—Corporate's management would own more than a third of the newly private firm. Perhaps the most striking aspect of the arrangement was that even though Bain Capital expected to earn high rates of return on its investment—as a rule, the firm aims for 30 to 35 percent—the true cost of capital to Corporate was lower than the cost of public equity. Bain Capital not only paid 30 percent above market price to purchase 100 percent of Corporate Software; it awarded 37 percent of the upside to management.

This kind of investment partnership brings value in addition to a lower cost of capital. It brings stability; the correct time frame for value creation; a deeper knowledge of the business than public markets can ever possess; and an expertise in building the kind of value that will carry weight with potential buyers in five or six years. And it brings alignment—a structure within which neither partner can succeed alone. The management teams at Bain Capital and Corporate Software must both succeed if either is to prosper.

Progress at Corporate Software came much more rapidly than anyone anticipated. In the first sixteen months after going private, Corporate's sales and profits almost doubled as a result of three acquisitions and growth in excess of 30 percent. In April 1995 the company merged with the global software services division of R. R. Donnelley & Sons to create Stream International, Inc., with combined sales of $1.3 billion. Morton Rosenthal is now CEO of a company positioned to be a global leader in software services, and Bain Capital's stake is on track to return many times the original investment.

Accuride

Another example of a company that was taken private in order to realize value it could not tap as a public company is Accuride, the leading North American manufacturer of steel wheels for trucks. When Firestone Tire & Rubber Company decided to divest businesses outside its core tire franchise, Bain Capital saw in Accuride a splendid opportunity—over time—to build market share, cut costs, improve management alignment, and increase value and profit. Bain Capital won the bidding partly on the basis of the price it offered and partly on its commitment to lay off none of the company's current employees. As we'll see, Bain Capital's strategy for cutting costs was not to eliminate human know-how and experience but to retain it and reward it more effectively.

The ideal LBO investor brings not only money to a company but skills and proficiencies as well. One of the important assets Bain Capital brought to Accuride was expertise in finding ways to deliver better value to customers. Accuride was already doing well on that dimension, with nearly 50 percent of the market. But the investment group helped management find creative ways of using value-sharing partnerships to win a 100-percent share of several large accounts. By carefully analyzing Accuride's plant economics, the investment team and Accuride's management realized that they could reduce costs 5 to 10 percent if they could increase run lengths (the number of wheels that can be made without tooling changes or production line modifications) by 50 to 100 percent. To make longer runs possible, management reviewed the potential benefits with customer executives and offered to pass along the majority of the savings if, in return, customers would award 100 percent of their business to Accuride.

Accuride's principal competitor was Motorwheel, a division of Goodyear. Because Goodyear, a public company, was under short-term earnings pressure, especially in its core tire business, Bain Capital assumed it would pressure Motorwheel not to cut prices. Since Bain Capital was quite indifferent to short-term reported earnings, it concentrated instead on how to build Accuride into the most valuable asset possible, encouraging Accuride to sacrifice immediate income for the sake of building customer share.

Bain Capital and Accuride's management team made several other improvements in the business. The company had two plants, one in Canada and the other in Kentucky, with very different labor rates, overhead structures, capacities, and raw material costs. With Bain Capital's support, Accuride completely reorganized production in the two plants to take advantage of their relative strengths and increase efficiency. Though the reorganization required a good deal of work and risk, the question is why it was never done before, while Accuride was a division of Firestone.

The answer to that question is that management never had the incentive. Firestone's compensation plan for Accuride's managers included a base salary plus an annual bonus based on performance against budget. This is the kind of incentive structure most U.S. corporations use. On the surface, it seems logical; in practice it is dreadfully inefficient. It motivates managers to negotiate low earnings targets, so they can easily exceed them and earn the maximum bonus. It also motivates managers to devote inordinate amounts of time and energy to the budgeting process, with top management demanding higher earnings and divisional management arguing the higher targets are unreachable. At the same time, of course, smart divisional managers are squirreling away opportunities to improve earnings, just in case the market or competitors should deliver some nasty surprises.

Firestone's bonus plan, like most other corporate bonus plans, topped out when divisional earnings growth reached 10 to 15 percent, giving managers no incentive to push themselves or take the kind of personal risks required to increase earnings growth to 25 or 30 percent. In fact, the bonus system gave them every reason to *avoid* pushing harder, by attaching a direct penalty to better results. In Chapter 5, we saw how Pizza Hut store managers suffered every time they outperformed their budgets; headquarters would just ratchet up the base for subsequent years, making it that much harder to meet the target. The "incentive" system at Accuride worked exactly the same way.

Bain Capital restructured Accuride's incentives to make them more like those at Chick-fil-A, which treats its store managers as partners and gives them an equal share of the value their units create. As we saw in Chapter 5, Chick-fil-A operators enjoy a twentyfold advantage over the competition in the benefits they earn for every extra dollar of profit they manage to generate. A similar system at Accuride took twenty managers with a previous average income below $100,000 and rewarded them with $18 million in shared earnings for taking on the risks and hard work required to transform their performance. Earnings grew by 25 percent per year over the period Bain Capital owned the company—a result Accuride managers never would have achieved without the incentive to reconsider their strategies for delivering value to customers.

The win-win-win economics of this approach, which shares benefits among customers, employees, and investors, really speaks for itself. Accuride's share of its target market grew from 55 to 67 percent. Customers took home price reductions ranging from 3 to 8 percent. Plant employment grew from 1,539 to 1,785. Management increased its compensation nearly ten times over. And Bain Capital, its limited partners, and co-investors earned a return of $121 million on an investment of $5 million. As we noted earlier, loyalty and alignment have the surprising capacity to produce results greater than the sum of their parts. Imagine how difficult it would have been to pull off this value-creating strategy at a company saddled with investors who concentrate all their attention on quarterly earnings.

HOW MANAGERS CAN FIX THE STOCK MARKET

As more and more industries enter periods of chaotic competition and restructuring—the very circumstances that create the greatest need for investor loyalty—the short-term focus of market investors is actually intensifying. The result is, first, that more and more companies have gone private (or have given it serious thought) and, second, that the high returns committed long-term investors so often enjoy have caused the private equity market to expand to meet the growing need for buy-and-hold investors. New inflows of private equity have grown from almost nothing three decades ago to about $8 billion in 1993 and $12 billion in 1994. New inflows of public equities, meanwhile, have been shrinking. The average for 1993 and 1994 was $71 billion per year, down from a peak of about $90 billion in 1992. So private equity is gaining share from public equity at a rapid rate, for the simple reason that it has delivered superior returns.

Many experts predict that the increasing inflows of private money will bid down returns. Perhaps so. But an equally plausible scenario is that if public ownership continues in its present direction—toward steadily higher churn and a steadily greater fixation on short-term results—the opportunities for private equity will multiply, far exceeding anyone's current expectations. Unless public markets change, in other words, more and more public companies will find that the only way they can compete effectively is to become private companies—at least during those financially awkward phases of competitive upheaval that require deep and expensive shifts in strategy. Private equity will continue to replace public equity wherever its greater relative stability allows companies to create value in excess of private ownership's targeted returns.

In this way, the market may self-correct and move back to lower levels of turnover, perhaps more quickly than we might imagine. Not only are some of the best value-creation opportunities migrating to the private equity market; so is some of the best talent. Many of the most capable investors and managers are moving toward private ownership. It's not just that the returns are superior; the ability to build value within a realistic timeframe makes a far more attractive career opportunity than the short-term, low-loyalty frenzy of public companies. Real partnerships are possible in privately owned companies.

Still, private ownership is not the right alternative for most companies. The level of debt is simply too high for the accompanying level of risk and uncertainty. In fact, most privatizations return to public ownership once their earnings have stabilized and the competitive turbulence is over. So while the current situation in the public markets hurts customers, employees, and long-term investors, the lasting solution is not to abandon public markets, but to fix them.

Surprisingly, the managers of public companies are in a position to take matters into their own hands, change the nature of public markets, and move them back in the direction of greater stability. Consider the facts: as a manager, you recognize the importance of stable, consistent investors who evaluate company performance not on quarterly results but on the basis of long-term strategies, investment policies, and value-creation potential. It's obvious to you that the market's evolution toward shorter holding periods works against the best interests of a great many companies, including your own. And it's easy to point the finger at increasing ownership by institutional investors. The biggest players in the growth of institutional stock ownership are pension funds, and most are managed in precisely the manner you find so destabilizing and destructive. On any given day, pension fund managers account for about half the trading on the New York Stock Exchange. It's easy to forget that your company, too, has a pension fund, and therefore employs the institutional managers who drive market churn. Since more than half of all pension assets are held by companies as sponsors, we might say that more than half the problem is the responsibility of the corporate managers who complain so vociferously.

There is plenty of evidence that the current approach to pension fund management—your own approach, in all probability—is bad business. *Fortune* magazine reported recently that over the past ten years, 74 percent of 2,700 retirement fund managers failed to beat the S&P 500 index. An article in the October 25, 1993, edition of *Forbes* claims that "overall, active money management is a losing game."[11] It cites a study by the Brookings Institution in 1992 which revealed that the average professional investment manager lagged the S&P 500 by 2.6 percentage points per year over seven years.

Besides the underperformance, there is the matter of fees and expenses. It costs a lot of money to trade stocks, hire money managers, and supervise them; *Forbes* estimates that American companies spend $9 billion a year on pension fund management. The article cites study after study showing that pension funds could earn far better returns by investing in low-cost index funds (which, by the way, have extremely low turnover rates). But adopting this simple strategy would put pension management bureaucracies out of work. How many jobs would disappear? *Forbes* notes that General Motors has an internal pension management staff of seventy and employs another seventy investment managers, plus numerous advisors and consultants, outside the company. Ford has achieved far superior results with its fund—approximately two-thirds the size of GM's—with just two employees.

Wasting $9 billion destroys a lot of value. Underperforming the market by an average of 2.6 percentage points per year for seven years destroys a great deal more. But what destroys the most value by far is the penalty this system assesses on companies whose management teams want to pursue long-term value-creating strategies but must instead spend their time and energy managing quarterly earnings, then explaining them to analysts and investment managers who care little about the businesses they invest in.

How *much* value does this penalty destroy? The drag on corporate earnings growth will vary by company, of course. But let's walk through the arithmetic for the universe of public companies in the United States to get a feel for the potential magnitude of the problem. In 1994, public companies earned around $250 billion in profits. Therefore, every percentage point of drag on earnings growth eats up $2.5 billion in annual profits. At a price/earnings ratio of 16, that's $40 billion in market value. Could the real drag be two percentage points, or three or even four? Bain Capital's record suggests it can go higher still. My own experience in consulting with public companies for nearly twenty years has convinced me that the drag could easily average two or three percentage points. If so, then the rate of value destruction approaches $100 billion per year, and that clearly deserves attention.

DUMB MONEY

It's hard to understand the logic of a system in which capital with the lowest short-term pressure (pension funds don't need liquidity in most of their investments for twenty or thirty years, when the average worker will retire) has the shortest investment horizon. Given the cyclical nature of business, every company's earnings will be squeezed periodically. The constituency with the greatest flexibility is investors. But in today's system, management is extremely reluctant to reduce dividends or earnings to investors. Most managers will raise prices or lay off employees so investors can enjoy a steady and predictable return, at least for the immediate future—despite the fact that the constituency with the *least* inherent flexibility is the workforce. Changing jobs or careers is a costly and painful process. At the same time, learning and stability—both critical to *future* profits—are least leveraged for capital and most for employees.

The paradoxes in this system are striking. But there are steps any CEO can take to eliminate the contradictions. Begin by walking down the hall to the office of your in-house pension manager. Check the average portfolio turnover rate. Find out if your company's pension fund is the kind of investor your company would like to have as a stockholder—one that cares whether the companies it invests in create long-term value.

Of course, you'll need to prepare yourself for a struggle. When you challenge your pension department's high-churn investment strategy, your pension manager will counter with some very persuasive arguments. You will be told that your company *does* select its investment managers on the basis of long-term performance, that their compensation *is* performance-based, and that your fund has outperformed similar funds as a result of its current investment strategies. Don't give up. Ask to be shown a credible study demonstrating that investment managers who perform in the top quartile over any given period exhibit anything better than average performance in the next such period. Tell your pension manager that good private equity investors earn 75 percent of their revenues in performance fees; ask how your investment managers compare. As for the argument that your fund outperforms its peers, that may well be true. But bear in mind that half of all pension funds are bound to be above average at any given moment, and that over the long haul the average fund underperforms the index funds. And don't forget that a creative analyst can make almost any fund look relatively successful by carefully selecting the time period and the funds to which it is compared, and by making "appropriate adjustments" for Beta risk, dollar- or time-weighted averaging, and more.

But remember, too, that since the objections raised by pension managers are perfectly sincere, you also need to consider their motivation. All bureaucrats, public and private, believe deeply that the work they do creates value. But all of them are firmly entrenched in the least efficient cell of the Friedman matrix, where effective resource allocation almost never occurs. Moreover, all of them are involved in a system designed more to protect their careers than to maximize investments.

Consider the way this system works. For the vast majority of pension fund balances, individual employees have little control over how their money is invested. That's the job of the in-house pension manager, a bureaucrat who lives by administering other people's money. But the system insulates the fund yet further from its owners because your bureaucrat delegates specific investment decisions to professional investment managers, who are supposed to have far superior expertise. Accountability is now two steps removed from employees. In larger funds, bureaucrats hire independent consultants to help them pick the fund's investment managers and allocate funds among them. This is the inefficient cell cubed—three layers of insulation between the money's owners and the people deciding how to invest it. (Of course, the growing shift toward self-directed employee plans—401Ks, for example—could begin to alleviate the problem over the next decade, but few of us can afford to wait that long.)

Remember, finally, that the Wall Street advisers who oil the wheels of this system are an extraordinarily talented and creative group of people. It was they who encouraged S&L executives to bet on interest rates, municipal treasurers to bet on derivatives, and corporate financial officers to bet on junk bonds. Since they are paid on the basis of transactions, not investment performance, their creativity is often misdirected.

While the stated logic of this system is to deliver superior investment returns, the real prime motivation of the corporate bureaucrat you've walked down the hall to visit is to advance or at least preserve his or her career by avoiding accountability. Great investment success doesn't make these people rich; the most it will do is give them a slightly higher annual bonus and some incremental career acceleration. More important, the system protects them from investment failure by giving them a buffer against criticism and responsibility. In cases of relatively poor performance, the bureaucrats work with their outside advisors and investment managers to develop plausible explanations. If these fail to satisfy company management or the investment committee, the investment managers and advisors get fired, not the bureaucrats.

Clearly, this system devotes more attention to the management of bureaucratic careers than to the management of pension funds. Consider, for example, the criteria bureaucrats and their advisors use to select the investment managers who churn accounts at the rate of 25 to 100 percent per year. Most decisions are based on a manager's recent track record. Firms like SEI and Russell monitor the quarterly performance of thousands of investment managers and rank them. Since the goal of investment managers is to stay in the upper deciles, their first concern is quarterly performance. Their second concern is the development of a compelling story line to explain away bad quarters and attract larger asset allocations to manage. An investment manager's compensation is based more on the quantity of assets managed than on the quality of their management. The key to success is client perception, not long-term performance.

The priorities of in-house pension managers are similarly skewed. They cannot afford to stick with their investment managers through thick and thin. Together with deeper investment analysis, such a policy might well lead to better long-term results. But it would inevitably lead to greater accountability as well, and accountability is perilous to careers. In this dilemma, long-term value-creating strategies are irrelevant.

So let's go back to the question we began with—how to fix such a system. The first step might be to follow the lead of Ford Motor Company and reassign your pension-fund bureaucrats to more productive jobs. Step two might be to encourage the remaining one or two employees to invest in index funds that simply track the market. This approach serves your employees two different ways: it minimizes the expense of managing their investments, and it beats the vast majority of active money managers with regard to long-term total return. It has another advantage as well. It's good for public companies in general, since indexing reduces market volatility and minimizes the distractions corporate managers have to cope with.

If you're intent on beating the market, just make sure you compensate your investment managers the way a good private equity fund compensates its general partners. Tie their income to performance. Pay them a bare minimum to cover administrative expenses, then give them a share in the surplus return they create. Over time, this system will support only those investment professionals who consistently outperform market indexes. It will also give investment managers a strong incentive to enter into productive, long-term relationships—the kind that would benefit *your* business—with corporate management teams at the companies they invest in.

A TAX ON POLLUTION

Of course, the strategies outlined here aren't going to put an end to short-term trading. Even if a large segment of business executives began to insist that their own pension funds adopt long-term investment policies, a great many more would do what they've done in the past. And what about the active traders who really *can* beat the market average? *Fortune* concluded that over a ten-year period, 26 percent of investment managers outperformed market indexes. If those 26 percent churned their portfolios at 100 percent per year or more, short-term investment would still constitute a major problem.

Unfortunately, this is one of those problems that free markets alone cannot solve. It's analogous to pollution. If one plant spews waste into the air and water and another invests in technology that eliminates pollution, the irresponsible plant can gain market share because its costs are lower. In a full-systems sense, of course, the costs at the polluting plant are higher, but much of that cost is borne by the people who breathe the air and drink the water and ultimately must pay to clean up the environment. It's only the polluting plant's customers, employees, and investors who get a break, and at everyone else's expense. Until the system costs are put back on the shoulders of the polluter, the whole community will suffer. Pollution is one of those rare problems that regulation and taxation address more effectively than the market.

High-churn investors are polluters. The cost of their pollution is the destabilizing volatility and short-term myopia of public company management. What's more, the polluters are gaining market share, and the cost of their activity is borne by the long-term stakeholders in public corporations. The only way to fix this problem is either to regulate the amount of pollution we allow—probably impossible in an economy as dedicated to market freedom as ours—or to estimate the true full-system cost of the pollution and charge an appropriate tax.

There is plenty of precedent for such a step. We already tax stock market profits, and for much of our history we have structured that tax to reward and encourage loyal investment. That's what a lowered rate for long-term capital gains is all about. Today, however, we need to do more than encourage long-term investing; we need to *discourage* speculative, short-term trading. And it seems reasonable to put at least some of the cost of fickle capital back onto the churners who create it.

The obvious first step is to correct the tax policy that lies at the root of burgeoning stock market churn. Congress was right to defer the tax on employee pension benefits until retirement. This policy encourages saving and protects the long-term security of older citizens. But it has had the unintended side effect of making pension funds immune to the taxation on realized capital gains that penalizes other investors when they engage in high-churn trading—which is one of the principal reasons pension fund managers churn their holdings at such astonishing rates. Their only frictional cost is the several cents per share in commissions that brokers charge them to trade.

A tax policy that encourages pension investors to churn their holdings makes no sense, especially in light of the destructive effect short-term trading has on public companies. The policy we now have is like a tax exemption for factories that pollute. As pensions continue on their actuarial trajectory toward complete domination of the stock market, moreover, the problem will grow increasingly more serious. We must either tax pension fund traders the way we tax all other investors (which would undermine the policy of tax deferment that has done so much to encourage saving) or levy a special tax on short-term pension fund trading—for example, 2 to 3 percent of the gross sale price on every share traded that is held for less than three years.

We must also alter our policy toward speculative traders who are not sufficiently discouraged by the current taxes they must pay on trading gains. One possibility is to further reduce the tax on long-term capital gains. Massachusetts recently passed legislation that provides an interesting model. Taxes on gains decline on a sliding scale based on how long the assets have been held. After one year, the rate comes down dramatically; after six years, capital gains are entirely tax free.

One problem with using tax policy to fight pollution is that while increased taxes or transaction fees will discourage trading pollution, the resulting revenue will do nothing to help the long-term stakeholders in the public companies that bear the costs of high churn. Conversely, a reduction in the long-term capital gains tax would subsidize long-term investors, but the cost of the tax cut would increase the federal budget deficit.

Another approach that might avoid the economic and political complexities of the tax code would be to create a transaction fee of, say, 2 percent on each purchase or sale of stock. The money, contributed disproportionately by churners, would go to the company that issued the stock, increasing its value to the remaining shareholders and compensating them for the pollution effect. Churn rates would surely decline. In fact, at least one tax of this kind already exists. Several funds in the Vanguard Mutual Fund Group assess a charge on new investments and put the money into the fund to benefit investment returns. In effect, this charge penalizes short-term traders and subsidizes returns for all fundholders who retain their shares longer than the average investor.

All these proposals need refinement and debate, but any one of them might be just what we need to return our capital markets to long-term thinking. Given the current hyperactive state of our investment industry, they may seem unrealistic and unrealizable. But even if they do sound utopian at the moment, serious need and relentless pressure can work wonders over time, especially when it comes to pollution control. Who could have imagined just twenty years ago that today we would enjoy a nearly universal ban on smoking in public accommodations?

The people who would be hurt the most are Wall Street brokers, who make a profit every time a share of stock changes hands. They would object strenuously, on the grounds of overregulation and the national interest. But pollution controls and taxes never seem like a good idea to the polluters. As for stockmarket analysts, if high-churn investors were hobbled, the analysts would have to refocus their talents on long-term value creation and performance, which would be no bad thing.

The tax would certainly not hurt long-term investors. It would actually make them more competitive against the mutual funds and pension funds that churn their portfolios so vigorously. Right now, you and your loyal customers, employees, and investors are subsidizing the profits of talented speculators, analysts, and their Wall Street brokers. You can continue to pay the implicit tax they charge, or you can lobby your representatives in Congress to put the costs they produce back onto their shoulders by means of a tax on transient investment.

SMART MONEY

All schemes to reduce the pressure on quarterly returns are open to the suspicion that managers just don't want their feet held so close to the fire. But if you believe that getting rid of short-term investors is a way of reducing the pressure to perform, then you haven't understood the message of this chapter. Loyal capital is more committed to your business, knows more about it, and therefore tends to demand more than the transient investors you never meet or hear from. Investors like Warren Buffett, Alfred Lerner, Paul Desmarais, Bain Capital, and State Farm insist on altogether exceptional performance. The difference is that they know what kind of performance is possible and understand the timeframe in which they can reasonably demand it.

It's not patient money you want but smart money. Smart investors know that the only way to maximize shareholder value is to earn the loyalty of customers and employees. That is increasingly true as businesses become more knowledge-based and service-intensive. As a manager, you must take steps to find smart investors, educate the investors you already have, and avoid the high cost of disloyal capital.

7

In Search of Failure

LOYAL CUSTOMERS, loyal employees, loyal investors—the system collapses without all three. In the preceding four chapters, we journeyed all the way around the virtuous cycle of growth shown in Figure 1-3. We had a good look at the whole conceptual framework of loyalty-based business systems; we saw some of the requirements for and benefits of getting and keeping the right customers, employees, and investors; and we had a chance to study some of the ways that customer, employee, and investor loyalties interact. What we need to do now is step back and consider how an organization can learn to use this conceptual framework to create more value for all three players—and in the process, vastly improve its chances of long-term survival.

One of the enduring mysteries of business is why established market leaders are so frequently elbowed aside by aggressive upstarts, and why, in general, big corporations die so young. Large companies should derive enormous survival advantage from the richness of their resources, the reach of their economic and political influence, the breadth of their experience, and the depth of their information about customers and employees. But the average Fortune 500 company has a lifespan of forty years. Most are outlived by a majority of their employees.

It's tempting to accept this high corporate mortality rate as the wholesome result of natural selection in the economic sphere. When companies fail to adapt to changing environments, they die—and a good thing, too. Otherwise, we'd be burdened with the kind of useless dinosaur industries that weighed down the Soviet Union. But companies are not species, and the Darwinian analogy doesn't really work. Genes can't learn; it's only the relatively glacial process of successful random mutation that produces adaptive change in species. Companies have free will. They can learn from their failures, and they can change—or they can decline to learn and refuse to change—the choice is theirs. They don't have to wait for random genetic events to alter their fate; they can alter it themselves.

So the question becomes, Why don't they? The answer is that they very often do, but because they misunderstand their mission, they alter their fates in the wrong direction.

EXCELLENT DINOSAURS

Darwin showed us that the true mission of a species is to produce offspring. Any species that got muddled on this point and decided that its real purpose was to bask in the sun or chase its own tail quickly vanished. In the same way, the true mission of a business is to create value. Any business muddled enough to believe that its real purpose is producing profit is probably not long for this world. Profit is absolutely essential, to be sure, but it is a downstream outcome of creating value, and so it functions very poorly as an objective in itself. One of the reasons so many businesses fail is that all their analysis and learning revolves around profit, so they become aware of problems only when their profits begin to decline. In struggling to fix their profits, they concentrate on a symptom and miss the underlying breakdown in their value-creation system.

They're a little like swimmers in an undertow, who can usually survive if they keep their wits, float with the current, and swim back to shore when they've drifted out of the current's grasp. Because they don't understand the forces beneath the surface, however, a lot of swimmers fight the tow head on, exhaust themselves, and greatly reduce their chances of survival. Businesses get caught in undertows as well, and the ones that don't understand the deeper economic forces sweeping them to ruin may spend their energy in ways that worsen their predicament. When profits are squeezed, it's safe to assume that something is wrong and needs fixing. But the core of the problem is usually insufficient value to customers. Managers who aim directly at higher profits by raising prices or slashing headcounts often exacerbate the original problem of poor value creation. They are sadly similar to swimmers who gradually succumb to fatigue without ever understanding what might save them.

And what *might* save them? Managers who focus on short-term profit are probably responsible for the death of many large corporations. In past centuries, physicians who thought blood was a carrier of contagion rather than the wellspring of health often killed their patients by bleeding them to death. Today, a lot of managers engage in corporate bloodlettings of much the same kind. They hope to cure a short-term profit illness by cutting costs, but by draining off the company's human assets, they often render a cure impossible.

Companies *can* save themselves. They can fix problems, alter course, adapt to new environments and new circumstances, even completely rebuild themselves. But the lifeblood of adaptive change is employee learning. (*Organizational learning* is a useful term, but it's only a metaphor. People learn, not organizations, and when people leave a company they take all their personal skills and much of their experience with them.)

Employee learning is the vital asset that allows companies to change and heal themselves. But even *with* a core of loyal employees, companies encounter immense barriers to change. This is because the most useful and instructive learning grows from the recognition and analysis of failure—and failure resists examination.

AVERSION TO FAILURE

There are two principal reasons why organizations do not study their own failures. The first is bureaucracy, which is almost perfectly designed to conceal mistakes and utterly disinclined to seek them out and lay them bare. The second is an almost universal fixation with success.

In a bureaucratic organization, the key to a career—to raises, promotions, funding for projects—is the boss. Bureaucrats can often succeed by pleasing their superiors in ways that have little to do with value creation—by doing favors, writing speeches, making the boss look good. Convince your boss that you're doing a fine job, and a lack of supporting evidence in the form of customer behavior may not matter for some time. Lose your boss's confidence, and even terrific numbers may not help. In this atmosphere, subordinates are understandably reluctant to share their failures openly with superiors. So people make a game of hiding or disguising their failures—or of fixing them before the boss finds out—until they get a promotion or a transfer. In a bureaucracy, in short, the most critical skills tend to be political rather than diagnostic. But to do any good, the goal of failure analysis must be learning, not concealment, and the boss must lead or at least cheer on the effort, not float in blissful ignorance.

Contrast this with a nonbureaucracy like Chick-fil-A, where only the customers vote on compensation and resource decisions. The good old bureaucratic skills—flattery, glibness, gamesmanship—just don't help. At Chick-fil-A, executives don't set the salaries of store operators, customers do. The executives are coaches; they can earn more only if their players can win more customer votes.

The second reason companies do so little failure analysis is that they are preoccupied with success. Undeniably, success has lessons to teach. By repeating behavior that succeeds, people develop good habits. By studying successful strategies to see what makes them work, companies can adapt them to win new victories in new circumstances. And by watching the triumphs of other companies, a business can occasionally pick up an insight or a useful idea. But business people today are *obsessed* with success—sometimes more obsessed with other people's success than with their own. Benchmarking has intensified into a feverish search for the nation's or even the world's lowest-cost manufacturing plant, highest-volume sales district, lowest-overhead distribution center. Academics and consultants scour the globe for approaches that have led to big profits in one business situation so they can reapply them in others. Executives search for "proven" successes that their own companies can emulate. The quest for best practice continues even when the results create little real value.

Take the phenomenal success of *In Search of Excellence*, first published in 1982. In the tradition of American management "science," this book, based on theories the authors developed by studying high-performance companies, became a bible for a whole generation of managers. It sold 5 million copies and spawned a whole new genre of business books claiming to reveal the key to business success. *In Search of Excellence* represented the best thinking of the business establishment. Its research included a painstaking analysis of twenty-five years' worth of data, and a Who's Who of business leaders contributed and endorsed the book's ideas.

But over the course of the ensuing ten years, who do you suppose would have become richer: an investor who built a stock portfolio out of the companies profiled in *In Search of Excellence,* or someone who merely matched the mediocre performance of the S&P index? Believe it or not, mediocrity trounced excellence. Two-thirds of the publicly traded "excellent" companies have underperformed the S&P 500 over the last decade. Several have stumbled badly, and a few are close to extinction. The authors acknowledge that only one-fifth of their original group remains excellent today, while the remainder fall somewhere on a continuum from merely good to downright bad.

Now, how on earth could this have happened? Success breeds success. How could *In Search of Excellence* turn out to be a castle built on sand? People who study systems can tell us. When a system is working well, they say, it's impossible to explain why. Its success rests on a long chain of subtle interactions, and it's not easy to determine which links in the chain are most important. Even if the critical links were identifiable, their relative importance would shift as the world around the system changed. So even if we could point to the critical links and more or less reproduce them, we still could not reproduce all the relationships between them or the external environment in which they work. This is precisely the problem with *In Search of Excellence.* While the book is undeniably entertaining, it cannot by itself help anyone to achieve or sustain the model of excellence it portrays.

What *can* help us to achieve excellence is the study of failure, a paradox that is intuitively obvious. Most people discover early in life that mistakes are better teachers than success, that more learning flows from failure than from good fortune. Systems experts attest that when one component fails, it can cast a spotlight on the workings of an entire system.

The airlines understand this. Airline performance in the United States, as measured by the fatality rate, actually exceeds six sigma—3.4 defects per million opportunities—which is the demanding standard of quality many manufacturers pursue but probably none have yet achieved. As far as we know, the domestic air transportation industry is the only one to *beat* six sigma, and it has done it by studying failure. When a plane crashes, investigators retrieve the flight recorder and spend whatever it costs to find out what went wrong. The result is that in a vastly complex and extremely dangerous operating environment, accidents have become relatively rare.

In a very different field, Warren Buffett, one of the world's consummate investors, has concluded that there is more to be gained by studying business failures than by examining business triumphs. In a speech at the Emory Business School, Buffett said:

I've often felt there might be more to be gained by studying business failures than business successes. In my business, we try to study where people go astray, and why things don't work. We try to avoid mistakes. If my job was to pick a group of ten stocks in the Dow Jones average that would outperform the average itself, I would probably not start by picking the ten best. Instead, I would try to pick the ten or fifteen worst performers and take them out of the sample, and work with the residual. It's an inversion process. Albert Einstein said, "Invert, always invert, in mathematics and physics," and it's a very good idea in business, too. Start out with failure, and then engineer its removal.[1]

Warren Buffett gained control of Berkshire Hathaway in 1965, and in the company's annual report for 1989, he published an essay called *Mistakes of the First Twenty-Five Years.* Just as Japanese manufacturers treat defects as a gift and use them to make continuous improvements, Buffett, by focusing on failure as the source of his learning, confounds those who try to emulate him by scrutinizing his successes.

FEAR OF FAILURE

This brings us back once again to the question we asked earlier: If failure analysis works so well, why don't more companies do it? In addition to the two reasons already mentioned—bureaucracy and the universal obsession with success—there are two simpler reasons that are less pleasant to confront: fear and incapacity.

Psychologically and culturally, it's difficult and sometimes threatening to look too closely at failure. Ambitious managers work diligently to link their careers to successes. Failures are usually examined for the purpose of assigning blame, rather than detecting and eradicating the systemic causes of poor performance. Underlying the airlines' outstanding safety performance is the courageous decision to install black boxes in the first place. Somehow, some airline people were able to overcome their natural human fears: not just the fear of failure, but the fear of analyzing failure, especially when the stakes are high.

Yet overcoming the fear is not, by itself, enough. A further obstacle to learning from failure is our inability to measure it on a useful scale. When you're on the edge of terminal failure, such as bankruptcy, it's probably too late to become a learning organization. So while the company is still relatively healthy, a manager's challenge is to find useful daily units of failure (as well as the right ongoing scale of failure). The trick is to set up a system to track, analyze, and gradually eliminate the failures that occur, then repeat the process with new units of failure.

Take a look at the NFL. Do coaches study a game's highlights as seen on the Ten O'Clock News—the breakaway scoring runs, the miraculous one-handed catches, the little victory dances in the end zone? Of course they don't. Highlights are entertainment. A good coach concentrates on failure even in victory. The relevant units of failure are penalties, bungled assignments, interceptions, miscommunications. It is these that coaches and players review and discuss, and that become the subject of the week's practice. Even a Super Bowl season is full of instructive mistakes.

If a football coach studied failure only on the scale of lost games, his learning opportunities would be few. He might be tempted to study the successes of the team that beat him and try to imitate its strengths. But the coach who's trying to copy someone else's winning system may find it completely inappropriate to the talents his players possess. A football game is a complex interaction of two organizations with very different characteristics. The long pass that wins the game may be principally attributable to the quarterback's superior arm, the defensive cornerback's inexperience, the receiver's speed and skill, the sluggishness of the defensive rush, the inadequacy of the losing coach's pass-coverage plan, or to all of these together—or to some other factor, like luck. In any case, you can't draw conclusions about a systemic failure from the results of just one play or one game.

The only way to know why the pass worked and the defense failed is to move to a higher scale of analysis than the single play or game. Knowing how often receivers were open on similar plays over a series of games will tell the coach whether this is a systemic problem that requires a change in strategy. The right subject of analysis is failures whose frequency and severity constrain the system's overall performance. Solutions must be appropriate to the system that adopts them, not simply mimic the team that won last week.

Warren Buffett believes that the tendency toward copycat strategies is one of the most common errors in business. That's why Berkshire Hathaway concentrates on the detailed analysis of failure, and why successful football coaches chart failure at the scale of fumbles and missed opportunities. But most businesses recognize failure only when it shows up at the level of disappointing earnings. Current profit may be a downstream consequence of value creation—and thus the wrong object of a company's efforts at improvement—but it is today the only kind of failure most business measurement systems track.

To implement failure analysis effectively, businesses need to train a microscope on the fine-scale realities of value creation and human loyalty, the organic building blocks of profit. The questions every company needs to answer are these: Which units of failure do we need to measure, and on what scale? How do we get a close focus on the fundamental causes of failure? How do we interpret what we find? And who in the company needs to learn from what we discover?

CUSTOMER DEFECTIONS

One of the most illuminating units of failure in business is customer defection, because it sheds light on two critical flows of value. First, a customer defection is the clearest possible sign of a deteriorating stream of value from the company to its customers. Second, increasing defection rates diminish cash flow from customers to the company—even if the company replaces the lost customers—as a result of reduced customer duration. For companies with the desire and capacity to learn, moreover, losing a customer is a fine opportunity to search for the root causes of the departure, to uncover business practices that need fixing, and sometimes to win the customer back and reestablish the relationship on firmer ground.

Let's look at a couple of examples.

MicroScan

MicroScan—formerly a division of Baxter Diagnostics, now part of Dade International—created its own opportunities in customer defection. A leader in the field of automated microbiology, Microscan vastly reduced the size of the unit of failure. It sought out almost invisible defectors and used them to uncover and correct a series of shortcomings, making itself even stronger and more profitable.

In mid-1990, MicroScan was neck-and-neck with Vitek Systems in a race for market leadership. Both companies made the sophisticated instruments medical laboratories use to identify the microbes in patient cultures and determine which antibiotics will kill them most effectively. Both companies were growing rapidly, converting customers from manual testing and edging out other manufacturers of automated equipment.

MicroScan had worked hard to improve quality and was thinking about applying for the Baldrige Award.

Perhaps because diagnostics was its business, perhaps because competition had heightened its quality awareness, MicroScan decided to do what it could to find and identify the microbes in its own system. The company asked its salesforce to identify customer defectors for study. The salesforce responded that there were no customer defections to speak of. A few customers had gone out of business, but in automated microbiology, defections were rare. In fact, defections are rare in many industrial businesses. Once companies have purchased equipment, they continue to buy consumables and service for many years.

Still, MicroScan was not getting 100 percent of subsequent sales on all its accounts, and under the circumstances, management chose to use this more demanding standard to measure attrition. In other words, management recognized that it could learn a lot by understanding why the company lost business, even if it lost very little. So the company began to analyze its customer base, highlighting accounts that had been lost as well as those that remained active but showed a declining volume of testing. MicroScan interviewed every one of the lost customers and a large number of the "decliners," searching for the root causes of each decision to change, especially when customers had defected to alternative testing methods.

The picture that emerged was clear, instructive, and painful. Customers were concerned about the reliability of MicroScan's instruments. They had complaints about certain features of the equipment, and felt the company was insufficiently responsive to their problems.

There is always a strong temptation to rationalize these kinds of complaints: these weren't good customers to begin with; it's not our fault that the customer's technical staff is less sophisticated than our instruments; customers that use our hotline all the time aren't profitable anyway. But rationalization is just a way of failing at failure analysis, and MicroScan's managers overcame their natural impulse to explain complaints away. Instead, they listened, learned, and took corrective action. They shifted R&D priorities to address the shortcomings customers had identified, such as test accuracy and time-to-result. Having learned that their instrument line was too expensive for many small labs, they accelerated development of a low-end model and brought it to market in record time. (Systematic analysis of billing records had shown that there were actually quite a few defections among small customers.)

They also redesigned their customer service protocol to make sure immediate attention would be given to equipment faults and delivery problems.

MicroScan's ability to learn from failure paid off. Two years later,
the company pulled away from Vitek to achieve clear market leadership; it now enjoys the bottom-line benefits that go with it. Tracking
and responding to customer defections, however uncommon—and they
are now less common than ever—has become central to MicroScan's
business.

From Small-Scale to Large-Scale Defections

MicroScan had a customer base of several thousand, so it could easily
afford to interview a few hundred decliners and defectors in depth. A
large bank we'll call Bank A was in a very different situation; more than
20 percent of its customer base was defecting or declining each year.
But with more than a million customers, Bank A needed to interview
several hundred thousand people, which seemed out of the question.
Instead, the bank administered a kind of satisfaction—or in this case,
dissatisfaction—survey to customers who closed their accounts. Unfortunately, the information it yielded was too superficial to be of real value
in pinpointing what was wrong with the business system. For example,
more than 50 percent of the surveys listed price or interest rate as the
cause of defection. But when the bank called up several of the price
defectors, it heard stories like the following:

Question: *How long had you been a customer at Bank A?*

Answer: *Twelve years.*

Question: *What caused you to close your account and move it?*

Answer: *Bank X was right around the corner and they paid a
           higher rate on my CD.*

Question: *Were Bank X's rates always higher or did they just change
           recently?*

Answer: *I don't know; I just noticed recently.*

Question: *What made you notice?*

Answer: *Now that I think about it, I was a little irritated at Bank
           A and then I saw an ad in Thursday's paper.*

Question: *Why were you irritated?*

Answer: *To be honest, it was being turned down for a credit card.*

Question: *Had you ever been turned down before?*

Answer: *Yes, several times, but in this case, the bank solicited me and gave me this big come-on about being a preferred customer—and then turned me down with a form letter!*

As it turned out, the rates at Bank X were almost identical to those at Bank A, except occasionally on Thursdays, because X changed rates on Thursdays and A on Fridays. But of course price had little to do with this defection. The real root cause was the credit card division's failure to coordinate its marketing and qualification efforts. When interviewers pushed the questioning far enough, *most* of the defectors who named price on their surveys turned out not to be price defectors.

Getting to the root causes of a problem takes a lot of time, effort, and experience. In a factory setting, where root-cause analysis has been perfected over decades, the process is known as the five why's, because you usually have to ask why something happened at least five times to get to the root of a failure. For example:

Question: *Why did the product get returned as defective?*

Answer: *The connector came loose.*

Question: *Why did the connector come loose?*

Answer: *The plug was out of tolerance with the specs.*

Question: *Why was the plug manufactured out of tolerance?*

Answer: *The intermediate stamping machine failed.*

Question: *Why did the stamping machine fail?*

Answer: *Routine maintenance wasn't done on schedule.*

Question: *Why?*

Answer: *There is an attendance problem in the maintenance department.*

After five why's, you begin to see what needs to be fixed, though it may actually take a few more questions to figure out the best solution. Since applying this type of rigorous analysis to every single defect a plant experiences would be absurdly expensive, smart companies first perform a statistical frequency analysis, so they can concentrate their efforts on the 20 percent of defect categories that account for 80 percent of the defects (Pareto's 80/20 rule).

The bank's dilemma was similar. Since in-depth root-cause analysis of all two hundred thousand defecting bank customers was not feasible, Bank A needed to interview a large enough sample of defectors to apply the 80/20 rule. Unfortunately, that was still far too many for the kind of thorough interviewing MicroScan had done. Yet the more affordable surveys were too superficial, and would almost certainly identify price as the principal root cause.

At this point, the dilemma deepens. The fact is, every defection is the result of inadequate value. And since value is the ratio of quality to price, price is always a factor in a defection. But so is quality. Understanding weaknesses in customer value is much more challenging than understanding why a part was stamped out of tolerance in a manufacturing plant. The quickie interview is almost certain to miss the essential subtleties.

Now, the level of value perceived by a customer can be defined as the time-weighted sum (more recent experiences are weighted more heavily) of all interactions with the company. Occasionally, a single event is so powerful it leads to defection all by itself ("The teller swore at me"), but that is the exception. In most cases, a series of events leads slowly to a decision to seek better value elsewhere. To assess the root cause, the interviewer must typically capture three or four disappointing events and weight them appropriately.

The bank solved its problem with a computer-assisted expert system for interviewing defectors. The first step was to invest in several hundred in-depth interviews. Experienced consultants spoke to defectors and reviewed the whole history of their interactions with the bank. They applied consistency checks to make sure, for example, that customers who claimed interest rates were the cause of their defection did indeed defect to institutions that were offering superior rates at the time. The consultants then captured the logic of the questioning process in a decision tree, and then translated the decision tree into a computer program conventional telephone interviewers could use at a fraction of the cost. The computerized expert system enabled interviewers to get to the root causes of defections in an average of twenty minutes, as opposed to an hour or two each for the initial customer interviews.

The new technology allowed the bank to question a large sample of defectors, concentrate on the right 20 percent, and dig deep enough to get to actionable solutions. Top managers were impressed with the new technology, but grew frustrated when the defection rate did not come down fast enough or far enough. The problem was not that they had the wrong learning tool. It was confusion about who in the organization needed to learn.

Who Needs to Learn?

Historically, one of the great failings of customer research has been that the people who learn most about customers are often the researchers—usually trained outsiders. They then direct their reports to senior managers, who may learn something. But by the time the information gets to front-line managers and employees, it is too general to be useful.

Bank A, as we've seen, had used new methods to study defections, and the information it had gathered was reliable. But branch managers had seen customer research before, regarded it skeptically, and doubted very much that these new root-cause interviews could tell them much they didn't already know about customers they'd worked with for years. They *knew* what the problems were; they just couldn't convince headquarters to invest in the required solutions. When the bank asked each branch manager to look at a list of individual branch defectors and suggest root causes, the branch managers asserted confidently that the great majority of defectors had left to get better rates or better products, or because backroom processing had made errors in their accounts—all reasons conveniently beyond the control of a branch manager.

The interviews and analysis showed something quite different. Though branch managers were placing nearly all the blame on factors controlled by the head office, about half of all customer defections actually resulted from problems at the branch level, such as customer service and problem resolution. Some managers were so skeptical of the findings, they insisted on listening to the interview tapes themselves. Others accepted the root causes identified by the study but refused to believe the defectors were desirable, profitable customers until they'd reviewed their past records. Gradually, evidence overwhelmed denial and persuaded the branch managers to open their eyes and ears and begin learning from their failures.

But then other problems arose. Many necessary changes affected several units in the bank, units that needed to learn from the defection interviews and then cooperate to create solutions. But cooperation across units was not a company habit. Worse yet, the failure-analysis team was itself something of a problem. Management had placed the team in the market research department, reasoning that the department's experience with satisfaction surveys made it a logical home. But the junior executive in market research couldn't get the attention of the other unit heads. The bank found that failure analysis needed the leadership of an executive with the power to assemble cross-departmental task forces.

For example, when the bank looked harder at defections among its most profitable customers, it found one important cause to be the bank's incidental fees. High-end customers felt that their large balances in multiple accounts delivered so much value to the bank that charging a $35 fee for bouncing a check amounted to gouging. Top management did the arithmetic on those customers, discovered that 0.2 percent fewer defections would more than offset diminished fees, and promptly reduced the fees. But the real problem went deeper and involved several organizational units. A new failure-analysis team, led by a senior executive, discovered that some of the offending fees were incurred because branch salespeople had steered clients into products that were inappropriate for high-balance customers. The right products—for example, a bundled checking, money market, and savings account—had no fees. The solution was to improve sales training in the branches.

The team also discovered that some of the fees were incurred because the marketing department had not included balances from certain products such as mortgages and credit cards in the packaged-product pricing formula. Finally, because of budget constraints, data processing had been postponing the implementation of a householding algorithm that would link all of a customer's accounts together. The final resolution of the fee problem involved training, marketing, data processing, the entire branch salesforce—and above all, of course, a failure-analysis team with the organizational clout to do effective root-cause detective work and implement solutions.

Who Wants to Learn?

Even if root-cause analysis *enables* managers to learn, they may ignore the lessons or never make the effort to understand them. The first rule in education is that the student must want to learn. In many organizations, the current incentives do little or nothing to make anyone care about fixing defections. Branch managers in a typical bank are paid bonuses on a variety of measures, ranging from budgets to satisfaction surveys. Learning why customers are defecting takes time and energy. So unless it's clear to branch managers that their annual bonuses are tied to reducing attrition, supplying them with world-class failure-analysis systems won't improve their decision making.

Likewise, the marketing manager whose bonus is based on the volume of "new deposit dollars" generated through CD promotions doesn't really care if those deposits defect next year. And the credit collections manager whose bonus is based on the balances collected from delinquent credit card customers doesn't long to learn more about customer defections from other bank products, like savings and checking accounts. Often the most important barrier to learning from defections is that employees can't see how it's relevant to their own success.

Thus the first step in unleashing the power of failure analysis is to make appropriate changes in measures, incentives, and career paths. Only senior executives can do this: they cannot delegate the process to a lower level of the organization. Bank A found it could evaluate cross-functional "defection correction" teams by measuring the ongoing frequency with which their target root causes recurred. Not surprisingly, when you measure individuals or teams and give them an incentive to learn, change begins to happen rather fast, even if the lessons to be learned are difficult. To find the necessary resources to fix the problem, team members at Bank A had to learn enough about retention economics to make the right cost-benefit tradeoffs. They did.

Even in companies that care enough about retention to engineer effective incentives, it's sometimes necessary to remind employees how important it is to continue *improving* retention rates. Even though State Farm's agent compensation structure was more heavily geared to retention than most competitors', headquarters discovered that some of its agents had grown complacent. To shake them up a bit, the company calculated what would happen to an agent's income each year for twenty years if that agent achieved a 1-percentage-point improvement in customer retention. The answer was just the tonic they were looking for: it turned out the agents could increase their average annual earnings by 20 percent!

Lexus is another company that has cared passionately from the beginning about earning customer loyalty. The new carmaker chose dealers who had demonstrated a commitment to customer service and satisfaction. But like State Farm, Lexus has found it very important to communicate the exact dollar value of improved customer retention to the dealer. The company has constructed a model that can be used to calculate how much more each dealership could earn by achieving higher levels of repurchase and service loyalty. These cash-flow calculations are important reminders, even for those who already believe in the importance of customer retention.

Levels of Precision

When managers realize that their bosses really care about (and are actually measuring) defections, they often discover that their root-cause analyses need to be more precise. On Bank A's computer-assisted survey, for example, credit collections (the process of collecting nonperforming loans) was one of the endpoints that occurred frequently enough to earn a high place on the list of root causes. But it told no one what was wrong with credit collections, or how to fix the problem. Did customers become irritated when they got a call from the collections department instead of the branch manager, whom they knew as a friend? Were the collections officers too brusque? Was the bank's information correct? Did the collector always know that the customer had, say, $200,000 in CDs at the bank, in addition to a nonperforming loan? Or was the problem that customers never talked to the same person twice, and so had to review the whole history of the account over and over again? Each of these explanations would require a different solution. The root-cause survey process needed to be precise enough to tell managers what action to take. At a bank, that might require more than 350 endpoints versus the typical 25 to 35 in a typical telephone survey. Clearly, computer assistance is indispensable, especially if you're dealing with a great many defectors.

Bank managers also learned that they couldn't rely on interviews alone. Even the most sophisticated and precise survey technology won't uncover every root cause, because some customers don't know why they defected. For instance, Bank A's branch managers knew that employee turnover had an effect on customer turnover, but few defectors mentioned it in interviews. A statistical analysis of the connection showed that personnel turnover could explain almost half the differences in customer attrition from branch to branch. Customers had a hard time identifying this factor, but they clearly perceived that employees who were less familiar with their jobs and their customers delivered lower value. (To isolate other improvement goals, the bank did subsequent interview studies at branches with similar employee turnover.)

Failure analysts also need to be on the lookout for customer categories with distinctive attrition levels. At Bank A, this kind of search led to several important discoveries. The first was that customers whose initial purchase was a particular money-market savings account showed loyalty well above the average. The bank redirected its new account promotions to feature that product. Another discovery was that customers who opened three or more different types of account at the same time had the highest retention rate of all. So marketing created a new product that combined checking, savings, a credit card, and an overdraft line, all with the same account number.

Conversely, the bank found that certain promotions—CD bonus rates, for example—produced customers with lower retention rates, so these programs were cut. The bank also found that highly transient neighborhoods exhibited consistently inferior retention rates, so it opened no new branches in those areas. Yet another discovery was that certain mergers and acquisitions brought in customers with very high attrition rates. Senior management adjusted its acquisition strategy accordingly.

This is Warren Buffett's prescription in action: identify failure—in this case, the defection of valuable customers and the acquisition and retention of unprofitable customers—and remove its source. The combination of root-cause analysis and systematic statistical analysis of high- and low-attrition customer segments can pinpoint business system failure so it can be fixed.

The Customer Corridor

Most companies have no experience measuring the value they deliver to customers, so it's hard to know where to begin. Some businesses we've worked with have found it helpful to map out the whole lifecycle of a customer's interactions with the company and its products. You can think of this lifecycle as a corridor like the one in Figure 7-1, which shows the customer corridor for a retail bank. Customers enter at one end, and each arrow along the top of the passage represents a doorway or interaction with the bank, beginning with the account application.

It's a good model for a study of customer behavior, because what determines value is the sum of relative benefits and drawbacks, advantages and disadvantages, that consumers experience at each doorway along the corridor. The model can also show the frequency of those interactions. Frequency combined with interview material can tell a company which interactions are the 20 percent that drives 80 percent of the differences in loyalty and value.

In many businesses, including banking, insurance, and other service industries, the customer corridor has a second set of doorways made up of the major changes in a customer's private life, shown here—along

Figure 7-1 The Customer Corridor: Retail Banking Example

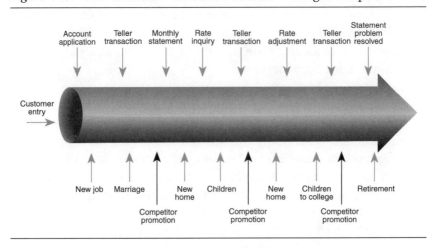

with competitors' efforts to lure the customer away—by the arrows below the corridor. Career moves, relocations, lifestyle changes, and almost any family watershed—a marriage, birth, divorce, or death—can be opportunities to deliver additional value to the customer. In fact, if a company does *not* gear its products and services to such events, family upheavals will almost certainly produce defections. Banks that have analyzed defection frequencies find that changes of this kind increase the probability of defection by 100 to 300 percent. For obvious reasons, relocation is a prime culprit; but root-cause interviewers looking only at the upper arrows would miss that cause. You can't save a customer who moves to Argentina. But a bank can easily develop a program that transfers customers who move locally to another branch. Several services now offer lists of households that will be moving in the next thirty to sixty days; smart banks buy those lists and contact customers before they can even think about defecting.

USAA uses this kind of corridor analysis to design its product and service offerings. Because the company tracks wallet share and retention rates separately by lifecycle segment, it can spot problems and opportunities early and develop solutions. USAA recognizes that any event on the customer corridor that produces a spike in defection frequency highlights a dimension of customer value that needs improvement.

In addition to its regular surveys of defectors, the company has built an on-line system called Echo that enables telephone sales and service reps to input customer suggestions or complaints as they occur. Managers analyze the data regularly to spot possible patterns, then review problems and potential solutions monthly with the CEO.

The Quality of Gain and Loss

Defections are not the only customer measure that needs systematic tracking with an eye toward failure detection and analysis. It's also important to measure the rate at which a company is adding good new customers to maintain a healthy level of growth. One valuable statistic for this purpose is the gain rate, the number of new customers added during the year as a percentage of total customers at the beginning of the year. Because of up-front acquisition and start-up costs, high gain rates usually penalize current-year earnings. But if the quality of the inflow is high—and if retention of mature customers remains high—then the future of the business is on solid ground. As MBNA's annual report put it, "Success is getting the right customers and keeping them."

Conversely, weakening gain rates are an early warning of trouble for a business and need to be watched as closely as any other unit of failure. Of course, gain rates will inevitably decline as a company fully penetrates the customer segments to which it can deliver superior value. USAA, for example, has largely exhausted its new-customer growth potential among military officers, active and retired. It now actively recruits their sons and daughters as associate (nonvoting) members. USAA has also devised a broader array of products in order to penetrate its present customer base more deeply.

State Farm faces a similar challenge. Because it now serves 20 to 25 percent of all the households in the United States, growth will come primarily from selling additional products to the customers it already has. Even a company like State Farm needs some real gain, however, to replace deaths and defections and keep the business viable.

Of course gain by itself is not enough; you need the right kind of gain. The business system that drops its customer standards in order to prop up a deteriorating gain rate is making a big mistake. As the credit card market matured, for example, companies that felt impelled to add new households were forced to relax both loyalty and credit standards, and profit margins began to spiral downward. Every company wants more customers, and if the sales force is paid for customer acquisitions, the customers will generally appear. But if standards drop, then the negative spiral takes over. Poorer customers cost more and yield less; the company raises prices and cuts service to save money; the value offered good customers begins to fall; defections surge; and earnings plummet.

The measures to keep an eye on are first, the early attrition rates of a new customer class, and second, the way revenue and profit curves for each new class compare with the same curves for older customer cohorts. Whenever these measures show deterioration, it's time to turn the spotlight of failure analysis in their direction. As essential as it is to track the quality of arrivals, however, it's equally essential to track the quality of departures, because if the quality of defecting customers goes up, then profits are going to go down. The best companies can compare the quality of defectors to the rest of the customer population, and first-class defections set off an alarm. At the other end of the scale, if the system indicates that defecting customers aren't really worth holding onto, then the indicated action is not to invest good money investigating and fixing the cause of their departure but to correct the customer acquisition process that attracted them in the first place. Every company has some customers it's better off without. They're unprofitable, they no longer fit the company's offerings (or never did), and managing their farewells—especially if they *want* to leave—is no loss to anyone. The danger, of course, is that on the basis of inadequate information, the company will mistakenly identify potentially valuable customers as marginal or dispensable. Unfortunately, such mistakes are easy to make, because some first-class defectors wear a kind of third-class disguise. They were once outstanding customers and could be again, but by the time they're ready to leave, they've already moved a substantial share of their wallet to a competitor. So they look like the kind of unprofitable, unwelcome customer you're eager to get rid of. Accepting the disguise at face value will not only lead to unacceptable defections, it can also tempt the company to underinvest in retention improvements.

These situations call for something resembling defection archeology—uncovering and analyzing several layers of historical and current-period data. One leading credit card company has built a system that lets its telephone reps instantly evaluate the quality of any customer who calls up to cancel an account. Because the technology is based on the potential profit from the customer's entire wallet rather than simply the company's present share, a shift of spending to a competitor won't fool the system. The phone rep can offer appropriate incentives to the best customers, and the company can watch to see whether the offers provide enough value to keep customers on board. Because of the inevitable tendency to dismiss all defectors as undesirable, knowing the true, sometimes hidden quality of a defector turns out to be critically important in activating root-cause tracking systems.

State Farm taught itself this lesson. The company had achieved a customer defection rate of less than 5 percent by consistently stressing customer service and value. But managers had come to believe that it wasn't possible to improve on that performance without keeping customers the company would be better off losing. State Farm was convinced that the customers who defected were vastly inferior to those who remained loyal. Then top managers decided to test their belief by carefully analyzing the driving records and historic profitability of defectors as compared to retained customers. They were surprised to find that the defectors were very attractive customers. As for State Farm's belief that disloyal customers were simply inveterate price shoppers that no company could hold onto for long, once again the facts were surprising. More than half the defectors had been with State Farm for more than five years.

Even a great company like State Farm can learn new tricks. The company has developed a powerful tool—called A Look at Your Book—that enables agents to apply failure analysis to their own customer inventories. A Look at Your Book not only examines customer defections, their root causes, and their effect on agent income; it also identifies current customers who are vulnerable to defection. By investing in learning tools of this kind, State Farm maintains and continues to improve its industry-leading performance.

One final reason for carefully tracking the quality of retained versus defecting customers is to make sure overzealous customer-recovery units don't spend money to save customers who are unprofitable or even costing the company money. A number of companies have launched indiscriminate defection-reduction programs, which not only offer discounts to negative-value customers (which exacerbates losses) but which also give equal weight to first-class and third-rate defectors in allocating resources to counteract defections.

EMPLOYEE DEFECTIONS

Customer defections are a practical unit of failure, because they reveal shortcomings in the flow of value to customers and can point to corrections. Employee defections are a useful unit of failure for much the same reason. When a valuable employee leaves, it's a signal that something in the system may need fixing. Of course, not every defection turns up something to fix—some are statistical outliers—but it's always a good idea to interview departing employees for a glimpse of their thinking, especially since their imminent departure may encourage them to say things they weren't willing to say before.

Because the decision to change jobs is so personal and complex, however, interviewing and analysis will often produce a confusing variety of apparently unrelated root causes. For this reason, root-cause analysis is often a less important tool than systematic statistical analysis for isolating useful—that is to say, correctable—insights into employee defections. Like a football coach or a Japanese factory worker, managers need to monitor statistical frequencies and focus on severe and recurrent failures.

Too Much Turnover

Consider the case of a large brokerage where broker turnover was so high, it created an enormous drag on company earnings. The company had been doing exit interviews with departing brokers for several years, but few cases appeared to have anything in common. Some of those who left were attracted to competitors by huge up-front bonuses; a few were unhappy with the performance of the firm's family of mutual funds. Several complained about the management and leadership skills of different branch managers. One or two mentioned the higher payout ratio at other firms, while others named the broader product line at one of the firm's competitors.

The head of the brokerage was firmly convinced that exit interviews were a waste of time. He believed that turnover was high in branches where the branch manager was weak, and that the solution was to upgrade the branch managers and train them to be better leaders. However, one member of his staff had worked with several competing firms over the years, and he pointed out that even firms with much lower average turnover had a similar range of strong and weak branch managers. Other factors must be at work.

Finally, the company's executives decided to try a new approach. Among other things, they examined the source from which each broker was originally hired. They found that attrition varied enormously by source, as shown in Figure 7-2. When the company hired brokers away from competitors, what seemed to matter most was how long the brokers

Figure 7-2   First-Year Attrition by Source of Hire in the
            Brokerage Industry

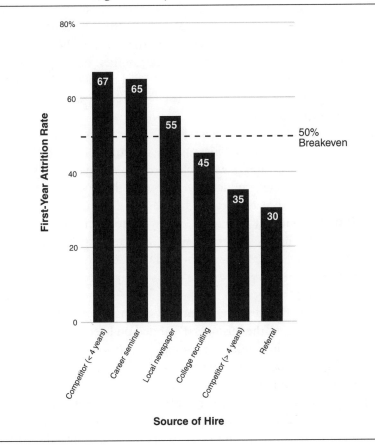

had stayed in their old jobs. Those who'd stayed less than four years
showed a high rate of premature defection. Those who'd stayed more
than four years also stayed longer in their new jobs. As for other sources,
people who answered newspaper advertisements were unlikely to hang
around long enough to repay what it cost to hire and train them; candidates from college recruitment programs showed greater loyalty; and
most loyal of all were the brokers who'd been referred to the firm by
present and former employees.

Too Many Hours

Despite the difficulty, root-cause analysis of employee defections is worth
doing. For example, it helped to unravel a persistent problem for

a sales company. Turnover among the company's salespeople was extremely high—more than 40 percent per year—and none of the company's improvement programs had helped. Then management began to interview departing employees in depth to identify the root causes of their defection. Most of the defectors complained that the hours were too long and that they hardly ever saw their families. Initially, managers dismissed the finding because they found it hard to believe that talented and ambitious salespeople—the kind they wanted most to keep—were leaving because of long hours.

But one of the beauties of rigorous failure analysis is that it allows you to test a hypothesis. In this case, a consulting team helped the company to divide the interviewed defectors into two groups, those who were above the average productivity level and those who were below. Analysts then looked at root-cause frequency distributions in the two groups. It turned out that management's hypothesis was dead wrong: it was precisely the best salespeople who were leaving because of the hours. Furthermore, the interviews showed that defectors had taken jobs requiring 20 percent less time on the job, so they were telling the truth in their interviews.

As it happened, this discovery put the company in something of a bind. The economics of the business depended on keeping facilities fully utilized, which made long hours unavoidable. A few maverick managers had tried to accommodate employees by allowing some of them to work their weekly hours in four days rather than five. The special hours were a headache to manage, but a lot of salespeople much preferred them. Because the company had established a failure-analysis database, managers could compare the defection rates of people in the special jobs with those of people working the old schedule. They found that the new arrangement cut defection rates by more than 15 percentage points. Since that kind of cut in turnover would increase profits 40 percent companywide, management strongly endorsed the experiment.

Unfortunately, not every facility was suited to the special schedules. So company managers undertook a systematic analysis of attrition by employee segment to see if it would be possible to hire more of the people who didn't mind, or at least could stand, the longer workweek. They searched the database for the characteristics of hires who'd exhibited better-than-average retention and productivity on the old schedule and made several discoveries. The first was that actions speak louder than words. All candidates said they were willing and ready to work the eleven- and twelve-hour days that the job required. But many had never worked days that long and didn't understand the toll it could take on their private lives. The database showed that the single factor that increased retention the most was hiring people who'd actually worked long hours in their previous jobs and had kept those jobs for several years.

A second critical factor managers uncovered had to do with the interviewing process. Candidates who were interviewed and approved by several people were more likely to last if hired. The success rate rose even further if candidates and their spouses were interviewed together— probably because it helped to weed out those couples who couldn't handle the job's impact on family life. Several other factors helped to explain retention rates, and management made sure local managers had plenty of incentive to learn the lessons the database had to teach. By combining interviews with systematic statistical analysis by employee group, the company can finally concentrate its efforts on the 20 percent of root causes that account for 80 percent of its defections. If companies understood the impact on profit of reducing turnover through failure analysis, they would put a high priority on building the database and developing the necessary analytical tools.

CREATIVE FAILURE ANALYSIS

As we saw earlier, the airline industry has achieved a sophistication and rigor in its analysis of airplane failure that is unmatched anywhere in the business world. But not even *airlines* apply black-box rigor to their analysis of business failures such as customer and employee defection. Why not? The quick answer is that death is so much more important than poor economic performance. But this explanation is inadequate. It takes nothing *away* from crash analysis to apply the same rigorous techniques in other areas. And once you understand the technology of failure analysis, why not use it?

The more probable explanation is that airlines have run into the same barrier that has stopped many other industries. Retailers, fast food chains, hotels, rental car agencies, airlines—none of them have been able to find a measurable failure to analyze. How do you define customer defection in those industries? What is there to measure? And how do you acquire the necessary information? Unfortunately, there's no black box for customer defection, and no FAA to require its use.

The right measure for airlines is probably their share of an individual's flights between specific cities—say, Boston and Chicago. By far the biggest driver of value for business travelers is convenience of departure, so one good measure of loyalty might be the number of minutes a typical business customer would rearrange a travel schedule in order to fly with a particular carrier. But if, for instance, American's frequent-flyer records show that a customer no longer flies American to Chicago from his or her home in Boston, the company doesn't know if that person has defected to United or simply stopped flying to Chicago. If American called every passenger whose usage dropped on a specific route, it would spend a lot of money analyzing false positives—people who look like defectors but aren't. And yet there may be an opportunity for American to create a defection database by making an arrangement with a group of travel agents or with one or more of the credit card companies business fliers charge most of their travel to. American could then apply Pareto's 80/20 rule, start asking the five why's, and begin taking steps to increase value and hence loyalty.

In businesses of many kinds, not just airlines and fast food, it takes a good deal of creativity to track defections and measure value delivered. In some cases, it seems nearly impossible, and yet with enough persistence, solutions do eventually present themselves somewhere along the spectrum from broad statistical analysis to individual root-cause interviewing.

Our own case at Bain & Company is a good example. It seemed to us that the durability of our client relationships was the only long-term measure we had of value delivered. But the picture that gave us was ambiguous. Consulting firms have long-lasting relationships with many large corporate clients. Each of those companies tends to have a complex portfolio of businesses and a steady stream of strategic questions requiring a relatively constant flow of consulting studies. Since the object of each individual study is the solution of an individual problem, however, it is often difficult to put specific projects into perspective and evaluate their contribution to the whole. Other companies have no ongoing need for consulting services, so the value of the projects done for them cannot be measured by how long we retain them as clients. They have a problem, we help them solve it, and that's the end of the relationship.

Of course, working with a client—even on a one-time project—puts us in a position to discover additional problems we could solve, so there is some relationship between how long a client stays with us and the success we have in identifying opportunities to create value. But here another difficulty arises, for we know that masterful salesmanship by a consulting partner is easily confused with true value creation, especially if the client is a large bureaucratic organization that may be buying consulting to please one of the bosses.

We needed a better measure than the length of the relationship. We needed a measure of genuine value creation that could also serve as a basis for failure analysis. After experimenting with a variety of peer review procedures and customer surveys, we found our answer. If we were truly delivering value, we reasoned, then it would show up in the long-term earnings and stock price of each client.

We decided to measure the stock price of each client from the time we started working together to the time we stopped, and to share that information throughout the company. No large consulting firm had ever done that before—probably because it makes failure so unmistakable, and so difficult to explain away. With Price Waterhouse auditing our methodology, we've been tracking our own client stock-price index since 1979, with the results shown in Figure 7-3. While our contribution to any company's success is obviously small in comparison to the unremitting efforts of the company's own managers and employees, we believe that over time and with hundreds of clients, this index must continue to outperform the S&P 500 or we will be failing in our mission to deliver value.

While no one measure perfectly captures all the important dimensions of value creation, this one has helped us to focus our organization on what does and does not create value. It has given us a common language and conceptual framework for discussing value creation. At the same time, its inadequacies have spurred our efforts to refine it.

FAILURE ANALYSIS IN A HURRY

Very few businesses have built the right measurement systems—a subject we'll take up in Chapter 8—or trained their people in the techniques of failure analysis. But when crisis comes, they need to figure out quickly which part of the business system is working poorly, or maybe not working at all. Fortunately, there is a shortcut, a process that can yield some of the critical benefits of failure analysis in a hurry, so you can take corrective action before it's too late.

Failure analysis demands a thorough understanding of the business system and its economics and a clear sense of what scale and unit of failure to scrutinize. The typical tree of possible failures in Figure 7-4

Figure 7-3   Client Stock-Price Performance as an Indicator of Value
              Creation

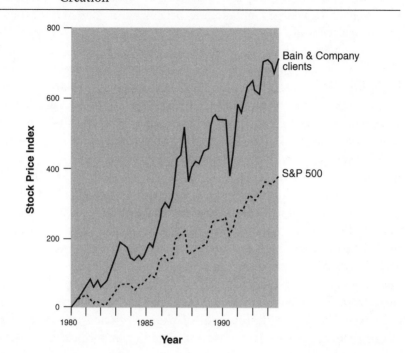

Note: Methodology and data attested to by Price Waterhouse through December 1993.

illustrates the difficulty. In any complex system, identifying root causes
requires training, experience, and judgment. So doing it quickly, and
with incomplete data, takes more than hard work; it takes senior management. You can't dish it off to a group of market research specialists,
because they simply cannot know enough about your organization and
its competitive situation, market and pricing strategies, cost position,
and capabilities. Failure analysis always requires the guidance of senior
management, but failure analysis in a hurry must be *done* by senior
managers. The process has four steps.

Let's take the case of a company that's losing market share and must
reverse the decline rapidly in order to survive. The first step is to gather
the senior management group (five to ten top executives) plus a sampling
of respected front-line personnel—branch managers, say, or leading salespeople. All these people will need quick training in the basics of failure

Figure 7-4   Failure Analysis of Customer Defection

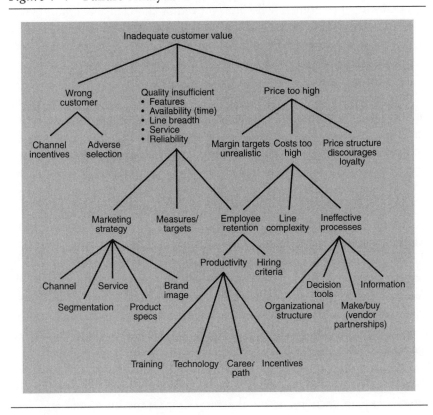

analysis—the five whys, root-cause analysis, and so forth. You must also convince them that this rapid diagnostic process is a top priority, and that by no stretch of the imagination will they escape without making personal phone calls to defectors. You will encounter great reluctance in some of them. Most people don't relish the idea of phoning strangers, let alone strangers who've been unhappy with the value they've received, and you will have to overcome that reluctance with leadership, peer pressure, and if necessary, a chair and whip. There is simply no substitute for having senior executives learn directly from defectors why the company's value proposition is inadequate.

The second step is to decide which customer defectors are truly critical. Obviously, you want to talk only to customers who genuinely represent the target segments of your future business. Waste no time talking to unprofitable customers or to customers who appear to be defectors but are really loyal customers who have moved or changed accounts. If your current information system is not up to the task of identifying key defectors, it is possible to hire professional telephone reps to call a large sample of apparent defectors and separate the wheat from the chaff. This is often a good investment, because the phone reps will not only collect basic data about each customer's demographics and true purchase history; they can also set up appointments for company executives to call back for a full root-cause interview. Most ex-customers will be so delighted at the prospect of a senior executive listening to their problems and complaints, they will seize the opportunity. Sometimes, of course, you will need to offer them an incentive. Go ahead and spend whatever it takes to talk with a true representative sample of your target defectors.

The third step is the root-cause interview itself. After an appropriate training session, each executive should be assigned ten to twenty-five defectors. The secret to success in these interviews is to probe into what drives customer behavior until you understand the root causes of each defection, then test various solutions to see which if any would have saved the relationship. After interviewing a quarter to a third of the targeted defectors, the executives should regroup to discuss what they're hearing, resolve any problems with the process, share best practices, and most important, develop a list of hypotheses about the corrective actions the company should take based on these early interviews. The remaining interviews can then focus on the most important questions and test various hypotheses.

The fourth step is the joint development of an action plan, based, of course, on the results of the defector interviews. The group will probably come up with some actions that require no major investment and can therefore be tested at once. Other remedies may require further research or analysis because of the size of the required investment. Including some front-line managers in the process will help to ensure that your interpretations of customer behavior are reasonable, and that your pro-posed improvements can be carried out.

As a shortcut, this four-step process has proven a great success. Most companies can carry it out in eight to twelve weeks, and it has repeatedly produced practical and effective solutions. Still, it's only a shortcut. Once you've laid the foundation for failure analysis by using it, you should set up an ongoing process that keeps senior management plugged into front-line customer feedback permanently. Lexus asks every member of its headquarters staff to interview four customers a month. MBNA asks every executive to listen in on phone contacts with customers in the customer service area or the customer recovery units. Some of those executives make the phone calls themselves. Every company benefits when executives learn lessons directly from customers and defectors. After all, the alternative is to depend on a second-hand interpretation— even if it is your own—of statistical research conducted by part-time college students who will never really understand the business, the competition, or the customers, and who will never really care.

FAILURE AND THE LOYALTY-BASED CYCLE OF GROWTH

The loyalty-based cycle of growth provides a template for searching out, prioritizing, and addressing failure of various kinds and on various scales throughout the organization. Each of the elements in Figure 1-3 can serve as a focal point for surveying and analyzing failure. The examples in this chapter have concentrated on the customer and employee sectors of the cycle, but the same lessons apply to investors.

As we have seen, there are several keys to organizational learning. The first is to understand that the true mission of any business, yours included, is the creation of value. The fact that most companies see profit rather than value as their primary business objective has inhibited their ability to learn in much the same way that the notion of an earth-centered universe stalled progress in astronomy. (Regrettably, management science has made essentially the same mistake. Business academics search out companies that look superior, usually on the basis of recent profit performance—and regardless of whether those profits were virtuous or destructive—then use those case studies to generalize about which management practices produce superior profit. As we have seen, this apparently reasonable approach has resulted in more science fiction than science.)

The second key to organizational learning is to grasp the value of failure. Only by measuring their failures can organizations unlock the doors to real learning. As Vilfredo Pareto said more than seventy years ago, "Give me a fruitful error any time, full of seeds, bursting with its own corrections." When it comes to value creation, the search for truth is a matter of looking inward, not of copying what appears to be excellence in others.

The third key to effective learning is to make sure that the right people in your organization learn to identify and correct the failures whose frequency and severity constrain your company's capacity to reach higher levels of value creation.

Finally, the best place to start monitoring failure is to watch defection rates for targeted groups of customers, employees, and investors. This practice will identify the hot spots that need attention in your value-creation system. Over time, of course, you will need to extend your system to cover other aspects of the system, including the volume and quality of new customers, employees, and investors. To systematize the learning process, most companies need to build new measurement systems that focus on all the upstream drivers of value creation. Otherwise they may analyze failure only when it shows up on the bottom line—by which time it may be too late. Chapter 8 will lay out the framework for the kind of measurement system that enables organizations to spot high-priority failures while there is still time to identify and eradicate the underlying root causes.

8

The Right Measures

THE MOST aggressive minds in an organization rarely focus on measurement systems. Years ago in Basic Accounting, measurement bored them. Now they have reached top positions in their companies, and measurement still bores them. Leaders, they feel, should concentrate on important, exciting things like vision and strategy, and let the people with the green eye shades worry about measurement.

The trouble with this attitude is that measurement lies at the very heart of both vision and strategy. It's hard to overestimate its importance in determining the future course of a business. As for excitement, it is measurement that allows managers to harness vision to the earthly realities of daily business practice. Measurement turns vision into strategy and strategy into fact.

Measurement is the business idiom. Just as language shapes thought and communication, measures shape the attitudes and behavior of a business organization. The choice of what a business measures communicates values, channels employee thinking, and sets management priorities. Moreover, through their inclusion in the feedback loops that underlie all organizational learning, measures define what a company will become. Deciding what to measure and how to link measures to incentives are among the most important decisions a senior manager can make. Yet most executives today work with inherited measurement systems that distort their business strategies. These systems, vestiges of

superannuated accounting traditions and outdated regulatory requirements, are practically useless for tracking the flow of value to and from
a firm's customers, employees, and investors. The vast majority of the
auditable measures used to run a modern company are embodied in the
income statement, which shows only one dimension of the business—this
year's profits. And the balance sheet, which tries to summarize the firm's
long-term value, is increasingly useless, especially in service businesses,
because it ignores the company's most important asset, human capital.
The result is that business leaders are like airplane pilots with nothing
but an airspeed indicator to tell them how they're doing. Which is to
say, most businesses today are like airplanes without fuel gauges, altime-
ters, or compasses—and many of them crash. The fact is, total reliance
on a single measure—current-period profits—is a form of flying blind.
But business leaders love the excitement of piloting, so few take the time
and energy to address the much more important job of designing the
airplane and its instrumentation. They believe that if they simply create
and communicate a compelling vision, the organization will stay on
course. But measurement is far too important to delegate, least of all
to accountants and MIS professionals. In a large, complex, far-flung
enterprise, measures are the only systematic means an executive has for
turning ideas into actions.

Our failure to develop new measurement systems has slowed the whole
progress of management science, for new techniques of measurement
have preceded most scientific advances. Physicians did not understand
the importance of blood pressure until a device was invented to measure
it. The ability to measure then led to discoveries about the causes and
effects of abnormal blood pressure, which enabled physicians to develop
treatments. It's very difficult to test a hypothesis unless you can measure
cause-and-effect relationships.

In business management, we have seen only a few advances in measurement, most notably in the area of process and quality control. Once
companies began to grasp the importance of defect rates, for instance,
they developed increasingly sophisticated statistical procedures for
tracking them. When the goal was reducing defects from 3 to 1 percent,
manufacturers could afford relatively sloppy measures. But taking defects
from 1 percent down toward six sigma (0.000003 percent) required a
whole new level of precision. The key that unlocked the door to the
quality revolution in manufacturing was the development of new, more

meticulous measures and of concepts that clearly linked those measures to the economics of the business.

The gateway to the loyalty revolution is developing the right kind of measurement system. Ideally, this new system should be compatible with the familiar profit-based measures most firms run on today. But it must also incorporate critical dimensions of the value-creation process that are hidden in the shadows of profit accounting.

In earlier chapters, we described a series of vital cause-and-effect relationships between loyalty and value creation. An understanding of those relationships is essential to successful management of the growth cycle pictured in Figure 1-3. If you turn back to that figure, you will see that the growth cycle consists of three sectors: customers, employees, and investors. Our new measurement approach will use two basic reports for each of the three sectors. They are analogous to the balance sheet and the income statement in financial accounting, but our balance sheet will cover human capital rather than financial assets, and in place of the income statement, we will develop a value-flow statement to show what drives the human-capital balance sheet. The second report will measure not only the flow of value to investors ("profit" on the accounting income statement), it will also monitor the other five streams of value that drive the human-capital balance sheet—the value flowing from the company to customers and employees, and the value flowing from customers, employees, and investors to the company. This new integrated system of measures will link each sector to the other two, permitting the organization to manage the entire value-creation spiral systematically.

Our aim is not simply to create a more balanced scorecard and to fill in the holes in the traditional income statement and balance sheet. It is to build the framework for an integrated scorecard linking the various components of the business together in relationships that can be quantified in cash-flow terms. This in turn will enable employees to establish goals, spot failures, use standard financial-analysis techniques, evaluate tradeoffs—and learn from the results.

We need to acknowledge at the outset, however, that there is a great deal of work still to do in this area. In contrast to traditional accounting, which has had centuries to resolve a long list of complex issues, like inventory valuation and the depreciation of capital assets, loyalty measurement systems are relatively new and untried. A few pioneering companies like USAA have seen the importance of managing value instead of profit, but most have yet to create their loyalty measures and will have to start from scratch using the guidelines that follow.

MEASURING WHAT'S IMPORTANT

The call for better measures is not new. The gaps in our information systems are too broad and egregious to have gone unnoticed. Many business experts have tried to devise new ways to gauge quality, teamwork, productivity, cycle time, workforce creativity, and customer and employee satisfaction. Yet most employees feel they already have more information than they can handle, and that cheap computing power simply swells the flood of indigestible data.

In fact, there has *always* been more information than the human mind could process. Our five senses bombard the brain with far more information than the brain can possibly assimilate. The answer is not to add a dozen new measurements but to help people filter out the irrelevant information so they can concentrate on the few dimensions that really matter.

First, we need exception-based measures that will draw people's attention to what's both relevant and pressing. In other words, we need to determine an acceptable target range for each variable, so we can focus our attention elsewhere unless a variable begins to drift. Second, we need not just more measures, but a simplifying paradigm that will let managers organize, categorize, and prioritize available data, old and new. We need a hierarchy of measures that fit together into a logical framework so that employees can dig only as deep as necessary to make a specific decision—without uncovering a mountain of buried detail.

An airplane pilot doesn't have to watch all the dials at once; many instruments have red lights that blink when their readings leave the acceptable range. But the pilot must understand not only what the instruments measure but also how the metered forces interact to keep the plane in the air and on course. In other words, the relationships among the variables are every bit as important as the variables themselves. A grasp of the physical forces governing the movement of the airplane is the right starting point for setting up a useful system of cockpit gauges.

Likewise, the right starting point for an effective loyalty-based measurement system is the set of forces that control the streams of value that flow to and from the company. We have seen that there are three twin streams of value—value that flows to and from customers, employees, and investors. Today's accounting systems measure some of these streams quite effectively, some partially or hardly at all. The unfortunate result is that businesses spend too much time trying to enhance the easily measured streams of value, and too little time trying to balance all of them for the sake of long-term growth and prosperity.

For example, we are probably best at measuring the value we deliver to investors—which after all is the focal point of profit accounting. This clarity of measurement is largely responsible for the fact that so many businesses work so hard to maximize shareholder value. Of course, conventional wisdom says we measure shareholder value because it's important, not simply because we know how. And the fact that all businesses do their best to maximize shareholder value is a strong argument for its fundamental importance. But it is equally true that all businesses work hard to do the opposite—that is, to *minimize* the cost of capital. It's just that we're not as expert at measuring the value we *receive* from investors, so we don't give it the same scrutiny we give to its mirror-image twin. The result is that many companies make foolish choices about their ownership and capital structures—as we saw in Chapter 6—with ultimately detrimental effects on all six streams of value.

Take another example. It sounds like a good idea to minimize labor cost. But we've seen that in order to maximize the potential for value creation, a business must find ways to pay its best people *more* than the competition. The problem, once again, is that we measure labor cost very effectively, but we have a cloudy notion of how well we deliver *value to* employees.

Even with customers, the situation is confusing. Common sense tells us to maximize the value we receive from customers—to raise prices until customers begin to wince. But it's just as obvious that customers won't keep coming back for more unless we're giving them good value—in fact, *best* value on at least one competitive dimension—so it's essential to pay as much attention to the value flowing out of the company as to the value flowing in.

The question is one of equilibrium: how to weigh and prioritize all these apparently conflicting imperatives so they balance out in a flourishing business system where value spirals upward and all players get a generous share. Oddly enough, the solution is to give particular attention to one measure, the net present value of the customer base, and place it at the top of the measurement hierarchy. This may sound counterintuitive, for it seems to set one stream of value above the other, value received from customers. But remember, we *have* to regard customers as first among equals, because their wallets are the source of all life-giving cash flow. Remember, too, that the only way to maximize the net present value of a customer base is to earn the loyalty of its most profitable members, which means giving them superior value. Finally, remember that only by orienting decisions and investments toward superior customer value can you ensure that there will be plenty of value left over for employees and investors.

In practice, the twin streams of customer value, to and from, are not independent. They are simply two hoses connected to the same hydrant. Both draw on the same source of value, and pricing is the valve that divides them. Value to the customer is the total value of the product or service less the price. Value to the company is the price less the cost. On the face of it, this is a very simple, almost simplistic equation, roughly as difficult as two and two equal four. Raising the price will increase value to the company and decrease value to the customer. Cutting the price will do just the opposite. But if we shift from a short- to a long-term view, something marvelous happens. Over the course of a customer lifecycle—indeed, *because* of the customer lifecycle—two and two begin to equal five or six.

Figure 8-1 illustrates this ongoing relationship. The uppermost line, called Full Value, is the price above which customers will defect—the price above which they get less value than they've paid for. The difference between full value and actual price is the consumer surplus described in Chapter 5. And of course, the difference between price and cost is profit.

The remarkable feature of Figure 8-1 is the way the lines move apart over time and the spaces between them grow. As a result of learning, familiarity, and the other factors we sketched in the economic model in Chapter 2 (Figure 2-3), the cost of serving the customer gradually diminishes. Simultaneously, as customers get to know their supplier and become more effective consumers, the full value they receive goes up. Over time, in other words, cost declines and value increases, so both profit and the consumer surplus grow. That usually means the price can rise as well. All these effects combine to create wider profit and value margins as customers mature.

Or perhaps we should say that they *can* combine to produce wider margins, because though the effect occurs to some degree whether one

Figure 8-1   The Dynamic Relationship Between Cost, Price, and
Customer Value

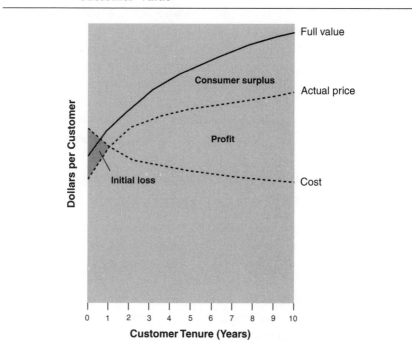

Note: Full value is the price above which the customer will defect.

seeks it or not, there is nevertheless a good deal a company can do to
encourage it. In general, there are three things you can do to maximize
the net present value of your customer base. First, you can search for
ways to cut costs without reducing customer value. Second, you can
search for ways to improve value to your customers at *increased* cost,
providing that increased cost is smaller than the increased benefit. Finally,
you can adjust prices to maximize profit, with or without a corresponding
increase in value. You just have to bear in mind that whenever price
exceeds the full value a customer receives, that customer will defect,
wiping out a stream of future profit. For that matter, whenever price
gets close to full value, the danger increases that a temporary lapse in
quality or service will generate a defection—or that a competitor will
push into that widening gap between cost and price.

Companies that consistently leave plenty of consumer surplus on the
table may hurt current-year profits, but they are building a level of trust

and loyalty that will insulate them at least partially from competitor attacks. They think of it as an investment in customer equity. State Farm, for example, has chosen to allocate to customers a substantial portion of the value its system creates. Instead of allowing price to drift upward over a customer's lifecycle, as in Figure 8-1, State Farm has chosen to do the opposite. It gives progressive rate reductions to its most loyal and consistently profitable customers. (We'll look at the formula in Chapter 10.) Such discounts are no way to maximize current profits. On the other hand, the policy of rewarding loyalty contributes powerfully to the customer retention that is such a big part of State Farm's competitive advantage.

THE MEASUREMENT HIERARCHY

Every industry and company will have its own unique circumstances to consider in trading off current profits against the increased security of future profits. For example, a high-tech company in a volatile market driven by technical breakthroughs will not want to invest as much in consumer surplus as a more stable insurance company. But without measurement tools that let you estimate the impact of various pricing and investment alternatives, it's difficult to make intelligent tradeoffs between strategies that increase this year's cash flow at the risk of decreased customer tenure (raising prices, for example) and strategies that decrease this year's cash flow in order to lengthen customer tenure (investment in improved service, for example).

In setting up the hierarchy of measurements in Figure 8-2, therefore, we have to put customer net present value (NPV) at the top. (Admittedly, *customer NPV* doesn't roll off the tongue as easily as the more common term, *lifetime customer value,* but that term has been used most often to mean lifetime revenue stream, as opposed to the discounted stream of profit net of acquisition investment.) On the next level down are the three measures that comprise customer NPV. Two of these, duration and lifecycle profits (how long your present customers stay with you, and the value they will contribute as they hang around) relate to the NPV of the *current* customer inventory. The third captures the rate of *future* customer acquisition, since customer NPV must also include the flow of value from anticipated new customers. (You must monitor the quality of these new customers to see whether they're enriching or diluting the loyalty and lifecycle cash flow of the current customer inventory. This

Figure 8-2 The Measurement Hierarchy

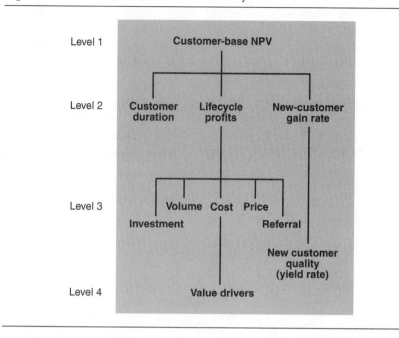

means that you must watch retention and cash flows very carefully for these new customers. Given the lack of a track record for these, new customers, it's important to use additional early indicators of quality whenever possible. We'll come back to this question later.)

Once your company has created a system for measuring all three factors—customer duration, lifecycle cash flow, and new-customer gain rate—you can begin putting them together to calculate the net present value of your customer base. (The process is described in Chapters 2 and 3.) You can also begin making decisions about how to increase this NPV.

THE CUSTOMER BALANCE SHEET AND VALUE FLOW STATEMENT

To study and manage its customer-base NPV in the manner just described, a company needs management reports of precisely the kind we spoke of earlier—a Customer Balance Sheet and a Customer Value Flow Statement. Figure 8-3 provides a template for each, showing the basic information any firm would require to make similar decisions.

On the balance sheet, the customer base is divided into new customers, gainers, decliners, and defectors. Gainers and decliners are current customers who are doing more or less business with the company than in previous years. Once you've divided your customer population into these categories, you can attribute revenue growth along the same lines. By combining this information with an estimate of future inflows of new customers, you will be able, using the techniques we demonstrated in Chapters 2 and 3, to estimate the NPV of your customer base. Tracking these balance-sheet items over time will show you your biggest opportuni-

Figure 8-3 The Customer Balance Sheet and Value Flow Statement

Customer Balance Sheet

Customer category	Number	Percentage of revenue	NPV
Beginning balance	–	–	–
+ New customers	–	–	–
+ Gainers	–	–	–
– Decliners	–	–	–
– Defectors	–	–	–
= Ending balance	–	–	–

Customer Value Flow Statement

Value Proposition
- Target customers
- Dimensions of value
- Measures
- Source of advantage

Value Delivered to Customers

	Company	Competitor A	Competitor B	Competitor C
Price	–	–	–	–
Quality drivers	–	–	–	–
Retention	–	–	–	–
Share of wallet	–	–	–	–
Gain	–	–	–	–
Yield	–	–	–	–

Value Received from Customers

	Company	Competitor A	Competitor B	Competitor C
New-customer NPV	–	–	–	–
Current-customer NPV	–	–	–	–
Defector NPV	–	–	–	–
Average profit per customer	–	–	–	–
Average revenue per customer	–	–	–	–

ties for improvement. For example, a simple variance analysis of year-to-year changes in customer-base NPV will spotlight how big the defector problem is in relation to a decline in new customers and gainers. If the decline in new customers and gainers is a $10 million problem and the increase in defectors is a $20 million problem, then the customer balance sheet has proved its worth by ordering your problems and investment priorities.

The balance sheet alone, however, will not give you enough information to manage the value-creation process. You need an accounting of the flows of value to and from customers, which brings us to the Value Flow Statement. The stream of value flowing to the customer is probably the single most important element in any business. As we have repeatedly emphasized, creating and delivering superior value to the customer is the center of the value-creation cycle and underpins all business success. Yet customer value can be quite a challenge to measure.

It is nearly impossible to measure unless a firm is very explicit about which customers it means to seek out, and how it intends to create so much value for them that a surplus will be left for employees and investors. Therefore, the first part of the value flow statement must be a brief statement of the company's value proposition. This statement should identify the company's target customers; articulate the dimensions of quality and service that will create value for those customers (relative to pricing and competitive offerings); specify the measures by which to gauge the value proposition's success; and finally, explain how the firm will deliver the value proposition in an economically advantageous manner, creating enough surplus value to provide superior compensation for employees and investors.

Below the value proposition, the value flow statement should list the critical measures that will be used to monitor the relative value of the firm's offering. One obvious measure to track is pricing in relation to competitors. Another is a set of benchmark statistics for the crucial dimensions of quality. In some businesses, timeliness is the critical dimension; in others, reliability. Still others find that fashion and features drive value. Sometimes the measures are simple and straightforward—the number of rings before a phone is answered, or the number of days to settle a claim. Other cases require more ingenuity. USAA, one of the most advanced measurers of value, has found that its customers care a great deal about getting their questions answered or their problems solved in one phone call. So the company has set a goal of resolving 87 percent of all requests on the first call and has developed the systems required to monitor its performance.

Few companies can continuously measure all the factors that drive customer value. There are too many customers and too many complex variables for constant oversight. Still, employees have to make day-to-day decisions. So what we need is a summary gauge—a light on the instrument panel that will blink as soon as the company begins to wander off course or run low on fuel. The best of these gauges are customer retention rate and wallet share. Though it is tempting to use customer satisfaction scores, that evidence isn't nearly as reliable as real purchase behavior, and should be used with considerable caution (a subject we will return to).

Customer retention and share of wallet are excellent summary statistics not only because they are reliable indicators of whether customer value is sufficient, but because they are key ingredients in the calculation of customer net present value. However, they can be tricky to measure. See the appendix titled "Measurement Pitfalls" at the end of this chapter.

GAIN AND YIELD RATES

Two more statistics appear in the second part of the Customer Value Flow Statement shown in Figure 8-3. These are the gain rate—the ratio of new customers to the current customer base—and the yield rate—the percentage of customers solicited who actually sign up. A healthy gain rate is evidence of a superior value proposition, especially if it is accompanied by good retention. As we pointed out in Chapter 5, growth in customer volume is absolutely necessary for a firm to improve its productivity. Making loyalty-based management work isn't merely a matter of holding onto present customers; acquiring the right new customers is equally important. Gain and yield rates are excellent measures of this effort.

Yield rates are also very useful as we move to the third part of the Customer Value Flow Statement, the flow of value from the customer to the firm. The ultimate statistic, of course, is the measure of net present value summarized on the Customer Balance Sheet. But it is impractical to track every element in the measurement hierarchy for every customer; we need summary statistics to tell us when to dig deeper. A high yield rate is a good leading indicator that at least the firm is attracting the kind of customer it's after. The risk of adverse selection—that deadly value killer we discussed in Chapter 3—is greatest when yield rates are low.

Average profit per customer and average revenue per customer are also practical statistics for monitoring the flow of value to the firm. But companies whose inflows of new customers have varied over time must be cautious and analyze these statistics one tenure group at a time. Studying the average profit and revenue of, say, third-year customers will filter out all the other tenure waves that can wash through a customer base and distort the broader averages.

One final dimension that can be revealing is the quality of defectors versus the quality of new customers. Ideally, defectors will be of low value and new customers will have high expected net present values, though that is rarely the case. Many companies find just the opposite—that defector quality exceeds the quality of new customers.

PUTTING CUSTOMER MEASURES TO WORK

The measures we have just described are not meant to be canonical, merely suggestive. The idea is to develop the best approach for each new situation. Let's look at a couple of examples to see how it's done in practice.

One discount brokerage house has approached the challenge of measuring gain rate and the quality of gain in much the same way a manufacturer might measure its yield rate—the value of labor and raw materials that goes into products that can be shipped versus the value lost in scrap, rework, and rejects. Most businesses could easily adapt this approach to their own circumstances.

The company's first step is to calculate its investment in each new customer. It allocates the cost of the advertising and marketing that brought in each new group of customers, then adds the cost of processing and setting up each new account. Close attention to product margins and activity levels then allows the company to calculate the yield it requires on these investments to bring each new class of customers to profitability.

With its investment per customer and its required yield nailed down, the company goes on to track new applications as a percentage of current customers. It watches the rate at which new applications turn into real accounts (i.e., accounts customers actually fund) and the percentage of those that become active enough to contribute to profits. Finally, using lifecycle profit and attrition patterns for similar older customers, the firm can quite accurately predict the percentage of any new class that will eventually produce a profit and a positive NPV for the company.

These measurement tools have enabled the brokerage to figure out which advertising campaigns generated the most applications and which produced the greatest number of good customers. (They were not the same campaigns.) Furthermore, when retention rates dipped, the brokerage could isolate the cause. Sometimes it was the quality of new acquisitions, sometimes service or product value. Every company should have a similar system to manage the process of investing in new customers. If banks had such a tool, they would probably stop trying to build a customer base by promoting CD rates. The system would make it clear that while the initial volume looks good, the new customers rarely stick around long enough to pay back the acquisition and set-up costs.

Another company that has used loyalty-oriented measures to manage and improve its value proposition is MBNA, which has made a systematic study of the kinds of customer behavior that drive lifecycle profits in its business. For example, one of the key profit drivers in credit cards is growth in average balance per customer. Since the way to get average balances to grow is to earn an increasing share of each customer's spending, MBNA surveyed customers with different levels of wallet share and discovered which dimensions of value were driving their purchase decisions. At the top of the list was the size of the credit line. Obviously, if one company offered a credit line big enough to cover 100 percent of a household's needs, it was easier to consolidate business with that company. So MBNA continued to refine its credit evaluation process to make sure each customer got as high a credit line as made sense. Another item high on the list was how quickly the company granted requests for credit-line increases.

MBNA established measures for each of the critical variables that drive customer value, then had employees in each critical area define superior performance and set corresponding goals. Now, on every day that at least 98 percent of those goals are met, the company contributes money to a bonus pool for nonmanagement employees. Scores are posted every day on a board outside the cafeteria. Since everyone in the company cares very much about hitting their targets, people work together to solve problems. For example, when the new accounts department was temporarily overwhelmed with new customer applications, other departments voluntarily pitched in to help out.

Other companies have tried to implement similar operational measurement systems, most of them less successfully. Some fail because they tie incentives only to the measures under each department's immediate control—with the result that each department cares too much about itself and too little about the rest of the organization. Frequently, however, there is another problem: measuring performance dimensions that aren't critical drivers of value to the customer. Companies gather perspective on customer moments of truth in their business processes, then establish measures and goals for each of them. They may even base their decisions on customer research. But they don't take the final and most important step; they never tie levels of performance on these moments of truth to the actual customer purchase behavior that drives cash flow and serves as the litmus test of customer value.

They assume, for instance, that one moment of truth is the customer's receipt of a bill, and that the number of billing errors is a key variable. But since they don't tie relative performance on this measure to customer lifecycle purchases, wallet share, or defection rates, they have no idea how important accurate billing really is or what improvements in billing might be worth. The fact is, drivers of relative customer value change over time as competitors' capabilities and customer expectations shift. The only way to be sure your employees are paying attention to critical variables is to tie the bottom of the measurement hierarchy back to the top—that is, to link practical operational measures to customer NPV by way of actual differences in customer loyalty and lifecycle purchase patterns. If billing errors can explain a significant share of customer defections, then employees know exactly how important those errors are. And if they also know the cash-flow consequences of a change in the defection rate, then they can figure out how much of an investment they can make to fix the billing problem.

CUSTOMER LOYALTY MEASURES AT LEXUS

One of the best indicators of customer loyalty is the purchase of service contracts, spare parts, and upgrades. In many businesses, these are also the sources of greatest margin, so they're critical not just as indicators of future equipment purchases but as profit drivers in their own right. Capital goods manufacturers in mature businesses (telephone switches and copying machines, for example) make little profit on the initial sale; they rely on service contracts to make the customer lifecycle profitable.

While it's probably necessary to keep sales separate from service from an organizational point of view, it is terribly important that their tracking systems be linked. They seldom are. The problem is that the information service representatives acquire in dealing with users needs to be cycled back into the measurements that drive product design and sales. Likewise, incentive systems should encourage salespeople to target buyers who have remained loyal service customers.

The automobile business has all these problems in exaggerated form. Most automakers haven't the vaguest idea which buyers are loyal service customers at their dealerships, delivering far superior margins to the system. On average, dealers retain only 30 to 40 percent of the postwarranty service dollars spent on the autos they sell. What's more, remarkably few dealers track service purchases systematically.

Lexus, a company that believes service loyalty is a key driver of both dealer profits and repurchase rates, has developed a computer system that estimates how much service work the cars a dealer has sold ought to generate. The computer compares dealers' service billings to its estimates; it also notices which customers have not returned for the first two checkups, which are free. Best of all, the system calculates how much additional profit a dealership might have earned if its loyalty performance had been in the top quartile. To help dealers manage their businesses more effectively and deliver better customer value, it also compares productivity levels.

The Lexus system has not come cheap. Each dealer has invested in an AS400 computer and a satellite dish to transmit sales and service information to the company's U.S. headquarters in Torrance, California. This unique network allows Lexus to track repurchase loyalty with a precision the industry has never seen before. Dick Chitty, corporate vice president of parts, service, and customer satisfaction, can review information with dealers and compare their service-loyalty records.

Some auto-service operations try to raise profits with higher prices and aggressive cross-selling. But tying individual employee incentives to the wrong measures can lead to customer defections—and worse. Sears Auto Centers ran into serious problems when its California operation switched from hourly pay to commissions based on sales volume. Since the number of customers was not increasing, the only way to increase bonuses was to raise the average ticket per customer. Employees began finding more and more problems with every car that came in, and the result for Sears was a public relations disaster. Customers went to the authorities, who launched investigations in New Jersey, California, and Florida. The debacle is a good example of what can happen when profit pressure focuses an organization on the wrong measures. Sears diagnosed the problem as not selling hard enough; the real problem was not delivering enough value to the customer.

If Sears had been measuring repeat business rather than sales volume, it would have seen the problem much sooner than it did. The keystone of the measurement system at Lexus is repurchase loyalty, the best possible indicator of how much value customers feel they've received. Employee learning revolves around the task of raising it. Lexus urges its dealers to review their service practices if pricing looks high. And dealers listen, because Lexus can show them what not listening will cost them in long-term profit. Dick Chitty can do more than share generic customer-satisfaction statistics; he can show dealers the names of defectors and calculate exactly how much profit each dealer is losing because of defections. The result for Lexus is a new auto-industry standard for service and repurchase loyalty.

THE CUSTOMER ACQUISITION/DEFECTION MATRIX

There is one final measurement tool that can be very helpful in managing the flow of customer value, especially when used in concert with the kind of failure analysis described in Chapter 7. It is called the acquisition/defection matrix, and Lexus provides a good example of how to use it. First, the company tracks defection rates and identifies the automobiles former Lexus owners buy. As much as possible, it does the same for its competitors. The results are then plotted on a matrix like the one shown in Figure 8-4, which summarizes the information, indicates weaknesses in the company's value proposition, and spotlights the competitive value propositions customers find more attractive. In the lefthand column are the cars customers trade in, and across the top, the new makes they purchase. By adding a row for new customers who haven't previously owned a luxury car, Lexus can analyze all customer movement in the luxury market, and avoid the pitfall of studying its own performance in isolation.

Most companies could (and should) construct this kind of matrix for their own industries. A further refinement involves tracking not just the number of customers, but the profits they generate, or better yet, their net present value. In many industries—banking, for example—the volume of

Figure 8-4   An Acquisition/Defection Matrix

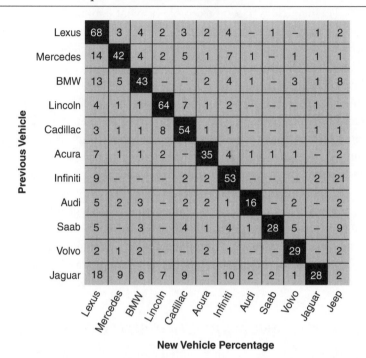

New Vehicle Percentage

How to read this chart: Of all Lexus owners, 68 percent repurchased a Lexus, 3 percent
bought a Mercedes, and 1 percent bought a Saab; of all Mercedes owners, 14 percent
bought a Lexus and 42 percent bought another Mercedes. Percentages do not total
100 because many auto makes are not listed.

Note: Data is out of date. Chart is intended only as an illustration of the format for
acquisition/defection data.

customer acquisitions and defections isn't nearly as important as the
flow of high-value customers. In these industries, root-cause analysis is
called for whenever any cell in the matrix indicates a large flow of
customer value (not just a large flow of customers).

THE SATISFACTION TRAP

One of the significant features of the measurement hierarchy and the
various individual measures we've looked at so far is that all of them
build on impartial fact. Customer retention, lifecycle profits, new-
customer gain rates, yield rates, customer purchases—these statistics

may be difficult to gather, but they provide real insight because they are objective and reliable. Even more important, they are linked directly to cash flows and customer-base NPV, as we saw in Chapter 2.

Not all the measures in use today are so dependable. One of the least reliable, and most common, is customer satisfaction. It's not that satisfaction doesn't matter; it matters a great deal. It's the manner, context, and priority of satisfaction measurement that has become a problem. And the problem is that if we fail to link satisfaction scores to customer loyalty and profits, they can all too easily become an end in themselves. In some organizations, they are considered a higher goal than profit. But managers who really understand the power of satisfaction surveys have also come to recognize their limitations. At Lexus, the consistent winner of auto satisfaction awards, surveys are not considered the best measure of satisfaction. In the words of Dave Illingworth, the first general manager of Lexus and now group vice president of Toyota, U.S., "The only meaningful measure of satisfaction in this industry is repurchase loyalty."[1]

Illingworth knows that the distinction between satisfaction survey scores and repurchase loyalty can be enormous. In the automobile industry, which pioneered the use of satisfaction research and probably spends more money on satisfaction programs and research than any other industry in the world, the dangers of the satisfaction trap are most evident. General Motors was one of the early adopters of satisfaction technology. The company committed itself to reversing the inroads of foreign competition by concentrating on customers, and its primary tool was the satisfaction survey. Management bonuses were based in part on improving satisfaction scores. In the 1980s, satisfaction scores went up—as did most measures included in management bonus calculations—but market share and profits went down.

Any company can fall into a satisfaction trap if it forgets that there is no necessary connection between satisfaction scores and cash flow. Early successes with satisfaction programs are often a matter of picking low-hanging fruit. GM's surveys identified some obvious sources of dissatisfaction—mechanics wearing dirty uniforms, customers not getting their cars when they were told they'd be ready—that could be fixed or improved with little expenditure of time or money. But once a company has made the obvious improvements, it's likely to find that the next level of enhancement requires a real investment. Is it worth $10 million to retrain all the service managers? Is it worth $10 million to increase the average satisfaction score from 85 to 90 percent? Is it worth $100 million? These questions are basic to delivering the best value, but satisfaction surveys cannot answer them. Employees will naturally search out the easiest ways to improve scores, but not necessarily the most profitable ones.

In fact, whenever bonuses are based on satisfaction scores isolated from repurchase loyalty and profits, the result is unproductive behavior. Many automakers now track satisfaction scores with statistical rigor and include them in their incentive and recognition programs. As a result, industry satisfaction scores have skyrocketed over the past ten years, to the point that more than 90 percent of customers today report they are satisfied or very satisfied. Meanwhile, repurchase rates for the industry remain mired in the 30- to 40-percent range. How can this be?

Evidence is piling up that dealers are responding to the satisfaction obsession in ways that don't necessarily improve customer value—or dealer profits. One Toyota dealership offered free detailing to every customer who agreed to return a survey marked "Very Satisfied" in all categories. The dealer even provided a preprinted copy of the survey showing the customer how to check it off properly. At another dealership, a recently hired salesman pleaded with a customer to fill out the questionnaire with favorable responses. "Both my wife and I just lost our jobs at a local computer company so my young family is depending on me—and I'll lose my job here if I don't get high satisfaction scores." These efforts may increase scores, but they probably won't increase loyalty.

Manipulating the system doesn't take place only at the grassroots level. Auto executives like to advertise high marks on the J. D. Power Satisfaction Survey, so some companies have figured out how to manipulate the scores. For example, calling customers immediately after they've bought a car and asking about their experience is one good way to keep scores high. This realization gave rise to boiler-room operations in which customers were telephoned after a purchase and asked questions related to satisfaction. Often as not, real feedback is ignored. The caller's primary purpose is to inflate the J. D. Power score.

Even when dealers try to implement satisfaction surveys for the right reasons, they run up against some of the inherent limitations of the technology. For instance, dealers are finding that an increasing number of customers are tiring of being surveyed. A Cadillac dealer tells this story:

One of my customers cornered me at a charity board meeting and told me, "I got a call after I picked up my car asking if I was satisfied with the sales experience. Then I got a call after the car was serviced, asking if I was satisfied with the service experience. Finally, another surveyor called several weeks later to check if I was happy with the ownership experience. So when I am going to get a call asking if I'm satisfied with the satisfaction survey experience?"[2]

One leading auto company admits that customers can get as many as six surveys or calls a year. Imagine how much this costs the company—to say nothing of the customer's wasted time.

Car companies serious about measuring the value they deliver to customers will not base their measurement systems on satisfaction surveys. They will recognize that measuring satisfaction—an inherently unstable and temporary mental state—is a tricky business, and that customer attitudes shift many times over the years between auto purchases. Instead, they will carefully track repurchase loyalty to determine the true value of their products and services in relation to competitors. When customers don't return to the dealer for service, when they replace their car with another brand—these are incontestable signs of unsatisfied customers.

Satisfaction surveys are a far less accurate test of satisfaction than behavior. In business after business, our research has shown that 60 to 80 percent of customers who defected had said on a survey just prior to defecting that they were satisfied or very satisfied. Some companies have responded by trying to increase the sophistication of their satisfaction measures. Most automakers have chosen this approach, investing heavily in their survey technology. The result? Ninety percent of their customers still claim to be satisfied, but only 40 percent come back for another purchase. Yet most auto companies are still putting more money into refining their satisfaction surveys than into developing reliable loyalty measures.

The exception is Lexus. Drive by a Lexus dealership and you'll see that satellite dish we mentioned earlier. It keeps the dealer in constant touch with Lexus headquarters, and maintains a steady flow of information in both directions about customer auto and service purchases. Lexus can track which customers are coming back for more and which are not. It can analyze the differences between the dealers who are earning superior customer loyalty and the ones who are not. It can then use satisfaction research productively to help understand customer purchase decisions.

Another advantage of watching what customers pay, not just what they say, is that it allows a company to track lifetime purchases. That forces a company to channel its customer-satisfaction investment toward customers with the highest potential value. Satisfaction research conducted broadly across the entire customer base—the statistically correct approach—will necessarily show the influence of unprofitable customers. For example, a branch bank manager might hear many complaints about long teller lines, but it's perfectly possible that the branch's most profitable customers do most of their business by phone, mail, and ATM. Investing in more tellers may inflate satisfaction scores but deflate profits by improving service and increasing cost in ways the best customers don't care about.

Another trap embedded in satisfaction programs not linked to loyalty and profit is that they may fall into disrepute just when improving value to customers should be a critical objective. One bank invested heavily in the development of a satisfaction tracking system, which it used along with other measures such as cost effectiveness and growth to compare performance across branches and evaluate branch managers. Then the bank decided to measure customer retention rates as well. To its surprise, it found that the branches with the highest satisfaction scores did not have the best retention rates. This led some managers to insist that the company eliminate satisfaction measures altogether and base more of a manager's bonus on cost effectiveness. Lacking a reliable measurement system based on loyalty and cash flow, many companies default to cost-reduction programs and layoffs.

The Baby Bells are another group of companies groping for the right management tools in an increasingly competitive environment. Most have developed satisfaction surveys to help focus their organizations on customer service. But few have yet built systems to analyze lifecycle purchases and profit from various types of customers. When they occasionally do this kind of analysis, they find that the top 10 percent of their customers are worth five to ten times as much in potential lifetime profit as the bottom 10 percent. If the telephone companies go the way of the auto-makers and implement increasingly refined customer-satisfaction systems, they are likely to fall into the same satisfaction trap. While they work at raising broad-based satisfaction scores, competitors will cull their best customers with focused marketing programs that deliver outstanding value to the most profitable market segments. Diminished cash flow will then make it more difficult to deliver good value even to average customers.

In depending so heavily on broad-based surveys, companies are letting too many defectors slip through the cracks. There is a better and a simpler way. Companies that want higher customer satisfaction (which they mistakenly equate with higher satisfaction scores) must know how much they can afford to spend to satisfy specific customers. That is, they need to measure the return on their investment. The only way to do this is to study customer lifecycle purchase patterns. But since they have to track lifecycle purchase patterns to determine customer profitability, why not simply use lifecycle purchases as the basis for measuring and managing satisfaction? Since repeat purchase loyalty is the goal, why not make it the basic yardstick of success? Companies can avoid the satisfaction trap if they remember that what matters is not how satisfied they keep their customers, but how many satisfied and profitable customers they keep.

YES YOU CAN—THE STAPLES EXAMPLE

Creating the kind of information and measurement systems we have described in this chapter may seem an impossible challenge to many readers, especially those in industries like retailing, where it is difficult to track individual customer purchases, let alone retention and wallet share. But auto-makers probably felt the same way until Lexus showed how it could be done—and how valuable the information could be.

Let's look at another example, a retailer that decided it had to find a way to measure customer value—and did it. The company is Staples, the office supply superstore mentioned briefly in Chapter 3. Founded in 1986 by Tom Stemberg, an executive with supermarket experience, and funded by venture capitalists, Staples decided early that it must find a way to track customer purchases. Its solution was to create a membership card good for discounts and special promotions. The company encouraged all its customers to sign up, then entered their membership numbers at the cash register every time they made a purchase. If the customer forgot to bring the card to the store, the cashier could access the account number simply by entering the customer's phone number.

This system allowed Staples to know its customers much better than the typical retailer. The membership application itself captured basic demographic information; cash-register data gave precise information about preferences, quantities, and frequency of purchase. Together the applications and purchase histories told management which customers and segments accounted for most of each store's volume. The company could then plan its stock and merchandising store by store, to meet the needs of its best customers. Staples had no need for expensive mass mailings to entire geographic markets, and it steered clear of generic coupons. Instead, it targeted coupons, mailings, and promotions to specific customer segments.

To create this system, Staples had to make a substantial investment at a time when venture capitalists were looking for at least a 35-percent return on their capital. But Stemberg believed this kind of customer data would give the company a critical competitive edge. He simply saw the world differently from other retailers, who underestimated or simply never saw the value of customer information systems.

It was a brave investment to make when the chain was still testing its basic merchandising concept, but it turns out to have been a remarkably clever move. The competitive battle has since heated up, and other office supply chainstores like OfficeMax and Office Depot have moved into Staple's territory, but Staples has more than held its own. One reason is that when a competing store is about to open, Staples' customer tracking system can produce a printout of its top one hundred local customers. The manager can then call on each of them, emphasize Staples' relative advantages, and customize special promotional packages to blunt the new store's appeal. Once the new store has opened, the Staples manager can watch purchase patterns to see which customers are defecting, then craft an effective counterattack and try to win them back. Results bear witness to the system's worth. Revenues have grown from zero in 1986 to more than $2 billion in 1994, and Staples' shares have more than tripled in value since the initial public offering in 1989.

In 1995, the Staples management team decided that it was time to redesign its customer tracking system. The original program included 90 percent of customers, and with Staple's rapid expansion, the database had ballooned to enormous proportions. Company managers reviewed what they had learned about customer lifecycle purchase patterns and took another look at how that data had helped them make decisions. The conclusion they reached was that their most critical insights all seemed to come from a better understanding of their best customers. The inclusion of vast numbers of small customers had not only overloaded the database, it had watered down the program itself. Instead of concentrating on the needs and behavior of its best customers, the company was offering equal rewards and incentives to everyone.

As a result, the original program was dropped in favor of a new reward structure for customers with more than $1,000 in annual purchases. The new program, called Staples Dividends, offered a tiered discount that rewarded larger cumulative purchases with larger rebates, giving good customers an additional incentive to consolidate their purchases at Staples. The more they spent, the lower the effective price. But of course the more they spent, the better the result for Staples. The change sharpened Staples' ability to measure, learn from, and manage the purchase patterns of its best customers. The result, in short, was greater value all around.

AN EMPLOYEE BALANCE SHEET
AND VALUE FLOW STATEMENT

This chapter has concentrated primarily on customer measures and how to use them to manage the value-creation process. But the need for improved employee measures is just as pressing. Since the employee measurements we will recommend are analogous to the customer measures we've just described, we can move more quickly.

The core of a sound employee measurement system consists of the Employee Balance Sheet and Value Flow Statement, samples of which are shown in Figure 8-5. The balance sheet tracks the volume and flow of total employees, new hires, and defectors. And as it does for customers, the value flow statement must begin with a value proposition. You can use it to identify target employees, define critical dimensions of value, explain how employees can earn superior compensation, and summarize the economic strategy that will help them create and share in a productivity surplus. As for actual measures, note that satisfaction scores are no more reliable for employees than customers. Here again, the best way to track the relative success or failure of the employee value proposition is to watch retention rates and hiring yield rates, then develop summary statistics for what drives this behavior. For most businesses, the drivers will include salary levels and compensation growth rates (per hour worked), investment in training and tools, and expenditures that create an attractive work environment.

Figure 8-5   Employee Balance Sheet and Value Flow Statement

Employee Balance Sheet		
Employee Category	**Number**	**Percent**
Beginning balance	—	100%
+ New hires	—	—
– Defectors	—	—
= Ending balance	—	—

Employee Value Flow Statement

Value Proposition
• Target employee
• Dimensions of value
• Source of advantage

Value Delivered to Employee

	Company	Competitor		
		A	B	C
Compensation per hour				
New	—	—	—	—
Fifth-year	—	—	—	—
Training	—	—	—	—
Tools	—	—	—	—
Yield rate	—	—	—	—
Retention rate	—	—	—	—
Referrals (% of new hires)	—	—	—	—

Value Received from Employees

	Company	Competitor		
		A	B	C
Revenues per employee	—	—	—	—
First-year	—	—	—	—
Fifth-year	—	—	—	—
Defectors	—	—	—	—
Profit per employee	—	—	—	—
First-year	—	—	—	—
Fifth-year	—	—	—	—
Defectors	—	—	—	—

Your value flow statement should also track retention patterns and lifecycle productivity curves (learning curves) for each group of new hires. In addition, you should track defection rates for employees of above- and below-average productivity, adjusted for seniority and experience. (An analysis of just such data led the brokerage in Chapter 7 to avoid certain hiring categories.) Finally, your company needs to benchmark all these measures against key competitors who hire from the same or similar talent pools. Figure 8-6 shows how these measures might be displayed.

One more dimension you need to track is the rate at which you are recruiting high-caliber candidates. Hiring rates as such are easy to

Figure 8-6   Employee Productivity and Defections

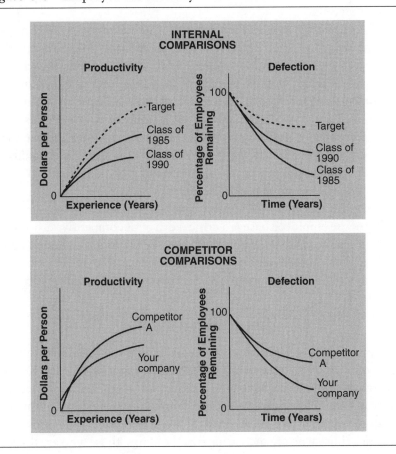

measure; it is harder to track the quality of new employees. Over time, of course, their actual productivity curves will tell you everything you need to know. But it is usually possible (and of course highly desirable) to estimate quality in advance.

At Bain & Company, we track the percentage of candidates who accept our job offers. We call this our yield rate. When yield rates are high, we are confident we are bringing the right kind of character and talent into the firm. But an even better measure is the yield rate we experience with candidates who have received job offers from our chief competitors. We believe it is important to win more than our share of these candidates if we are to maintain or improve the overall quality of our employee base.

Harvard College predicts the quality of its incoming freshman class the same way. In 1993, 74 percent of the applicants Harvard accepted accepted Harvard. The next highest yield rate—20 points lower—was at Princeton, which had 54 percent of its admission offers accepted. If top students are accepted at an average of three colleges, then any yield rate above 33 percent means the school is doing well. Yield rates of 50 to 75 percent give a stunning advantage to the institution that earns them, since the quality of the student body is critical to the quality of the undergraduate experience—to say nothing of the future stream of alumni donations that successful careers produce.

Yield rates this high are a great benefit to businesses, too, since the quality of the employee base is a critical driver of competitive advantage. Yet very few companies watch these statistics, and almost none report them in their annual reports—further evidence that most companies don't understand the importance of employee quality and loyalty.

INVESTOR MEASURES

In Chapter 6, we saw the importance of finding the right investors (the ones who behave like partners) and of increasing their loyalty. Keeping those goals in mind, we have put together an Investor Balance Sheet and Investor Value Flow Statement (see Figure 8-7). Instead of lumping all investors together, we have divided them into four categories—new investors, those who are increasing their holdings, those who are decreasing their holdings, and defectors—to highlight progress toward the creation of a stable, low-churn investor group.

As before, the value flow statement should begin with a clear statement of the value proposition for investors, describing the company's target investors, what they value, and how management means to recruit them. This will help to clarify which investor statistics you need to watch. Most companies track dividends and share-price appreciation against comparable investments in the shares of other companies. But they also need to monitor the long-term drivers of share price, which are not as mysterious as some people make them out to be. Warren Buffett often quotes his mentor, Ben Graham: "In the short term, the market is a voting machine . . . in the long-run [it] is a weighing machine."[3] What the market weighs is the company's ability to generate cash and reinvest

Figure 8-7 Investor Balance Sheet and Value Flow Statement

Investor Balance Sheet				**Investor Value Flow Statement**				
				Value Proposition • Target investor • Reinvestment hurdle rate • Timeframe (target holding period) • Key elements of partnership				
Category	Number	Percent	Percent of Dollars					
				Value Delivered to Investors				
Beginning balance	—	—	—				Competitor	
+ New	—	—	—		Company	A	B	C
+ Gainers	—	—	—	Profit/cash generated	—	—	—	—
– Decliners	—	—	—	Return in excess of capital	—	—	—	—
– Defectors	—	—	—	Dividend rate	—	—	—	—
= Ending balance	—	—	—	Stock appreciation	—	—	—	—
				Value Received from Investors				
							Competitor	
					Company	A	B	C

				Defection rate
				  Your stock
				  Their portfolios
					—
					—
						—
						—
							—
							—
								—
								—

				Average holding period	—	—	—	—
				Half-life	—	—	—	—
				Reinvestment rate	—	—	—	—
				Target Investors (% of total)	—	—	—	—

it in projects that continue to generate returns superior to an investor's alternatives. What a company must measure, therefore, is the rate at which it generates cash and the returns it earns when that cash is reinvested.

Value received from investors must take investor stability into account when calculating the cost of capital. Measures of investor stability might include half-life, churn rate, or the average holding period for your stock. To get a better read on the quality of your current investors and their probable future loyalty, you should also monitor the rate at which they churn their entire portfolios. And since management needs to know what percentage of company ownership is in the hands of target investors, one final, somewhat subjective measure is the percentage of ownership that in senior management's judgment understands and endorses the company's value-creation strategy and time frame.

THE METAPHYSICS OF MEASUREMENT

Measurement is an unforgiving task. Too little and too much are both wrong, but the golden mean is elusive. It should be clear by now that we are against measuring too much—which is one of the reasons we introduced summary measures to serve in place of the more elaborate and sophisticated measures. As we pointed out at the beginning of this chapter, measurement can, under the worst circumstances, consume a large helping of company resources while providing information too extensive and detailed for any practical use.

Having said that, we should emphasize that some details are indispensable. Measurement systems create the basis for effective management. Companies that want the benefits of loyalty-based value creation have no real choice but to invest money in measurement, and—much more onerous for those who find measures boring or beneath the dignity of top executives—to put in the time and effort it takes to develop a thoughtful, effective, well-proportioned measurement system.

Most firms have a long way to go to develop a full set of integrated measures for tracking customer and employee value creation. The truth is, today's loyalty leaders (with the possible exception of USAA) did not rely on scientific measures to achieve their current loyalty advantage. Most were lucky enough to have leaders with an intuitive grasp of loyalty's worth. Their insistence on giving top priority to creating value for customers produced decades of sound business decisions.

Today, many of those companies are facing increasing challenges in volatile marketplaces. What's more, their leaders are beginning to retire, and a new crop of executives is taking over. At A. G. Edwards, for example, seven of nine people on the executive committee will reach retirement age over the next two years. Sometimes leaders can pass on their intuitive wisdom to a new generation of managers, but the risk is great that in today's accounting-oriented world, less experienced executives will make the wrong choices. What will happen when investors complain that the stock price is rising too slowly? If younger managers allow conventional measurement systems and the pressure to maximize profit to take priority over the tradition of creating and allocating value, they will hasten the day when their companies slip back down into the mainstream of business activity, where loyalty and returns are perpetually mediocre.

The right measures are even more important in companies where the importance of loyalty and value creation are not yet widely understood or accepted. Such an organization has to build the right loyalty habits and traditions, internalize the economic insights they produce, and learn how to operate according to new principles. A thousand executive pep talks and mission statements won't communicate this shift in strategy as clearly as the introduction of a few new loyalty-based measures, closely linked to incentives. But changing measures is a task that takes years to carry off. Agreeing on goals and definitions; designing rigorous measurement systems to provide the input for effective failure analysis and learning; linking measures to incentives; allocating the large sums of money required to create these systems; and training employees to use them effectively—the burden of change on this scale falls to senior managers.

Appendix: Measurement Pitfalls

Measuring customer loyalty seems a simple matter, at least in concept, but it's full of snares and thickets. Here are some of the most common pitfalls.

SLOPPY DEFINITIONS

An obvious candidate for use as a loyalty bellwether is a company's average customer retention rate—but make sure you know what you're measuring. Banks, for instance, use the number of closed accounts as a percentage of total accounts. When they dig deeper, however, they find that many such accounts are closed by a customer who immediately opens another. In other words, a great many closings are bookkeeping entries, not defections. At the other end of the spectrum, a customer may maintain an account but transfer the bulk of the balance to a competing bank—a real defection that completely fails to register.

Insurance companies have a similar problem in that their accounting systems track policies, not customers. Many insurers use policy lapse rates as their summary measure for customer loyalty, and some even compensate their agents on that basis. But here too, a closer look shows that most lapses are not genuine defections. Many are policies that have been canceled because customers haven't paid their bills on time. Two months later, when the customer does pay, the company issues a new policy and counts the whole transaction as a lapse and a sale. Or take the family that drops an auto insurance policy because it sells one of its cars. This too shows up as a lapse. Now compare the family that buys an extra car and insures it with a competitor. Though a real defection has taken place, no lapse shows up on the computer.

Another critical dimension to consider in building a set of measurement statistics is the number of customer segments that need to be tracked separately. In banking, for instance, a small percentage of customers create most of the value for the bank. Banks that track broad defection rates miss this point, even if they define defection thoughtfully. To get around some of the most obvious problems, one large retail bank grouped all accounts into households, then defined two levels of defection— households that closed all their accounts, and households that reduced their total balances by 50 percent. It turned out that even this refinement was insufficient, however, because less than 20 percent of the defectors accounted for more than 100 percent of the reductions in customer NPV.

The bank needed to concentrate its measures on this small troop of once highly profitable customers, and avoid letting vast numbers of unprofitable defectors cloud the summary statistics. Though many banks today are trying to increase customer loyalty, in all too many cases their broad, unsegmented measurement systems cause them to spend too much time and energy on unrewarding customers. If the goal were to *minimize* customer NPV, this would be an excellent method.

DANGEROUS AVERAGES

Average loyalty measures are not useful when customer segments are hugely different. The same goes for averages that include customers of different tenure, even within the same segment. Companies need to track each incoming class of customers separately, at least for the first few years when defection rates are highest. Mixing incoming classes together to calculate an average retention rate can muddy the waters enough to hide most of the valuable insights loyalty measures have to offer.

Figure 8-8 shows a typical defection pattern for an insurance product. Many insurers examine policy lapse rates by agent or geographic region to find best practices to share with others in the system. We've seen the danger of relying on lapse rates. There is a second danger, even when defection rates are correctly tracked. It is the danger of drawing false conclusions from a comparison of the defection rates for customer groups of differing tenure, as the following example illustrates.

Imagine two property and casualty agents in the same town. One has been in business for thirty years, and his book consists almost exclusively of customers who have been with him five years or longer. (In Figure 8-8, notice how low the defection rates are beyond the fifth year.) In fact, this agent rarely solicits new customers; he just makes sure there is plenty of time in the afternoon for golf, and relies on his staff to solve customer problems. The other agent is young and energetic. She provides outstanding service all day long, but she is relatively new to the job, so her customers are more likely to defect.

Now consider these three questions. First, how will average customer retention rates compare for these two agents? Are they genuinely comparable? Will they teach us anything useful about the agents' relative merit in delivering value and earning their customers' loyalty? Purely as a result of customer tenure, the older agent's average retention rate will be at least five points higher than the younger agent's. The only good way to compare these two agents is to move beyond overall averages

Figure 8-8   Defection Pattern for a Typical Insurance Policy

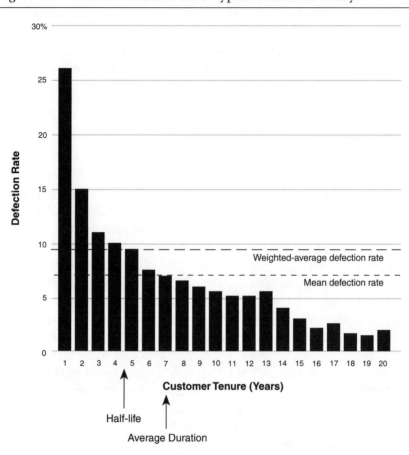

and look at the defection rates for customers of similar tenure. Comparing each agent's retention rate for customers in their third year would almost certainly produce quite a different, more accurate picture. Another approach might be to examine the two-year persistency of the new business each agent writes.

Average retention rates can make for perilous comparisons not only between agents of different tenure in the same company but between different companies that have been acquiring new customers at different rates. It's a dangerous business even when the same company has been acquiring new customers at different rates through the years. It's a little crazy to celebrate historical improvements in your average customer retention rate when you are simultaneously slowing your rate of new-customer acquisition. Fewer new customers in your book will inevitably raise retention, because new customers have inherently higher defection rates.

Any number of summary statistics would make a better indicator than average retention. For example, one insurance company adopted a ten-year standard after determining that a policy must be in force for at least ten years before the *customer* receives good economic value. It now tracks ten-year customer persistency for all its agents and has begun to tie agent compensation to that measure.

Since ten years is a long time to wait, other firms want a summary statistic that captures essential differences in customer loyalty in the critical early years of the relationship. Average customer duration does this to some degree, but a handful of 30- or 40-year customers can still inflate the averages for some of the older agents. One solution is to track customer half-life—the time it takes for half the customers in an entering class to defect. Physicists use this measure to describe the decay rate of radioactive substances, and it works just as well for summarizing the decay rate of a firm's customer inventory. It works better than annual defection rates, because it seems to create a more urgent call for action. State Farm, for example, loses only 4 to 5 percent of its customers annually—a modest, undisturbing rate—but the half-life of its customer base is only twelve years, which sets off alarms at a company that would like to do business with customers for thirty-five or forty years. For State Farm, the half-life calculation was a dramatic reminder of how much room there was for improvement.

Finally, raising annual retention rates just a few points doesn't seem to impress people, though it should. Perhaps we ought to multiply all our summary statistics by 100 or 1000. Every baseball fan knows there's a world of difference between a .280 hitter and a .320 hitter, but the actual difference is only four percentage points. Businesses need a similar way to dramatize the enormous disparities inherent in four percentage points of retention.

NONANNUAL PURCHASE CYCLES

While the general attrition pattern shown in Figure 8-8 is typical of many industries and companies, the relevant cycle is not always one year. In some businesses, repurchases or renewals occur at very different intervals. At the grocery store, people buy cornflakes once a week, but when a family decides to buy a new Ford, they probably won't replace it for at least four years. If Kellogg loyalists are 99 percent loyal in their weekly purchases, and Ford's repurchase rate at the end of four years is 45 percent, how do we compare the two retention rates? The second cycle is more than two hundred times longer than the first. And how do we compare either one of them to a 90-percent retention rate for a life insurance policy that renews annually? Or consider a product with a *really* long purchase cycle: John Deere lawn tractors. The company makes an outstanding product—so good, customers keep their tractors for an average of eleven years—but when it's time to replace them, 77 percent of customers buy another John Deere.

The way to make all these numbers comparable is to convert them to annual rates. A weekly retention rate of 99 percent comes out to 60 percent annually. A repurchase rate of 45 percent at the end of four years is the same as 82 percent annually. And while annual retention of 82 percent is not very impressive, John Deere's 77 percent repurchase rate after eleven years equates to an annual rate of almost 98 percent— and that's world class.

CUSTOMER LIFECYCLE PROFITS

In some businesses, neither retention rate, nor duration, nor half-life is an adequate indicator of customer loyalty. A manufacturer, for example, is less likely to drop a supplier completely than to cut back its share. A supplier might maintain all its accounts from year to year, but if its share of some customers' spending is declining, that's trouble, the kind of trouble a measurement system needs to catch early.

For these kinds of businesses, it makes sense to move directly to the second ingredient of customer NPV—customer lifecycle profits. Figure 2-3 shows the economic components of this calculation. But since it's impractical to measure all those dimensions continuously for every customer, again we need a summary statistic. For most businesses, the single most important factor driving lifecycle profits is the so-called purchase volume effect—a consequence of a customer consolidating an increasing share of business with one supplier, presumably the one that gives the best value. The summary statistic that captures this effect is the share of spending the firm earns from its customers—what we call share of wallet.

As a measure of loyalty, wallet share is superior to both annual retention rates and half-life. USAA is one company that uses this approach.

It believes the right target to shoot for is 100 percent of its customers' lifetime purchases in product categories in which USAA can deliver superior value. USAA tracks retention rates for core members and associate members separately and monitors the wallet share it earns from each. It also tracks these measures separately for five separate life stages *within* each segment. It knows, for instance, that 1 percent of its associate members in the mid-career stage (ages 40 to 54) bought a life insurance policy from Northwestern Mutual Life within the past twelve months. Top-flight companies like USAA must track not only their own share of each customer's wallet, but the shares of competitors who are beating them. USAA's measurement system provides this information so management can channel organizational effort toward the right competitors and the right customers. Lexus, too, knows which brands its defectors are buying.

But knowing the name of a successful competitor isn't the same as winning back lost business. So the next task is to pinpoint the nature of the superior value that is luring customers away. To do this, you must understand the performance dimensions that drive customer value and learn to recognize early warnings of competitive trouble. (Value drivers make up the fourth level of measures in Figure 8-2.)

EARLY WARNINGS

The best measurement systems also try to anticipate defections before they occur. In the credit card business, for example, the key drivers of lifecycle profit are the amount of customer spending and the size of the balance on which a customer pays interest. As a general rule, balances and usage decline for some time prior to a customer defection. By the time customers cut up the card and cancel the account, in other words, most have long since shifted a big share of spending and credit to someone else. Once customers cancel, it's extremely hard to win them back.

The most advanced credit card companies track the share of balance they receive from customers through credit bureau reports. When this measure begins to deteriorate, they look for the source of their disadvantage versus competitors that are gaining share. The solution may be a pricing change, or it may be that competing companies are offering new benefits that the company simply has to match. Or perhaps credit lines need to be increased. Without a trustworthy measure of wallet share, it's impossible to catch these problems while there's still time to fix them.

9

Transforming the Value Proposition

MOST BOOKS about business performance begin with this chapter. The authors have a tool for improving results—a tool so powerful it can create value in just about any business system—so they get right down to the business of promoting it. The tool kit for company improvement is now chock full of these devices, from the flat organization to cycle-time reduction to total quality management.

As companies skip from one cureall to another, desperate for results, each of these tools has its vogue. Some are nearly as powerful as advertised; some are harebrained. Most of them fulfill at least part of their promise, at least for some businesses, at least for a time. But nearly all exaggerate their own potential, because nearly all ignore the ultimate foundation of the value proposition, which is human capital. Most of these tools offer technical solutions to what are human problems. And by ignoring the human context, they fail to ask and answer crucial questions: Why are people defecting? Why doesn't the present system deliver better value? Is the company bringing in the right customers and employees? Has management built a genuine partnership for creating and sharing value? Does this partnership align individual and organizational interests?

Companies often use the tool of the day to address symptoms—high costs, for example, or poor revenues—without understanding that they *are* symptoms, second- or third-order effects in the value-creation system. Most of these tools address the profit problem rather than the value problem that underlies it, and no company can get where it wants to go by making incremental improvements in a flawed value proposition. Doing the wrong thing well is still doing the wrong thing.

Even companies that recognize their problem as poor customer loyalty often try to fix it with specific programs to improve retention. But to treat loyalty as a program or a tool is a sure sign that the company doesn't really understand the power of loyalty or the way it can enhance performance. Is it reasonable to expect GM's credit card operation to improve the value GM delivers to customers when the dealer network is terribly misaligned? Can frequent-flier programs really increase customer loyalty when almost every dimension of airline service is undifferentiated? Can a cardholder recovery unit stanch the flow of customers away from a credit card company that is still charging 18.9 percent interest? Any one of these actions might work well as part of a systematic strategy to improve customer value, but as isolated efforts, none of them has much chance of forestalling customer defections.

The first question a company must ask itself is whether its current value proposition is basically healthy (in which case, management can concentrate on incremental improvements) or whether it is so seriously flawed that it requires transformation. Chapter 1 put the same question a different way: When your organization executes its strategy well, does it create so much value for so many customers that plenty of value spills over for employees and investors? If the answer is no—and for a great many businesses the answer *is* no—then your value proposition needs revitalization.

On the other hand, you cannot revitalize a value proposition until you *have* a value proposition. And that's why the first seven chapters of this book concentrated on the strategic foundation on which a successful value proposition must rest. Without that foundation, *value* and *loyalty* are apt to become buzzwords and slip into the tool-of-the-day category, alongside management by walking around.

THE AUTO INDUSTRY

The U.S. auto industry is an excellent example of a value proposition in desperate need of revitalization. Customer repurchase rates of 30 to 40 percent show clear dissatisfaction with the value provided by most of the major makes. Dealer loyalty is even worse, with only 20 percent of customers returning to the same dealer to purchase their next car. The service picture is equally dismal. Two-thirds of nonwarranty service revenues go to mechanics outside the auto-dealer system. With this sad record, continuous incremental improvement is probably not a sufficient solution.

American automakers have made great strides in improving the quality of their products, but like manufacturers of other durable goods, they continue to focus on new-customer conquest instead of customer retention. It's true they have set up extensive customer satisfaction programs, and the Big Three have experimented with some parts of loyalty programs—direct marketing campaigns using new-customer databases, credit cards with buyer discounts, expanded leasing programs. (Leasing tends to increase retention rates by 5 to 10 percent over purchases, partly because the company stays in touch with customers through the monthly billing process and knows when they'll need a new car.) Still, loyalty rates remain abysmal. In fact, auto manufacturers don't measure their retention rates very carefully, and few see them as a critical problem. Average return on equity for the Big Three has been a negative 2.8 percent over the past decade, but only a few executives see the link between low brand loyalty and low profits or understand that the industry must correct fundamental flaws in the value proposition before it can realize significant improvements in value, loyalty, and profit.

Carl Sewell, one of the nation's leading Cadillac dealers (and a Lexus and Oldsmobile dealer as well), wrote a book called *Customers for Life* in which he calculates the amount of revenue an auto dealer could realize from an average buyer if the dealership could keep the customer for life. The total is $332,000. Having captured the reader's attention, Sewell goes on to explain how dealers can earn this kind of customer loyalty, and his advice is excellent. The only trouble, as Sewell himself points out, is that dealers can't fix all of what's wrong with the auto industry's value proposition. Manufacturers have set up a number of counterproductive systems that only they can fix.

For example, customers buy a car only once every four or five years, so they don't much care about the convenience of the showroom location. But they have to get the car serviced every six months or so, and the aggravation of dropping it off, arranging for substitute transportation, and picking it up again suggests that an ideal service network would have convenient locations all over town. Yet manufacturers require every dealer to provide service and sales at the same location, which virtually guarantees that auto dealers will have too few service points, too many showrooms, or both. Actually, this arrangement suits the manufacturers just fine. Their historical approach to market share has been to franchise a great many dealers—far more than the system really needs—on the theory that putting lots of inventory at lots of dealerships will keep prices down and the metal moving and that the resulting volume will give manufacturers the economies of scale that are the key (they think) to long-term competitive advantage.

Automakers *might* look on their dealers as partners whose success is important to the company, the customer, and the entire value network. They've chosen instead to oversaturate the market, wish everyone good luck, and let the best dealers win. The result is a dreadfully inefficient distribution system that finances too much inventory on too many streetcorners and service on too few. The vast majority of customers take their service dollars to the corner garage or the large chains like Midas, Goodyear, Firestone, or Sears. Dealers wind up with pinched margins and a belief that they can't afford to pay good wages to their sales and service staff.

As a result, very few talented people want to sell cars for a living. The benefits are poor, and compensation, based almost entirely on commissions, averages $20,000 to $25,000. Add low status and long hours, and it's no wonder turnover rates of 30 to 50 percent are fairly common. But let's take that turnover a step further. Compound this rate over a four- to five-year repurchase cycle, and clearly the odds are minuscule that a salesperson will ever see the same customer twice. Now factor in a compensation system that pays everything for the sale and nothing for customer retention, and you wind up with a sales force that will do almost anything to close a deal, even if it means alienating customers so badly they'll never return to the dealership. With this system in place, the only surprise is that as many as 20 percent of customers eventually do return to buy another car.

Since mechanics' jobs are not much better, turnover is a serious problem in the shop as well. And poor shop productivity exacerbates the economic disadvantages dealers already suffer from inefficiencies of size and location. For customers, the result is pricing that seems out of line. So they defect to the corner garage, where they get not only better prices but better quality as well, since corner mechanics stay in their jobs and get to know customers and their cars. By the way, most manufacturers happily provide name-brand parts to these garages—and to Kmart—so the dealers have no special advantage in quality or availability. And as manufacturing quality has improved, there has been less warranty work—indeed less service work in general—so dealers must also cope with a shrinking market. Given all the disadvantages of the system the manufacturers have created, is it any wonder car dealers provide poor service and poor pricing? The system delivers inferior value; inferior value generates low customer and employee loyalty; and low loyalty weakens the foundation of the system.

HOW LEXUS IS REVOLUTIONIZING THE VALUE PROPOSITION

Toyota knows about loyalty. Toyota's repurchase rates in the domestic market in Japan exceed 70 percent, compared to an average of 50 percent for its principal competitors. Toyota's outstanding dealership system gets credit for a big share of this advantage. In setting up its new Lexus division, Toyota decided it had to make fundamental changes in its U.S. dealer system in order to realize its marketing objectives. The goal of the new division was not only to maximize sales volume and profits, but to earn breakthrough levels of customer satisfaction and loyalty. Lexus took Sakichi Toyoda's philosophy of "Customer first, dealer second, company third" and pushed it one step further. The new covenant reads "We will treat each customer as we would a guest in our own home . . . and we will do that by having the finest dealer body in the industry."[1]

The executives who planned the new division saw that they'd have to make changes in the traditional auto-industry value proposition. First, they recognized that the product itself had to be truly outstanding in design, quality, and value. But they knew that a great product by itself would not be enough. With the goal of understanding their target customers' value equation better than anyone else, they studied every interaction the company and its dealers would have with customers. The lead engineer for the LS400 left Japan to spend three years in the United States. There he joined the rest of the Lexus management team in scrutinizing the whole experience of shopping for, purchasing, and owning a luxury car, in order to uncover every source of customer dissatisfaction.

All functions worked together to do the research, and together they developed systems to optimize the value delivered at each step in the customer lifecycle. They detailed processes, created performance measures, and established performance goals. Company research indicated which interactions were the primary drivers of lifecycle value for the customer. They include the sale itself, delivery of the vehicle, the driving and operating experience, service (routine and emergency), company communications, and the residual value of the car when the customer decides to trade it in. The company crafted satisfaction surveys to monitor sales, delivery, and service. It set goals for residual value (the best in the industry) and developed programs to buy back, recondition, and warranty used Lexus cars. The buyback offer strengthened value for customers (whose cars retain a higher residual value) and for dealers (who profit from both the reconditioning and the sale of the "pre-owned" car).

But the most important statistics for gauging the new division's success at delivering superior value would be the repurchase rates for service and new cars. Remember the words of Dave Illingworth: "The only meaningful measure of satisfaction in this industry is repurchase loyalty." With that thought in mind—and wanting very much to break the record for customer loyalty set by Cadillac back in its heyday—Lexus set itself the seemingly impossible goal of 75 percent repurchase loyalty.

Customer Selection

As Lexus began the design work on its first car, the LS400, it faced a difficult decision—which customer segment to shoot for. The young fashion-and-performance crowd seemed a logical choice. Being younger, these customers would be inherently less loyal to their BMWs and Jaguars, so Lexus had a good chance of winning them over with stunning design. Moreover, their youth gave them a longer lifetime in which to buy more cars.

But fashion-and-performance customers tend to be fickle. The obvious danger was that one day soon they would jump for the next hot new design, the same way they had jumped to Lexus. On the other hand, the more staid and conservative Cadillac and Mercedes buyers had already demonstrated superior brand loyalty—which admittedly would make their business more difficult to capture, but would probably also make them loyal Lexus customers if and when the company could win them over.

Lexus decided to take on what it saw as the greater challenge with the greater rewards. It designed the LS400 to attract Cadillac and Mercedes core customers. Nissan's Infiniti division, which copied almost every other element of the Lexus system, decided to pursue the BMW and Jaguar segment, as we mentioned in Chapter 3. Now, five years later, both divisions have had stunning success with their initial product offerings and customer conquests. But Lexus has repurchase rates 21 percentage points higher than Infinitis—63 versus 42 percent—largely because of initial customer selection.

Where are the Infiniti defectors going? The biggest single group seems to be buying that last word in suburban-cowboy vehicles, the off-road 4 × 4. Infinity plans to introduce a sport-utility vehicle to capture those defectors, but who knows how long before the next fad sweeps the market? By seeking out customers with inherently high loyalty coefficients, Lexus has built an enormous economic advantage and can afford to worry less about novelty.

Dealer Selection

It took guts and self-confidence to introduce a new brand in a mature auto market suffering from excess capacity. The decision to create an entirely new dealer network as well must have struck some industry experts as ludicrous. Toyota already had one of the strongest dealer systems in the country and could easily have used it to distribute Lexus. But Dave Illingworth and his executive team wanted to achieve a level of relationship marketing the U.S auto industry had never seen, and they decided that their breakthrough aspirations required a completely new system. They believed the key to an unprecedented relationship with customers lay in an unprecedented partnership with dealerships. Looking back, Illingworth sees that partnership as the single most important element in the Lexus success story.

The search for dealers generated more than 1,500 applications, which the company screened down to 150 on three principal criteria: financial strength and stability (each dealer had to invest from $3 million to $5 million in the dealership); a demonstrated ability to earn top satisfaction scores; and a track record as a loyal dealer (about half the winners were Toyota dealers). Lexus paid close attention to every detail of the new dealership facilities, from landscaping to wall decor. For the first time ever, an automaker used the same designer for the dealerships and the automobile. Building layout was based on the preestablished sales process. Near the door of each showroom is a marble receptionist's desk. Sales consultants may not approach a browsing customer unless requested to by the receptionist. The sales presentation area is open, with three chairs and an oval table instead of a desk. The idea is to make customers feel like guests.

Because Lexus expected a lot from its dealer partners, it recognized that the company had to deliver a lot in return. To begin with, Lexus believed its partners had to earn a healthy profit. So instead of saturating the market with three hundred to five hundred dealers, like BMW and Mercedes, after six years in operation, Lexus has fewer than two hundred dealers, and expects never to exceed that number. Consider what this means for dealership profits. BMW and Mercedes have nearly twice as many dealers but sell fewer units than Lexus; so the average dealer's sales volume is much lower. This productivity advantage lets Lexus dealers charge lower markups, provide extra amenities, and still earn superior profits. Attention to dealer economics is evident even in the facilities design, which recognizes that most locations are built on expensive real estate, and so keeps overall square-footage to a minimum. Service-quality pundits often mention the luxury loaners, free car washes, and flower arrangements at Lexus dealerships, but dealers couldn't afford those gracious touches if it weren't for the company's superior economics. As one of Illingworth's successors as general manager explained, "Our special customer handling is fueled by good dealer profitability—you can't have one without the other."[2]

Profitable Service

Service is a key part of the profit formula for most auto dealers, even at the dreadful retention rates most of them achieve. High markups, aggressive marketing (often after your car is on the lift), and warranty requirements all help to keep the service dollars flowing.

Service is a critical profit factor for Lexus dealers too, but the cash-flow equation is a good deal different. In the first place, a Lexus requires very little maintenance, which is one of its selling points. So Lexus has engineered a system that keeps service loyalty much higher than the industry average—in fact, more than *twice* as high—at the same time that it holds costs down and raises productivity. By helping dealers to a less expensive and much larger slice of a smaller service pie, Lexus more than compensates for the fact that its automobile requires less attention than many others.

One of the keys to this system is the satellite-based communications network that connects all dealerships with national headquarters in

California. Other keys include customer satisfaction, diagnostics, training, and expert help with problems. The satellite system gives Lexus service departments several unique advantages. For one thing, every car's maintenance record is tracked on-line, so any dealer in the country can instantly access the service history of any vehicle—a valuable tool for delivering outstanding customer service and for spotting cars that aren't getting fixed on the first try and figuring out why. The communications network is also hooked into an ultramodern parts inventory that saves dealers money and eliminates the inconvenience of waiting for parts deliveries.

In *Customers for Life*, Carl Sewell calls this system "the best automobile parts inventory management system in the world. It allows us to reorder what we need daily. This means higher availability and lower inventory costs for us—and them."³ When it comes to the more expensive parts, Lexus manages a dealer's inventory centrally through the information network. The company has developed a just-in-time system for shipping parts by next-day air freight, which keeps dealers' inventories small and economical. The average Lexus dealership has $100,000 tied up in its parts inventory, compared to an average of more than $200,000 for the industry as a whole, and a Lexus dealer's parts inventory turns over nearly eight times a year, as opposed to an industry average of four.

Lexus wants its dealers to earn 80 percent of its cars' postwarranty service revenue (compared to the industry's 30 to 40 percent), so not only does it provide superior information systems but the company has developed state-of-the-art diagnostic equipment to improve efficiency and productivity in its service departments. It also created a detailed flowchart for every service job, to permit more effective training and certification of dealer personnel. John Lane, service manager at South Bay Lexus in California, reported in *Fortune* magazine that he had "received more training in the first month at Lexus than in his entire 18 year career at Cadillac."⁴

But even when service quality and value are extraordinary, customers have to be broken of their assumption that only a fool would service his car at a dealership. Therefore, Lexus reimburses dealers for the expense of a free one-thousand-mile checkup and another at seventy-five hundred miles. This gets customers to come in and experience the superior service that is so critical to earning their postwarranty business. When some dealers failed to persuade a high percentage of their customers to come in for the free service visits, Lexus created reminder postcards that could be designed, printed, and mailed out via the dealer's AS400 computer. It taught service managers how to time the mailings to smooth the flow of customers into the service bays, which enhanced customer satisfaction (no long waits) and improved dealer economics (well-utilized bays boost profits).

Lexus also sends out teams of service consultants to customize improvement programs for dealers whose service departments are underperforming on profitability or customer frequency. One such team discovered that a dealer's service technicians were failing to write up certain procedures, with the result that customers were underbilled. In another case, service writers were not pointing out all the preventive maintenance cars required. In both cases, the root cause was that service representatives feared customers would resent the larger bills and give them lower scores on satisfaction surveys. Obviously, those dealers needed to reduce their reliance on satisfaction scores.

To address the inconvenience of fewer locations, Lexus helps dealers with the cost of free loaners and free pick-up and delivery. Of course, those services cost money, but not as much as saturating the market with low-volume service locations. And the expense is more than offset by breakthrough rates of customer loyalty on nonwarranty service, which have reached nearly 84 percent, and by a doubling of lifecycle revenue per car.

Dick Chitty, Lexus' vice-president for service, parts, and customer satisfaction, believes that the service experience is even more important than the sales experience as a driver of repurchase loyalty. "A customer buys a car only once every four years," he says. "But he'll have it serviced 6–12 times before he buys again."[5] This explains why Lexus has put so much energy into transforming the service portion of the value proposition. Chitty's organization tries to make sure that dealers' service departments are highly profitable and deliver outstanding service at a fair price. To that end, the company has used training, job-process redesign, computerized diagnostics, parts inventory control, and satisfaction surveys—most of which the competition has now copied, or soon will. But Lexus has one weapon that no one in the industry has tried to match.

Measuring Loyalty

Lexus is the only car company in the world that can track service retention rates for every one of its dealers, every day of the year, on-line. As mentioned in Chapter 6, part of the dealer's initial investment goes to pay for an AS400 computer and a satellite dish that connects the dealership to Lexus headquarters in California. Lexus created a system that not only tracks all service work done anywhere in the system for every vehicle; it tracks the percentage of each dealer's customers who return for the one-thousand-mile checkup, the seventy-five-hundred-mile checkup, and all subsequent services.

Lexus dealers can see how their own performance compares with that of other dealers locally, regionally, and across the nation. Each dealership gets a monthly report summarizing its service retention by model year, both for free checkups and for the later work that customers pay for. The report includes all relevant comparisons to other dealers and provides diagnostics to help dealers and their employees perform failure analysis and recover the missing customers.

Since every dealer reports service-department revenues and costs as well as sales, Chitty and his staff can show each franchise how much profit it leaves on the table by not performing as well as the best of its peers. For example, they can prove to a dealership that lower retention rates on customer-paid service are depriving it of the $500,000 extra per year that dealers with similar satisfaction scores and similar sales volume—but higher service loyalty—are taking in. When less productive dealers wonder what needs fixing, service consultants from Lexus go to work with a set of diagnostics and failure-analysis tools. In one case, they discovered that sales consultants were not taking the time to introduce new customers to the service manager, especially on busy Saturdays. So the dealer instituted an extra commission, paid only when customers actually came in for their free service checkups. Immediately, salespeople began finding creative ways to make sure customers met the service manager and came in for their free checkups—including follow-up phone calls if they didn't. The AS400 computer allows dealers to print out weekly lists of overdue customers for salespeople to call when showroom traffic is slow.

Effective learning requires motivation as well as tools. Lexus provides the motivation in two ways. First, it appeals to dealers' pride by comparing their performance to company targets and to the results of dealers that are top performers. Second, it appeals to the dealer's pocketbook by demonstrating the economics of loyalty and letting dealers devise their own employee incentives. The company's unique information system provides all the necessary tools and measures. While some bugs in the system have yet to be worked out—for example, some dealers in Phoenix have to figure out how to account for the false defections of customers who live there only in the winter—Lexus is constantly refining and improving its measures to make them more accurate. For instance, the company now uses surveys to determine repurchase rates but is developing a more rigorous system to track the rates by dealer. Lexus is also developing programs to teach dealers and their employees how to do failure analysis, including a simple flowchart that walks them through the process step by step.

When asked to compare his experiences with Lexus and Cadillac, Carl Sewell commented, "Lexus has done a lot of things very well—but perhaps most important, they convinced us to set much higher standards for our performance than we ever thought possible—and we did it."[6]

Future Challenges

Lexus did set the bar high for its first set of jumps, and the results are striking. The company has achieved unprecedented levels of excellence and has dominated industrywide satisfaction contests. Its dealers have been at or near the top of the industry in profitability since the car was introduced. Nearly 84 percent of its customers—the highest rate in the industry—visit a dealership every six months for customer-paid service, and repurchase rates hover around 60 percent. Toyota is pleased with the results. Some industry experts estimate that while Lexus accounts for only 3 percent of unit sales at Toyota, it has contributed approximately 30 percent of Toyota's corporate profit.

But it's still early in the game, and some serious challenges lie ahead. When the flagship LS400 was introduced in 1989, for instance, the price tag was $35,000. Now that the yen has appreciated against the dollar, the new LS400 will carry a ticket price of about $50,000. Sticker shock may cause a lot of potentially loyal customers to reconsider. Because the price problem has already begun to squeeze unit sales and dealer margins, Lexus may have to struggle to persuade dealerships to maintain free loaners and car washes in the face of lower profits. When cash flow tightened at one Southern California dealership after the 1993 earthquake, the controller tried to scrap the flowers and free doughnuts. But customers noticed right away.

There are other challenges as well. Competitors have copied many elements of the Lexus system. And Lexus has not gone far enough in fixing one of the greatest and most widespread flaws in the system, the high turnover in dealership staff, especially the sales staff. While the turnover at Lexus dealerships is below the industry average, it is not far below. If Lexus is to weather the storms of an occasional weak design cycle, or another run-up in the yen, it must find a way to change the nature of the partnership between dealers and their employees.

Perhaps Lexus did not go far enough when it established its new dealership system. It has kept the number of dealers down, but it has chosen to appoint multiple dealers in many markets, causing price wars and other confusing marketing tactics. In soft market cycles, sales consultants have even reverted to the invidious practice of negotiating deals with customers, a throwback to the old tactics that earned the industry its 40 percent repurchase rate. General Motors' Saturn division took the next logical step and appointed one dealer to cover each market. Saturn dealers operate more like true partners, opening the right number of sales and service locations on their own initiative. But while Saturn has done well with its distribution strategy, it has not offered a broad enough product line to earn customers' loyalty as they grow older and more affluent. Some GM executives expect that satisfied Saturn customers will trade up to Pontiacs, Oldsmobiles, Buicks, and Cadillacs, but that is probably wishful thinking. The dealerships have nothing in common.

All in all, Lexus has done an impressive job of transforming the value proposition for luxury autos. It conceived an entirely new system, oriented toward breakthrough levels of customer value and loyalty, then demonstrated that the economic advantages of loyalty can revolutionize value for the customer, for dealers, and for the company. And it is a difficult strategy to copy. According to one senior Lexus executive, "There's no one answer on owner loyalty. If you look at what we do, we do a hundred little things. Duplicating that is difficult, because the difference is in how they all fit together."[7] The way Lexus went about looking for its answer, however, is no secret. Dick Chitty, who was there at the beginning, describes the process. "We looked at the way cars were sold and serviced, we got all the problems and failures on the table, and then we built a system to eliminate every one of them."[8] Sounds a lot like Warren Buffett.

Yet it's easier to create a breakthrough value proposition from scratch than to take a huge, established system and transform it. What Toyota did with Lexus was not to fix an old system but to build a new one. And one of the great remaining challenges for Lexus may be the challenge of transferring its technology and business systems to the parent company, because even successful value propositions need revitalization if companies are to continue to grow and flourish. Can the parent learn from the child? Sometimes the most practical way to change an established business is to create a completely new system to serve an important customer segment, then transfer the experience back to the core once the new approach has proved itself. Dave Illingworth has been promoted from Lexus U.S. general manager to the same job at Toyota; he is in a perfect position to judge how many of the lessons he learned are relevant to the task of improving Toyota's value proposition. Asked if loyalty was less critical in Toyota's system with its more than 1,200 dealers targeting middle-income buyers, Illingworth replied, "There is no difference. People are people. Whether they earn $200,000 or $10,000 a year, they want to be treated with respect."[9]

THE LIFE INSURANCE INDUSTRY

When a value proposition is flawed on a grand scale, correcting failures in specific parts of the system will not rescue a company from its inevitable fate. It's like ordering drinks on a sinking ship. They may make you feel better, but they're not going to keep the enterprise afloat.

Consider the case of a leading life insurance company—let's call it Eastern Insurance—with a number of identifiable problems and a practical, pragmatic improvement program for each of them. Eastern introduced a reengineering program to slim down a bloated cost structure. It allocated capital to each of its business lines in accordance with sophisticated risk-based hurdle rates, which put money where it will produce the greatest benefit to the company.

Eastern even learned enough failure analysis to do a systematic study of customer and agent defections and uncovered several areas where it could improve performance. The company learned that many of its agents were going after precisely the wrong (that is, the least loyal) customers. It discovered that agents were attracting new business with a product that appealed most strongly to disloyal customers. It identified the agents who were writing policies with low persistency and recognized that certain techniques for generating new customers (Yellow Pages advertising and seasonal volume bonuses for agents) were lowering the company's overall persistency rates.

Eastern used these insights to develop practical programs that can lead to substantial improvement in customer and agent retention. It implemented a persistency incentive program that rewards agents for achieving predetermined customer-retention levels. It set up training programs to teach agents how to prospect for the right customers, and repriced the product agents had been using as a come-on so it would no longer attract the wrong customers. Finally, Eastern altered its agent recruiting to emphasize the candidate pools that had shown the highest loyalty over time (principally older, second-career candidates) and to avoid the pools that had demonstrated high attrition.

But even with all these improvements, Eastern Insurance is not likely to achieve the performance gains it's after. To understand why, we have to step back a bit. We have to stop looking for blemishes in the plasterwork and start looking for cracks in the foundation—that is, in the company's value proposition. Incremental change is not enough.

Some of the biggest cracks that ever appear in a value proposition are the defection rates for key customers and employees. For Eastern, as for most insurance companies, these cracks are wide. One of the best measures of customer loyalty in life insurance is lifetime wallet share, or the percentage of a customer's lifetime insurance purchases the company earns after selling that first policy. More than two-thirds of the lifetime purchases of Eastern's customers go to its competitors. This kind of abysmal performance is not unusual in the insurance industry, even though a few top companies like Northwestern Mutual and State Farm earn more than twice that level of loyalty.

Agent attrition levels indicate that Eastern isn't delivering good value to its agents, either. For every hundred new candidates it recruits, only twenty are still with the company four years later. Most of the 80 percent who quit do so because they can earn a better living elsewhere, given the time and energy they're willing to invest in their work. But many quit because they see that the value the company offers its customers is nothing to be proud of. In the case of the standard policy the company wants them to push hardest, they know customers have to keep it in force for at least eight years to get a good return—that is, a higher return than they could get simply by buying cheap term insurance and investing the difference in a no-load mutual fund. For customers who let their policies lapse before that time, the policy is a value destroyer. Regrettably, the vast majority of customers—more than 80 percent—lapse well before their eighth year, which means that about 80 percent of Eastern's customers are receiving bad value. Remember, too, that about 80 percent of agents quit their jobs prematurely. Could these two statistics have anything to do with the weak performance and deteriorating capital ratios that Eastern—and the whole insurance industry—now suffers?

Most insurance companies are in denial about the severity of this problem. They point to other industries with high employee turnover. Public accounting firms, for example, lose 80 percent of their people in the first five years. One important difference, however, is that many accounting trainees sign on because of the valuable training they receive. Life insurance trainees are not so lucky. Unintentionally, they end up learning how to sell a product that will destroy value for 80 percent of their customers.

When turnover rates for customers and salespeople are that high, it is almost certainly a sign that the value proposition needs rebuilding. The insurance industry is a leading practitioner of many of the new management techniques—name one insurance company not currently being reengineered—but a lot of these techniques are like those drinks at the Titanic's bar. They won't save the enterprise. What will is some fundamentally new thinking.

The New Proposition and the Old

A few firms have already rethought the traditional value proposition and are achieving high rates of customer and agent retention. State Farm has integrated its life insurance into a family of personal property and casualty products so its agents can offer customers excellent value over a lifetime. Northwestern Mutual has taken a somewhat different approach. Instead of broadening its line, it has singled out customer segments with inherently superior economics (high average policy size and high loyalty), paid close attention to cost management, and shared the extra value with customers and agents.

If other companies want to tap into the cash-flow surplus that higher customer and employee loyalty produce, they need to offer the same kind of superior value. When most of the value propositions for life insurance were created fifty to one hundred years ago, there were few alternatives offering tax-deferred saving or investment, and term life—pure insurance against premature death—was unavailable. These days, we have municipal-bond mutual funds, annuities, IRAs, 401ks, and a lot of other employer-sponsored retirement plans and subsidized insurance benefits. So to sell an individual customer a life insurance policy today—or at least to do so responsibly and in a manner that might create value and *earn* customer loyalty—it is absolutely essential that the policy fit with the customer's saving, investment, retirement, and estate plans, along with his or her tax circumstances and risk preferences.

But this kind of integrated approach is inconsistent with the skills and capabilities of most of today's sales force. Analyzing a customer's financial condition is a lot of work, and the commission on a single policy is simply too small to be worth the effort. The only way an agent can recover so large an investment of time and energy is to sell the customer a variety of products over a period of many years. But that solution requires a low-turnover, career-oriented sales force, and an inventory of insurance, saving, and investment products varied enough to meet the needs of a lifetime. Indeed, it requires more than that, since customers have any number of distribution channels open to them, and the competition for their business is intense. Those who don't need much in the way of advice will find they can get the lowest prices by buying financial products over the phone, or through the mail. Customers who do need personal counseling will tend to select the advisor who best understands their needs and charges the least. That successful channel—usually but not always an agent—will achieve superior productivity through a combination of the broadest possible range of products and the deepest possible knowledge of customer segments.

For the insurance companies, this question of the distribution channel is of great strategic importance, because the integrative activity just described takes place in the channel, not within the company—except, of course, in those exceptional cases where a very large and versatile insurer does its own distribution. In other words, the individual insurance company does not need to offer its preferred channel a full range of financial products, but the line it does offer must fill out and fit into the inventory that the agent (or other channel) offers, understands, and is prepared to work with.

The trouble is, few insurance companies *have* a preferred channel. Most have recognized the inadequacies of their old channels, but their solution has been to sell through lots of new ones rather than to concentrate on fixing the one preeminent channel on which their fortunes are most likely to rise or fall. This scattershot approach seems logical, because the additional sales maintain the volume that the home office was built to serve. It also spreads risk by putting the company's eggs in several baskets. But the lack of commitment to any one channel will almost certainly diminish the loyalty of all channels, especially—and certainly most critically—the loyalty of the old-line sales force. When a customer can buy the same brand-name product from an agent, a bank, a stockbroker, the benefits office at work, or through the mail, then that brand will no longer support the margins required to fund the direct sales force. The sales force will weaken, its quality will diminish, its loyalty will wane, and the economics for everyone involved will deteriorate. In order to earn a living, some salespeople may even resort to desperate and misleading (or even illegal) sales tactics, and that will eventually ruin the brand's good name.

The history of this dilemma is long, involved, and unhappy. Some of the blame goes to the increasing variety and complexity of insurance products, some to the old manufacturing mentality that gives top strategic priority to market share. Great old firms like Metropolitan, Prudential, and Equitable grew to their current stature over the course of a century by delivering excellent value to policyholders and agents. But then the relative value of traditional life policies began to decline. First, life insurance came unbundled—that is, the investment and pure term-insurance components were separated. Next, alternative saving and investment products—IRAs, tax-free bond funds, unit trusts, and mutual funds—proliferated. Finally, low-cost distribution channels—employee-benefits departments, telemarketing organizations, banks—put additional pressure on margins and volume.

As agents' incomes began to suffer, they pressured the insurance companies to offer more competitive products. The companies obliged with a plethora of new and complex policies, such as variable life and single-payment deferred annuities. Some of these new products truly added value; others simply allowed agents to offer better deals to new customers without destroying the pricing levels on the old product lines.

The companies also pressured the agents. They wanted continued growth so they wouldn't lose the bragging rights that are based on industry rankings. The companies turned up the heat on their sales incentive programs, which pushed agents to sell to more marginal customers and employ more marginal sales tactics—which sowed the seeds of increased customer turnover in the years ahead. Since the pricing for the new policies needed to be aggressive, some companies let the returns on old, established policies slip a bit. No one thought those loyal old customers would notice that their returns were becoming less competitive, but the defection rates for mature policies increased. As agents responded to their front-end-loaded sales incentives, the churn of new policies replacing old ones camouflaged much of the erosive activity, but more and more damage was quietly taking place.

As time went by, the sales job became increasingly difficult. After all, the underlying value of the product line was diminishing in relation to the alternatives, so only the most gifted salespeople (the ones who really could sell icemakers in the arctic) prospered. Agent turnover rose, which led inevitably to further increases in customer attrition. (To everyone's surprise, customers eventually got fed up and defected when they called the company repeatedly with questions about the policies they had bought, and the new agent they left a message for—the one who replaced the agent who sold the insurance and received the commission—never found the time to call back.)

On top of all this, expense ratios continued to worsen—an inevitable result of the rising cost of recruiting and training a steady stream of new agents and of selling, underwriting, and administering a growing array of increasingly complex customer products. Because generally accepted accounting principles disguise much of the damage done by deteriorating agent and customer retention rates, many insurance companies fail to realize just how much trouble their value proposition is in. An accurate cash-flow analysis would reveal that business written in recent years has a negative present value and is actually destroying their capital base.

Death or Transformation

The summary statistics are gruesome. These grand old companies are destroying value for 80 percent of their new customers and 80 percent of their new agents, and of course their investors will suffer too as markets begin to reflect the cash-flow consequences of decreased retention. To break out of this downward spiral, these companies need to transform their value propositions, and the right place to start is the same place Lexus started. Select customers carefully; learn more than any other company about what those core customers value through the whole cycle of shopping, purchase, ownership, and replacement; then redesign channel partnerships, sales and service processes, communications, product lines, and logistics to deliver outstanding value. The new value proposition must provide better value than anything the competition can offer.

If for any reason the net present value of a customer is higher to a competitor than it is to you, your value proposition will eventually fail. Your competitor will be able to reinvest more cash flow in the continuous improvement of its value proposition than you can afford to reinvest in yours.

Transforming the value proposition is never easy, but it is the only way out of the insurer's downward spiral. While the creation of a new value proposition is complex and arduous, requiring a great deal of strategic experience and the integration of extensive knowledge about customers, competitors, and system economics, it is quite easy to tell whether or not the transformation is working. It is working when the company's wallet share begins to climb over 30 percent and head toward 60 percent, and when retention rates rise to the point that new customer NPVs are once again positive.

RECLAIMING SUCCESS AT AMERICAN EXPRESS

Not one of the major insurers we've been looking at has yet reversed its downward spiral because none has successfully transformed its value proposition. American Express, another large financial services company, makes an interesting comparison. Amex found itself facing a similar competitive challenge but has begun to turn the situation around.

Founded in 1850 as an express company to transport freight, packages, and money, American Express introduced traveler's checks in 1891 and enjoyed extraordinary success through the 1970s and early 1980s. Profits grew from $100 million in 1970 to $1.25 billion in 1985. By the mid-1980s, however, American Express had penetrated most of its targeted customer segment of upscale business executives and frequent travelers, and its bankcard competitors, envious of such success, were mounting an unprecedented assault on these highly prized customers in an effort to steal their spending. Amex's competitors introduced gold cards, cards with no annual fee, cards with frequent traveler rewards, and they cosponsored cards like the GM card that offered special benefits. As bankcards extended their customer reach upward, the distinction between the two products began to blur. Some core customers became less loyal, shifting a portion of their plastic spending to bankcards, and some began to defect.

The bankcards challenged merchant loyalty as well. Because of the revenue advantage consumer interest charges gave them, bankcard issuers could offer some merchants a lower price for processing customer transactions. Merchants chose to accept American Express, even at a premium price, because its cardholders spend more money on more profitable merchandise and are in general very attractive customers. But now there was a risk that merchant perceptions—and behavior—would change. As the percentage of Amex cardmembers who also held Visa and MasterCard grew, there was a danger that some merchants would become less willing to pay higher American Express fees and begin encouraging customers to use a bankcard instead. The value proposition that American Express could offer merchants was being publicly challenged by Visa and needed a shot in the arm. As in the insurance business, churn roiled the cost structure and made growth even more difficult to achieve.

When Harvey Golub became CEO, he and his executives recognized that short-term, incremental solutions would not be enough to protect and enhance their leadership position. They revisited the economics of their business and thought hard about how they could revitalize the value proposition both for their core members and for merchants. Golub and his team wanted to know which segments were in a position to repay clearly superior value with a conspicuously greater share of wallet, so they built up a detailed picture of the lifecycle plastic spending and lifetime profitability of various customer segments.

American Express had always maintained a powerful and highly respected marketing capability, but its traditional diagnostic tools were insufficient to the task of searching out the ultimate root cause of rising defections. Recognizing that it had to dig into the available data more aggressively, the company embarked on a two-stage analysis of its card business.

First, Amex segmented its target market on the basis of the net present value—to itself and its competitors—of current and potential customers. For example, customers who carried large credit balances were historically more valuable to bankcard competitors, while high spenders who preferred to pay in full each month were more valuable to American Express. This segmentation gave the company a picture of how vulnerable some of its current customers were to competitors' value propositions.

The second stage was an in-depth root-cause analysis of customer behavior that enabled American Express to understand what drove the most critical customer decisions—share of wallet, usage frequency, and defection. By combining this analysis with a clear understanding of

competitors' capabilities, constraints, and intentions, American Express
was able to design truly world-class value propositions for the customer
groups it wanted to retain and attract. It tested these value propositions,
revised them on the basis of customer feedback, and has begun to roll
them out around the world.

Senior management mobilized the organization with a visionary goal—
100 percent of its target customers' plastic spending. While it may take
years to achieve or even approach this ambitious target, the vision itself
commits the company to earning the strongest and most sustainable
loyalty in its industry and has helped the company to move from product-
based systems to relationship-based systems. For example, if customers
need a Gold Card, a Corporate Card, and an Optima Card to cover
100 percent of their spending, the company now communicates with
them as individual customers who happen to have three products rather
than as three customers of three product lines.

The company is also developing more value-added services for merchants worldwide, including a program that will allow them to sign up
as "loyalty partners" so their customers can earn points based on the
purchases they charge on their Amex cards—points they can redeem for
a broad range of incentives, including frequent-flier miles and merchandise. American Express now also offers an improved billing statement
that allows merchants to communicate more efficiently with their customers.

American Express has already made substantial strides toward the
100 percent objective. It has launched a number of innovative new credit
cards. It is signing up new merchants worldwide at the rate of one every
two minutes. It has learned a good deal about what its name represents
in the minds of its core customers and has developed a much clearer
strategy for building its future. Together, these efforts have contributed
to a substantial increase in card-business profits.

American Express responded to competitor forays on its customers
with an ambitious set of changes and is now tracking its progress by
rigorously measuring customer loyalty in all its targeted customer segments. It has recognized that loyalty is more than products and programs—it is the core of a competitive strategy.

Earning customer loyalty in any business requires intense focus, careful
analysis, consistent actions and investments, and a passionate concern
for customers—but the benefits of success can change a company's overall
trajectory and potential. Companies that ignore customer loyalty in order

to shore up their short-term profit margins are choosing a far riskier and ultimately more arduous future. The symptomatic relief they seek often merely aggravates the illness, because the management tools that fix profits were not designed to examine, correct, or for that matter even uncover the potentially much more serious flaws in a company's value proposition. On the contrary, concentrating on immediate profit improvement tends to undermine whatever value the company still *can* deliver to customers and employees.

Companies cannot succeed or grow unless they can serve their customers with a better value proposition than the competition. Measuring customer and employee loyalty can accurately gauge the weaknesses in a company's value proposition and help to prescribe a cure.

10

Partnerships for Change

In BUSINESS, change has become rampant. Over the last twenty years we have seen revolutions in dozens of areas, from global competition and information technology to customer service, employee empowerment, and corporate governance. As a group, corporate executives have probably lost a century of sleep trying to make sense of it all and keep their companies on course and a step or two ahead of chaos. Indeed, change management has become a discipline in its own right, the subject of an endless stream of expert advice—one more skill to be mastered and then constantly adapted to new conditions. But change management is by definition an elusive goal. For that matter, *change* management is an understatement. *Turmoil* management would be closer to the truth.

So what you and most other managers now do is try one new approach after another (without ever quite achieving the advertised result) in an effort to address the long list of fundamental shifts and alterations your company *must* make if it is going to survive and flourish. The last thing you need right now are three *new* change programs for customers, employees, and investors. What you *do* need is a framework for simplifying, coordinating, and prioritizing all the indispensable changes you already have in the works throughout your organization.

This is precisely what loyalty-based management provides. And once again, it is the loyalty leaders that can show you how it's done. It's easy to dismiss loyalty leaders as models. After all, they've been working on value creation and loyalty for decades, so while they present a clear picture of the ultimate goal, that goal is a long, long way from the challenges you face today. What you need to know is what to do next week and next month in order to begin reducing defections. But when you look at loyalty leaders you see ends, not beginnings—or so it seems. In fact, loyalty leaders are superb models of change management. They've been able to build winning management systems by aligning all the components of loyalty and then keeping them aligned through twenty or thirty years of rapid, confusing change. What lies at the root of their ability to cope with constant change is not something they did years ago; it's what they are doing right now and have always done—things all companies need to do to keep on a steady course and an even keel.

Loyalty leaders follow two basic precepts. The first is to nurture a clear sense of company mission based on value rather than profit. The second is to use the power of partnership to align, motivate, and manage the members of the business system. Together, these two principles make up a navigational regimen as dependable as any compass.

TRUE NORTH

The first critical advantage loyalty leaders enjoy—in an environment about as placid and predictable as the mid-winter North Atlantic—is a steady and unchanging reference point for navigation. No matter how bad the weather, a company with one eye on the North Star need never experience confusion about where it is and where it wants to go. Of course, no company ever actually *reaches* a safe harbor. In business, there is no such thing. In business, the journey is everything. But the difference between sailing and drifting is precisely this strong sense of basic direction that guides daily decision making and long-term strategic planning. For loyalty leaders, the sense of direction can take a wide variety of forms, but all come down to the same underlying principle: the creation of maximum value for customers. Let's look at a couple of examples.

Northwestern Mutual

Over the past decade, the life insurance industry has seen chaotic and pervasive change—new products, new regulations, new competitors, volatile interest rates and investment markets—and yet a few companies continue to prosper. One of the best examples is Northwestern Mutual.

According to CEO Jim Ericson, the company prides itself on being "the policyholder's company" and believes that the best measuring stick with which to track its success is the policyholder persistency rate. By this measure, the value Northwestern Mutual delivers to its customers continues to improve, because customer defection rates continue to decline. Today, only 4.2 percent of first-year customers and 3.4 percent of renewal customers let their policies lapse. This is less than a third of the industry average.

The secret to this success is a strong awareness of true north. Jim Ericson puts it this way: "We have to deal with all kinds of change, but the one thing we're never going to change is our values. This place really is based on the loyalty of the employees to the idea that we are here to deliver value to the policyholder."[1] It's easy to talk, of course. There are probably thousands of CEOs who will tell you what Ericson told me. The difference is that Ericson and Northwestern Mutual work constantly to make the talk come true, and they use defection rates to measure their progress. In executive meetings at Northwestern, the principle of customer value creation repeatedly pops up in difficult discussions, where it actually shapes decisions. The investment group is evaluating, say, a complex derivative product when one person suddenly interrupts the discussion with the question they've all momentarily forgotten: "But how will it create policyholder value?" The discussion immediately refocuses on that one familiar question; when the answer is unsatisfactory, the group drops the idea.

This question and the answer to it seem to be the critical reference point in all the company's strategic planning as well as in its day-to-day decision making. Many years ago, for example, the company asked itself this question about product distribution. It came to the conclusion that the best way to deliver consistently superior value to customers was to sell only through its network of exclusive general agents, who are committed to the company's strategies and ideals. At the time, sales through independent brokers accounted for 40 percent of revenues. It's not hard to imagine the kind of compromise with principle most companies would make in such a situation. But Northwestern chose the more courageous course and phased out broker sales, sacrificing a great deal of short-term cash flow for the sake of long-term policyholder value.

Or take a more recent example. In the 1980s, surging interest rates gave most life insurance companies an earnings windfall as investment yields soared. Some firms used the surplus to acquire more new customers. Others went on shopping sprees, buying banks, brokerage houses, finance companies, and credit card companies. Many awarded big management bonuses. But Northwestern Mutual directed the windfall right back to its existing customers. *Forbes* magazine commented at the time: "It is rare indeed to find a company devoting such effort to a program whose primary purpose is to improve the position of existing policyholders rather than to attract new policyholders."[2] Northwestern explained its decision by pointing to the credo adopted by its executive committee in 1888: "The ambition of the Northwestern has been less to be large than to be safe; its aim is to rank first in benefits to policyholders rather than first in size."[3] Despite that lack of ambition, the company today has more than $300 billion worth of life insurance in force.

Northwestern Mutual has been sailing by the same star for more than one hundred years. Founded in 1857, the company faced its first crisis two years later, when a passenger train was derailed after striking a cow near Johnson's Creek, Wisconsin. Fourteen people died, including two Northwestern Mutual policyholders. The claims amounted to $3,500, but the total assets of the two-year-old company came to only $2,000. The policies specified a grace period of sixty days before the company was required to pay the claims. Instead, Northwestern's president borrowed the extra $1,500 on a personal note so he could pay the beneficiaries immediately.

A. G. Edwards

While Northwestern's legacy of putting the policyholder first goes all the way back to 1859, most loyalty leaders have much younger traditions. Lexus and MBNA are newcomers. A. G. Edwards and USAA operated for decades before shifting to a loyalty-based orientation. At each of these companies, however, it was commitment to the notion of value creation that formed or eventually came to form the cornerstone of the business system.

Ben Edwards III, the current CEO of A. G. Edwards and great-grandson of its founder, described how his management team came to focus on loyalty long after the firm was founded. In the mid-1960s, when the firm had about four hundred employees (it now has ten thousand), Edwards' father developed heart trouble and moved to Florida, leaving young Ben Edwards in charge of a company that was, in Edwards' words, "drifting and vulnerable." The executive team held a series of off-site retreats to reconsider their core partnership and the company's strategy and operating principles. After several emotional sessions in which members addressed their own management styles, relationships, and personal objectives, the ten executives agreed to spend two days a month at a Ramada Inn outside St. Louis discussing the company's strategy, direction, market position, and fundamental objectives. What emerged over the next two years was first, a consensus about the firm's mission—to deliver financial services of superior value to customers—and second, a growing conviction that to act as the best possible agent for its clients, the company would have to fundamentally redefine the broker's role.

Historically, the primary corporate goal had been to maximize profits. But it became clear in the meetings in St. Louis that that goal was inconsistent with the new mission. At a typical brokerage house, the trading desk acts as an important profit center, and corporate executives earn an override on those profits. The trading desk tries to make as much as it can on each customer trade, rather than give the absolute lowest price to the customer whose interests the company is pledged to promote. The conflict of interest is obvious. As profit to the trading desk grows, value to the customer diminishes. As we pointed out in Chapter 4, in-house mutual funds create another conflict by encouraging brokers to push company funds even when better alternatives are available and appropriate.

Having made a commitment to act as the customer's true agent, A. G. Edwards now took the radical step of eliminating all these practices. Headquarters ceased to be a profit center. Financial incentives that worked against the interests of the client were weeded out; the firm stopped manufacturing its own products. According to Ben Edwards, "We decided to view profits as a necessity, but not as a goal. Committing ourselves to our customers allowed us to have fun running the business as well as we possibly could. Our top managers began to like and respect each other more, and we all felt energized, often putting in fourteen hour days. We also decided to put all the cash we generated back into the business. To our surprise, when we removed profits as a goal, profits went up!"[4]

This new view of its mission prompted A. G. Edwards to redefine what it meant by loyalty. "When most brokerage houses talk about broker loyalty," Edwards explains, "they mean that their brokers are being loyal to headquarters by pushing the more profitable in-house fund groups. But to us, that is *disloyal* behavior because it means the broker is not acting in the customer's best interests."[5] Loyalty leaders like A. G. Edwards tend to think of loyalty not as loyalty to the company but as loyalty to a set of principles that stand ahead of profit. It is this higher-order loyalty that energizes employees, builds customer retention, and, paradoxically, generates cash flow and profits.

The firm's basic principle is that it exists to deliver value to the customer, and its dedication to this principle produces the kind of behavior guaranteed to mystify and depress competitors. A. G Edwards is still the only brokerage that refuses to sell in-house products. In Chapter 1, we saw how State Farm paid more than its policies required to bring hurricane-damaged homes up to code, because as CEO Ed Rust, Jr., explained, "Our goal is to take care of our policyholders. That's what we're driven by."[6] As Dave Illingworth of Toyota/Lexus pointed out, "The more you focus on the bottom line, the harder it is to hit."[7]

USAA

Another company that has earned its way into the front ranks of loyalty leaders by adhering to the principle of putting customer value first—followed closely by employee value—is USAA. Founded in 1922 to provide auto insurance to military officers, USAA's performance was lackluster for decades. Always good on claims and on price, the company was dreadfully weak on customer service. When retired general Robert McDermott took over the helm in 1968, policy paperwork and service commitment were in such a mess, he almost changed his mind about taking the job. On any given day, the chances of finding a particular file were only fifty-fifty, and the company employed twenty to thirty college students to come in every night and search for missing records in the piles of paper that covered hundreds of desks. Moreover, morale at the company was abysmal. The average employee stayed with the company only eleven months, and many did little but punch their timecards in and out.

McDermott made radical changes. The first was to give an unequivocal top priority to customer service. He implemented a set of programs to automate policy and claims processing; greatly expanded the list of financial services the company offered; and broke the bureaucracy up into five groups that competed with each other on service quality and productivity. McDermott spent $130 million on technology to produce a nearly paperless company in which every service representative has instantaneous access to every customer's records—including computer images of hand-drawn sketches of accident scenes. Above all else, however, he insisted on delivering value, service, and loyalty to the customer.

For example, nearly every life insurance policy in the world has a so-called war clause, which lets the company off the hook in the case of combat deaths. USAA policies have no such provision. That may seem obvious in a company that serves military officers, but USAA pushes the logic of loyalty a step further. During Desert Storm, the company allowed policyholders to *increase* their coverage and actually sold new policies to people on their way to the war zone. (Of the fifty-five officers killed in that war, every one was a USAA member.) At the same time the company encouraged members to downgrade their auto insurance policies, since cars that sit home in the garage don't need liability coverage. USAA set up hotlines to serve members with special needs associated with the emergency and went out of its way to assure them that their insurance would not be canceled because of late payment due to the war. When auto losses turned out to be even lower than expected, the company declared a 25 percent rebate on auto policies for everyone who served in Desert Storm.

The second thing McDermott did was invest heavily in employees. USAA spends $19 million (2.7 percent of its annual budget, double the industry average) on training and education. The company's seventy-five classrooms are filled every evening, and some 30 percent of employees take courses in any given year. Furthermore, the training has a goal. New skills and increased competence lead to promotions for almost half the workforce every year. USAA has also pioneered progressive employment practices, like the four-day workweek for virtually all employees. The company's 286-acre headquarters includes tennis courts, softball diamonds, jogging trails, a driving range, and three artificial lakes. USAA has become probably the most desirable employer in San Antonio.

McDermott retired in 1993, but the company's new CEO, Robert Herres, another ex-general, is equally committed to USAA's concept of true north. McDermott enriched jobs with education, career opportunity, empowerment, greater job content, decentralization, and a battery of extra morale-boosters. But at the root of his and now the company's view of work is the conviction that what makes people happy in any job is doing better work—giving customers more value, creating stronger bonds with them. In short, what drives USAA is value, not profit. In an interview in the *Harvard Business Review* in 1991, McDermott said, "The mission and corporate culture of this company are, in one word, service. As a company objective, service comes ahead of either profits or growth."[8]

In general, loyalty leaders feel that their commitment to an ethical mission—placing customer benefit above their own short-term profit—gives them an advantage in coping with change. Whereas academics have turned business ethics into a complicated debate, loyalty leaders see it very simply. They do what they say they are going to do; they live up to their commitments, and often exceed them. Most important, they always try to act in their customers' best interest. This behavior not only energizes the organization, it gives everyone in it an easy-to-read road map in times of confusion and heightened competition. Knowing who you are and where you're going is not just ethical window dressing, it's a competitive advantage.

Northwestern Mutual's CEO Jim Ericson recently attended a roundtable on ethics at the Harvard Business School. When he said he saw ethics as a strategic advantage for his company, most of the other participants were skeptical. Doing business ethically was desirable, they all agreed, but there was no denying that it often constrained profits.

Ericson *does* deny it, and Northwestern's experience bears him out. In fact, superior ethical underpinnings give all loyalty leaders an advantage among employees and customers that translates into higher profits, not profit constraints. Ericson recalls that when he was recruiting young lawyers for Northwestern's legal department, one of the key benefits he stressed was integrity. "Our morals at this firm stop us way before the law does," he used to tell recruits. "You'll never lose any sleep here, because this company is going to do the right thing."[9] He wasn't talking only about following federal guidelines. He meant that employees could rely on the company to dedicate itself to a higher mission than profit—the mission of creating value for customers. That mission is a big part of what customers are buying when they do business with the company and one of the principal reasons they come to Northwestern Mutual to stay.

PARTNERSHIP

The second big advantage loyalty leaders enjoy in coping with change is their ability to align the objectives of different members of the business system. A solid fix on true north lets them steer the ship, but this second advantage helps them sail it effectively.

The secret to alignment is partnership, and the secret to partnership is compensating each partner with a shared interest in the value he or she helps to create. Partnership in this sense—the partnership of all the long-term players whose compensation rests directly on the value they help to create—is unrelated to the legal distinction between partnerships and corporations, which has more to do with tax consequences and liability limitations than with value-sharing. There are partnerships in the technical sense of the word that don't genuinely share value and decision making, and there are corporations that do. In one of Berkshire-Hathaway's annual reports, for example, Warren Buffett says, "Although our form is corporate, our attitude is partnership."[10]

The advantages of value-sharing partnerships are enormous. To begin with, all the partners are motivated to create as much value as possible. In addition, the system promotes self-motivation, self-governance, and self-correction. You don't have to tell people what to do or when to do it. Partners deal with change as necessary to maintain growth in the pool of value they all share. Loyalty leaders have found that they can most effectively manage every one of a business's constituencies—customers, employees, and investors—through partnership.

Customers

Some of the best and most familiar partnership success stories revolve around so-called vendor partnerships. (Seen from the vendor's point of view, of course, these are *customer* partnerships—a point we made in Chapter 1. In any case, it is often loyalty-oriented vendors who must take the initiative in creating them.) The Japanese auto industry pointed the way, but now many U.S. companies have taken on the challenge of transforming arm's-length, adversarial relationships into long-term partnerships, in the process creating enormous value for suppliers as well as customers. Sharing information makes it possible for vendors and their customers to identify opportunities for systems improvements. Sharing the benefits of the improvement motivates both partners and tends to cement and steadily improve their relationship. Little of this was possible in the old system, when each side tried to maximize its own value on every transaction—bidding and negotiating fiercely, hoarding potentially productive information, playing the price and profit game to the hilt for the maximum short-term, one-time benefit. No vendor could afford to customize its products and services for better long-term value to the customer, because the customer might suddenly switch to another vendor. No customer could afford to give a vendor deep insight into its production capacities and weaknesses for fear the information would find its way to a competitor.

Breaking the old mentality made it possible for customers and vendors to work together and uncover enormous opportunities for value creation. Internal functions that are difficult to manage can often be greatly improved by outsourcing, which forces them out of the bureaucratic nest and into the open air of clear measures and accountability. The trend has revolutionized many businesses. Leading hospitals have essentially subcontracted their supply and logistics functions to the companies that supply them with medical products. Automakers now allow vendors of windshield wipers to design and manufacture not just the wiper but the entire assembly. Companies like Accuride work with committed long-term customers to develop mutual economies in plant configuration and run lengths.

Leo Burnett is an excellent example of a vendor that works hard to build customer partnerships. While most advertising agencies strive only to provide clients with effective advertising, Leo Burnett goes much further. When Burnett was about to sign his name to the firm's first contract with its first client, Green Giant—still a client today, sixty years later—he penned an additional paragraph that enlarged the standard vendor agreement about producing ads, buying space, and maintaining confidentiality. It read: "Counseling with you in regard to your advertising and sales efforts, seeking new ways of supplying ideas to improve your advertising, make it more productive, and in every way within our power, working with you to advance your business."[11]

To this day, Burnett chooses customers with whom it can earn the right to act as a partner. In 1994, of the 54 companies that invited the agency to talk about a business relationship, Burnett pursued only 5. Of its 33 current clients, 12 have been with the firm at least twenty years, 10 for more than thirty years. Current CEO Bill Lynch says, "We try to earn our client's loyalty by devoting the resources and people required to completely understand the total business. We try to involve ourselves in the total marketing of their products, and we try to help them grow their businesses."[12] The vast majority of new billings come from established clients whose business growth creates additional demand for advertising.

Lynch also takes the long-term perspective when a client's business is not going well. If a loyal customer runs into a bad year and has to cut back on its advertising—let's say by 50 percent—Burnett doesn't automatically cut back its services by 50 percent and pull half its management off the account. The company is willing to lose money on an account over the short term. In Lynch's words, "We try to be a partner and invest ourselves in the business."[13] One of the reasons Burnett can take this kind of long-term view is that it remains a private firm. The two hundred fifty stockholders are all active managers in the company, and all believe that the value of their stock will grow as the result of building and maintaining superior client partnerships.

Another loyalty leader that sees partnership with its customers as a basic operating principle is State Farm. Decisions like the one to bring houses up to code after Hurricane Andrew are a good example of the company's long-term view. Even State Farm's pricing is designed for partnership. At the end of three years, accident-free customers get a 10 percent discount, followed by another 5 percent discount three years later. Another four years of good driving and customers earn guaranteed insurability for life. This straightforward mechanism shares value with the customers who helped to create it.

Employees

In the case of employees, partnership produces a long array of benefits in the management of change. We will take up three in particular: alignment, flexibility, and talent.

First, alignment. State Farm refers to its agents as marketing partners, and that's more than just a pretty phrase. Neither agent nor company can survive without the other; for either to prosper, both must meet their separate responsibilities with energy and skill. The company must provide competitive products, efficient overhead, and smooth, rapid claims service. Agents must find and sell the best possible customers and then give such good service that they retain them. State Farm could never overcome the turmoil of the insurance business by trying to manage its eighteen thousand agents as individual employees. But by structuring partnerships with the right value-sharing incentives, the company has managed to thrive for more than seventy years, creating the largest network of independent business locations in North America—half again as many as McDonald's or 7-11.

Well-structured partnerships are also the key to another benefit of alignment, superior levels of productivity. After all, most productivity advances come from front-line learning, not from headquarters. In Chapter 5 we saw how State Farm's value-sharing compensation and career management policies gave its front-line partners an incentive to maximize the loyalty surplus. And State Farm's gross commission structure encourages agents to treat expense dollars as if they were their own—because they are.

Northwestern Mutual has a similar partnership arrangement with its one hundred seven general agents. The company and the general agents are completely dependent on one another for success. Northwestern pays them only for the business they generate, and there are none of the fixed fees or management pass-throughs that are standard at most other life insurance companies. This means that all sales and distribution costs are variable expenses, managed at the local level by a partner who shares in the benefits of efficient management. Since they also share in the profits, general agents invest carefully to grow revenues and recruit and train high-caliber agents, with whom, in turn, the general agents form a kind of partnership. The result is an alert, self-managing network of partners and general partners who adjust quickly to changing competitive conditions.

The second benefit of value-sharing in the management of change is flexibility. Networks of partners are much more nimble than bureaucracies. Look at Chick-fil-A, whose store managers split profit fifty-fifty with the company. Suppose headquarters conceives the idea of creating satellite lunch operations in high-traffic pedestrian areas outside the malls where the restaurants are located. All management has to do is describe the opportunity to operators. They will implement it themselves whenever they believe it will help them to build profits. These operators know their territories, allocate their own time, and share the profits—and therefore the expenses—of their own shops. So every operator applies his or her own judgment and knowledge to make the best possible decisions about creating value and managing change.

Contrast this scenario with what would have to take place in a restaurant chain like Pizza Hut, where store operators are not partners but employees. To begin with, the human resources staff at headquarters would not tolerate a revision of the bonus formula in mid-cycle, so any change would have to wait until the following year, when it could be folded into a new compensation plan. And given that most of the store managers expect to be in their locations only for another year or two, not many would do handstands to make the new satellites succeed. Significant change of any kind would require a lot of preparation that wouldn't pay off for at last a couple of years. Obviously, only partners who know they will be around to reap the benefit are going to dedicate time and energy to make an innovation work. In the Pizza Hut system, which represents the American norm, top management has to decide what changes to make, who's to make them, how they're to be motivated and compensated, and how to make sure they implement the changes effectively.

The third great benefit of partnerships in managing change is this: the opportunity to earn one's way into a partnership attracts better people. The fact is, smart, creative people are better able to understand and cope effectively with change. The best people want to be judged and rewarded on performance, so they avoid bureaucracies and organizational pyramids. Look at the jobs taken by the best business talent over the past twenty-five years. The majority of MBAs at the top ten schools—especially those at the top of their class—passed up the opportunity to join Fortune 500 corporations. They chose instead to work in consulting, investment banking, real estate, venture capital, leveraged buyouts—anywhere they could find a decent prospect of earning money and responsibility on the basis of merit and hard work.

Some deans and professors wring their hands over this migration away from the historic backbone of corporate America. But there's no getting around the natural tendency to pursue the most attractive careers. The tide continues to flow toward partnership structures, not only because they're performance-based and thus more motivating, but because partnerships are expandable. A partnership can accommodate any number of outstanding partners, not just a few senior executives. Besides, in a corporation, every one of those senior executives has a boss—except of course the CEO. As for the CEOs, they're usually elected by a set of outside directors, who in most cases are securely seated in the worst possible cell of the Friedman matrix. They are not value-sharing partners, yet they're picking the bosses for senior management teams. In a partnership, the partners either elect their *own* managing partner, or at the very least, are closely consulted on the decision. In a partnership, delegation of such a critical responsibility to an outsider would be unthinkable. The partnership structure offers not only a superior degree of independence and control over one's destiny but superior opportunities for compensation as well. In a well-structured partnership, compensation is limited only by the partners' ability to create value for customers.

(One obvious key to an effective partnership is to structure incentives so that partners focus their energies on fashioning the biggest possible pie for the group, not on increasing the size of their own slices. Equally important, partners should agree in advance on the basis for measuring and sharing the value created. At A. G. Edwards, the allocation of the bonus pool is set at the beginning of the year so that during the year, officers will work together to maximize the size of the pool. At Price-Waterhouse, bonus allocations are fixed in advance every two years. At Bain Capital, partners agree at the time they raise a fund how they will split the carried interest—20 percent of investment profits—so that throughout the ten-year life of the fund, they can further their own interests only by furthering those of the partnership.)

The talent advantage can work for any company in any industry, not just for consulting firms and buyout funds. It works for State Farm, which attracts talented agent candidates who want to become independent business partners rather than members of a sales force. It works for Chick-fil-A, whose fifty-fifty profit-sharing draws better operator candidates than the bureaucratic hierarchies that run so many fast food chains. And it works for Leo Burnett, which is a good example of a corporation that behaves like a partnership. Recruits who perform well over their first eight to ten years and demonstrate a consistent contribution to client and agency success are invited to buy shares in the company. So far, each generation has made certain that its investment prospered over time—and has resisted the temptation to make a quick killing. Every set of managers since Leo Burnett himself has had the opportunity to take the firm public and raise enormous amounts of cash to distribute among current owners, and every generation has chosen not to. Instead, managers continue to sell their shares back to the company when they retire, and at book value—a very conservative price.

Why? Bill Lynch, the seventh CEO, believes that public ownership would make it more difficult to take the long view and invest in people and clients as assets. He also believes that as CEO of a public company, he would have to spend a lot of time with analysts and pension-fund managers instead of clients. "I think going public is a short-term move for current management to make a lot of money," he says, "but I don't think it's in the best long-term interests of the company."[14] This philosophy of business has built a partnership across generations that helps the firm to maintain its edge in recruiting and keeping young managers, who can see that the firm's superior economics are likely to continue into the future. It also reinforces the loyalty and commitment of senior managers, since a large part of their ultimate compensation—the buyout of their shares when they retire—depends on the firm's continuing success. They worry less about this year's compensation and more about the firm's future health.

Truett Cathy, CEO of Chick-fil-A, has taken his firm down a similar path. Cathy could probably sell the company today for more than $1 billion. Instead, he keeps the company private, and he nurtures the people who will carry it into the future. He is grooming his two sons to carry on the tradition he established. Of course, all this makes Chick-fil-A that much more attractive to current and potential operators, improving its choice of talent and bettering the odds that it will continue to meet tomorrow's challenges and make the most of tomorrow's opportunities.

Investors

In Chapter 6, we studied the ways investors can create or eliminate value. We urged you to seek out investors who will make a clear contribution to the value they will share in. But you need to ask yourself an even more basic question: Do you really need outside investors at all? State Farm, Chick-fil-A, Leo Burnett, and others have grown very large without outside capital. Well-structured partnerships can generate surprising amounts of cash flow that you can use to grow the firm or take it private.

Still, a handful of companies have demonstrated that loyalty-based management is possible even under public ownership. We described a few of them—MBNA and A. G. Edwards, among others—in Chapter 6. Another notable example of a public corporation that has managed to put customers and employees ahead of profits and stockholders is Johnson & Johnson, the health-care giant. J&J's famous credo, carved in stone at the company's world headquarters in New Jersey, declares that shareholders will get a fair return only after the company has ensured outstanding value to customers, employees, suppliers, distributors, and the communities in which J&J operates.

So it can be done. At least, it can if you're as old and as big and successful as Johnson & Johnson. If you're not, the pinch will come the minute short-term earnings hit a bump, or the instant your industry enters a period of great change. Pressure on quarterly earnings is guaranteed to bring out the worst in public investors and to underscore their lack of concern for the company's future. Their demands for short-term earnings improvement will sharply increase the danger of shortchanging customers and employees, and of initiating a downward spiral into mediocrity.

Executives who build successful companies around their own vision earn a rare privilege—the opportunity to perpetuate their aspirations and ideals in an institution. Selling out to the highest bidder often means selling that opportunity. Not even great companies can survive managers who aren't willing to subordinate their desire for maximum compensation to the long-term health and viability of the organization. Selling out to public investors is often the quickest way to get rich, but the wealth is often purchased at the expense of customers, employees, and managers for generations to come.

Of course, some firms have no real choice. They require access to public equity markets because their need to finance rapid growth or global expansion—or their inability to carry additional debt—denies them the luxury of private ownership. For these companies, the key is to attract public investors who bring more value than their cash, who act like long-term partners, who believe that their own best interest is most effectively served by attending to the best interests of customers and employees. It's not all that hard to figure out whether investors are inclined toward partnership. Check the average churn rate for their investment portfolios. Listen to their views on allocating value among customers, employees, and investors. (For example, do they favor allowing managers and employees to share in long-term profits beyond a base rate of return on capital?) Look at the kinds of management incentives they prefer. If they endorse long-term partnership structures like the ones favored by Warren Buffett, chances are they're the right investors for you. In times of trouble, these are the investors who will help to solve problems instead of bolting for the exit.

HOW PARTNERSHIP ACCELERATES CHANGE

It may seem that building partnerships involving customers, employees, and investors is just too time consuming to solve the pressing needs of a business like yours. But partnership structures can generate improved performance very quickly. The Accuride case is one good example of how rapidly change can occur when a company shifts to partnership structures and a commitment to creating value for customers. Let's look at two more: the case of Carl Sewell and Curley Crawford, and the case of Andrew Banks and Royce Yudkoff.

Carl Sewell's Cadillac dealership had a service department that was losing money. Sewell thought he'd found the man to fix it, a promising young transmission specialist named Curley Crawford. Before promoting him, however, he first restructured compensation for the job to make it a value-sharing partnership. He offered Crawford a base salary of $27,500 plus 10 percent of any profits the department generated. And he gave Crawford free reign to make all the changes he thought necessary to run a high-quality operation.

Crawford seized the opportunity with both hands. He hired first-rate technicians, demanded superior workmanship, and relentlessly increased his team's reliability in delivering cars to customers on time. By the end of the second year he had turned the shop around and was earning a combined salary and bonus of $75,000. That was more than Crawford had dared to hope for, and a lot more than Sewell had expected to pay. But instead of restructuring the formula, Sewell confirmed it. After all, why not? Sewell was getting the other 90 percent of the profit, so there was no reason to complain.

Two more years and Crawford was making $150,000—outrageous compensation for running a garage. But Crawford continued to refine his operation, listening closely to customers and employees about how to improve service further and create more value. By the time he retired, Crawford was making more than $250,000. And Sewell, of course, was making nine times that much—more than $2 million a year from a service department that had once been losing money.

Sewell estimates that comparable dealerships were earning about $500,000 a year from their service departments. He attributes his success to two factors, picking the right man and sticking with a partnership compensation formula. Sewell made a great deal of money; Crawford remained loyal to the dealership until his retirement; and best of all, with a self-managing partner, Sewell was freed to spend his time on other parts of the business. The experience reinforced his belief that everyone in the organization should be paid like a partner and that salaries are not a good thing:

The only people I have on salary are staff types and controllers. It takes a little bit of work initially to set up a partnership pay plan. To make sure it is fair and effective, you have to figure out a logical

*way of quantifying the amount of work a person does. But doctors
get paid this way, and so do lawyers. Hell, if they can figure it out,
anybody can.*[15]

THE ABRY STORY

Another example of the huge potential of loyalty-based strategies to
manage rapid change involves a company called ABRY Communications.
Andrew Banks and Royce Yudkoff (the AB and RY of ABRY) were
partners in Bain & Company's Boston office when they decided to go
into business for themselves. Few of Bain's consulting staff mean to
spend their entire careers as consultants, so it is not unusual for the firm
to back its people when they create new companies. In the case of Banks
and Yudkoff, Bain Capital and about 20 consulting partners provided
funding. The business plan was to raise enough capital to purchase
several television stations around the country, increase their value with
operating improvements, and then sell the stations and return the money
to the investors. The time range was five to ten years.

Once the capital was assembled, the two partners purchased five
second-tier stations (with no major network affiliations) in Baltimore,
Cincinnati, Kansas City, Birmingham, and Milwaukee and began to
reorient management practices. In a few cases they had to replace managers, but in every case they immediately restructured the compensation
arrangement. At the Baltimore station, for example, the general manager
had always been paid like an employee—a salary of $125,000 plus a
bonus of up to $25,000 for meeting annual budget goals. ABRY replaced
this standard deal with a multi-year commitment. The manager would
earn a base salary of $125,000, but instead of an annual bonus, he
would receive a portion of the value he helped to create—that is, a
portion of the future sale price of the station, after investors received
their capital plus a reasonable rate of return. Over a five-year period,
the manager vested into the arrangement and became a real partner.

In many cases, general managers changed their behavior significantly
when they became partners rather than conventional employees. As
Royce Yudkoff puts it, "In almost every case, we saw these individuals
become more effective negotiators with vendors, customers, and bankers.
People always seem to be smarter negotiators when it's their own money
at stake."[16] ABRY also noticed that they stopped hiding failures. For
example, they began to bring up budget shortfalls far enough in advance

to adjust cash-flow projections and lending agreements. And according to Yudkoff, "when one of them makes a hiring mistake (which we all do from time to time), instead of trying to cover it up, managers share their concerns openly so we can help them find the best resolution for everyone involved."[17] Finally, Yudkoff and Banks noticed that people felt more responsibility to help out across department lines, since their own success was a function of how well the company did as a whole.

One of the interesting characteristics of a television station is that the only way to increase the value of the company is to increase the price of advertising to customers. Operating costs are relatively small and more or less fixed. There are always some opportunities for cost reduction, but they're dwarfed by the opportunities for revenue enhancement. Another unyielding figure, however, is the number of advertising minutes the station can sell. So increasing revenue has to mean increasing price per minute—and to increase price per minute, you have to find a way to increase the value an advertiser receives from a minute of advertising. Whereas many businesses try to increase value by adding capacity and acquiring new customers—or perhaps by reducing costs—TV stations are not distracted. They know that value creation is a matter of increasing the benefit the product delivers to current customers and then of realizing a share of that added value by means of higher pricing.

Increasing viewer loyalty was the core component of ABRY's strategy. As Banks and Yudkoff saw it, the audience they wanted to serve was that small group of people who watched the station intensively. By concentrating on that core group, they would be able to tailor their programming precisely. When a station consistently delivers programming that appeals to its target viewers, it reduces their inclination to reach for the remote. And getting the same group of customers to stay tuned creates enormous economic advantages for the rest of the business system. One of the largest expenses of running a station, for example, is the promotion budget—the cost of advertising the station and its programs to attract new viewers. At the Baltimore station, promotion ate up 20 percent of sales revenue in the first year of ABRY ownership. By the fifth year, the proportion had declined to 4 percent. An intense focus on the preferences of the core segment of viewers made the improvement possible.

ABRY chose different groups of target customers in each market, basing the selection partly on each station's historic viewer base and partly on an analysis of local market segments. In Milwaukee, ABRY singled out young male sports fans. In Cincinnati, Banks and Yudkoff noticed that the level of video rentals was extraordinarily high and decided to target movie buffs. In Baltimore, ABRY chose African-American viewers, whom the national networks underserved. (Nationally, African-Americans comprise 15 percent of the TV market, but in Baltimore they represented 40 percent of local viewership.) ABRY learned as much as it could about customer preferences. Through focus groups, for example, it discovered that blacks saw the station as second rate. So the company upgraded graphics, improved the on-air look of station identifications, and raised promotions to national standards.

The most important learning, however, came from failure analysis. With Nielsen ratings available for every major market, the television industry does not have to rely on satisfaction scores. Managers can track actual viewing patterns by demographic segment and by time slot. ABRY studied the data to see which programs were most popular with black audiences, then loaded the Baltimore station's schedule with those shows. They also studied specific viewer patterns for the Baltimore station to watch for ratings dropoffs from show to show. When they spotted defections between time slots, they adjusted their lineup to hold on to as many viewers as possible.

By building a core of loyal viewers at each station, ABRY created a more valuable medium for advertisers who wanted to target those groups. Smart advertisers don't just buy Nielsen points, they buy results. ABRY's predictable audience enabled local advertisers to fine-tune their promotions to gain the best possible sales impact.

ABRY also created programs to develop advertiser loyalty. One effective device was the award of a trip to customers who remained loyal to the station and were willing to commit to a larger advertising budget for the next year. The trips were impressive; ABRY could arrange for events that individuals would have found difficult to duplicate. At the end of a private boat trip down the Danube, for instance, the group toured the Imperial Palace in Vienna, serenaded by the Vienna Boys Choir singing "America the Beautiful." One customer, a prosperous auto dealer, told Yudkoff and Banks that he could easily afford luxury-class travel but had come to appreciate the station's trips because they gave him a chance to get to know station managers on a level that would otherwise have been impossible. He said that in the past, it had been all too easy to work through the year and skip his vacation entirely. Now he put the trip on his calendar almost a year in advance, and all the planning was done for him.

The annual trip met a number of needs. It was a way of recognizing the station's most loyal customers for their valued partnership. It was also a way for station managers to spend time with advertisers, to reach a better understanding of their needs and dissatisfactions and develop more effective programming for the year ahead. Furthermore, the time to qualify for the next year's trip began shortly after the group returned home, with the experience fresh in memory. As stand-alone promotions, the trips would have been not much more than marketing gimmicks. But as part of an overall loyalty strategy based on the development and continuous refinement of a superior value proposition, they were extremely effective.

The result of ABRY's partnership strategy was to substantially improve the performance of its stations over a five-year period. Audience share increased by 52 percent, profit margins by 200 percent, and operating cash flow multiplied 17 times! ABRY sold the stations somewhat sooner than expected when one buyer offered to acquire all five—at a price that gave investors a 64 percent annual rate of return. ABRY had raised a total of $30 million from investors and realized $210 million from the sale. For every $50,000 committed, investors received $350,000 in distributions.

All the partners shared in the success. For example, the general manager in Baltimore had been making $150,000 a year before his association with ABRY. Over the five years of ABRY's ownership, he made $125,000 a year; his stake in the sale was worth $2.5 million (taxed, of course, at the capital gains rate).

Yudkoff and Banks, still in their thirties, earned more than enough to retire. Instead, however, they have just raised another fund with which to buy more stations, build new loyalty-based partnerships, and create and share more value. But as they raised the second, somewhat larger fund, Banks and Yudkoff did not forget the investors who backed them originally. On the basis of their track record, several big institutional investors wanted to buy up the whole fund. Though it would have been easier and cheaper for ABRY to deal with only one or two big institutions, Banks and Yudkoff made certain their original backers had the opportunity to reinvest.

The ABRY story demonstrates that the benefits of loyalty apply equally to customers, employees, and investors. By striking the right value-sharing partnerships across those three groups, a company can create enormous value relatively quickly. At ABRY, the entire process took five years.

11

Getting Started:
The Path Toward
Zero Defections

LOYALTY-BASED MANAGEMENT is hard work. No one can transform measures, incentives, customer lifecycles, employee career paths, and capital structures overnight. Yet you can begin making impressive loyalty-based progress in as short a time as it takes to build some well-aligned value-sharing partnerships. We saw in Chapter 10 that Corporate Software nearly doubled its sales and profits in the first sixteen months after going private. At Sewell Cadillac's service department, the profit turnaround was evident in the first year, and the company was making a healthy profit by the second year. At ABRY, each of the individual TV stations showed significant progress by the second or third year, and the whole process—from raising money to selling the five stations and returning a 700 percent gain to investors—took only five years. At Accuride, profits grew more than 20 percent in the first year after acquisition. Performance can improve rapidly when companies begin to concentrate on creating value for customers through a network of value-sharing partnerships.

It is equally true, however, that loyalty-based management is a slow, steady, never-ending process. Companies like State Farm, Leo Burnett, and Northwestern Mutual Life have pursued the ultimate goal of zero defections for decades, continuously improving their companies, their profits, and the benefits they offer their constituents. What these venerable companies demonstrate is that loyalty-based management is not a fad; if anything, it is remarkably old-fashioned. And yet it continues to produce remarkable results, even in an age when loyalty is said to be dead.

These remarkable results make it tempting to borrow a few tools and techniques from the loyalty leaders, without bothering to address the question of basic values and philosophy. Unfortunately, that's like trying to borrow the engine from a Lexus and put it in a Chevy. Unless all systems are designed to work together in harmony, you won't see much benefit. The key to ultimate, lasting success is how the parts of the system fit together. Therefore any practical improvement program must focus on specific components. In this chapter we will review the principal messages of the first ten chapters. In the context of this big picture, we can suggest a road map to guide you on the path toward zero defections.

THE BIG PICTURE

We began this book by arguing that loyalty must be viewed not as a tactic, but as a strategy. Customer, employee, and investor loyalty are so thoroughly intertwined that to understand and manage one, you must understand and manage all three. But while loyalty is indeed strategic, its implications transcend strategy and point to a philosophy of business that places people above process. The central tenet of this philosophy is that the purpose of a business is to create value, not simply to create profit. The value-centered business model we introduced in Chapter 1 (Figure 1-3) shows how the economic forces of loyalty explain and predict growth and profit.

Loyalty is not only philosophy and strategy; it speaks also to operations, because it offers a set of practical measures for implementing strategy. By observing the behavior of customers, employees, and investors (do they or don't they come back for more), you can quite straightforwardly determine where value is being delivered and where it isn't, and by extension, whether a business is succeeding or failing in its mission to create lasting value. Loyalty thus provides a standard for measuring business performance and a framework for pursuing it.

Loyalty leaders—the companies that have achieved the highest standard of performance in their industries—provide important insights into how companies must operate if they are to earn superior loyalty. While every loyalty leader's strategy is unique, all of them build on the following eight elements:

1. *Building a superior customer value proposition.* Every one of these companies centers its strategy on the development of a value proposition that offers key customers truly superior value in relation to competitive offerings.

2. *Finding the right customers.* Loyalty leaders understand who their target customers are and develop systems to acquire them selectively. Getting the right customers often depends more on the magnetism of the value proposition and the referrals it generates than on brilliant salesmanship. In fact, loyalty leaders often care more about filtering new customer flow than about increasing its volume, because adverse selection can seriously diminish the value available to core customers.

3. *Earning customer loyalty.* Loyalty leaders treat customers like assets, and do everything possible to retain these assets and increase their lifetime value. Pricing policies, product line, employee incentives, and service levels are all engineered to enhance customer loyalty.

4. *Finding the right employees.* Successful loyalty-based businesses tend to be as selective in their choice of hires as they are in their choice of customers. They look for people with character who share the company's values, recruits with the talent and skills to achieve the levels of productivity that make for satisfying, long-term careers.

5. *Earning employee loyalty.* Loyalty leaders invest heavily in the development and training of their employees and construct career paths and organizational structures that enable them to make the most of their education and abilities. As employees stay on, they get better at their jobs and become better acquainted with their customers; employee loyalty and customer loyalty reinforce each other, making jobs more satisfying and further increasing the potential for superior customer value. Loyalty leaders share the resulting productivity surplus with employees in the form of higher compensation, which feeds back into the growing loyalty spiral.

6. *Gaining cost advantage through superior productivity.* The productivity surplus that grows from better customer and employee

loyalty produces a cost advantage. Employees may earn better salaries—often 10 to 50 percent higher than the competition— but as a percentage of revenues, the cost of their higher salaries is actually lower. What's more, loyalty leaders structure incentives so that employees treat expense dollars as if they were spending their own money.

7. *Finding the right investors.* To stabilize their business systems and enable themselves to respond to competitive threats and industry turbulence, loyalty leaders need to attract the right kind of investor. This often means nontraditional capital structures such as mutual or private ownership. For public companies, the right investors are those who are predisposed to long-term relationships, who pick investments carefully and stick with them, and who believe they will prosper only when customers and employees prosper. The growth targets for loyalty leaders are based not on Wall Street's expectations but on the creation of sufficient opportunities for people within the business system.

8. *Earning investor loyalty.* Loyalty leaders are managed by partners who prosper only when other members of the business system prosper. In other words, investors must earn a fair return on their cash before any bonus is paid to management. This gives managers a strong incentive to reinvest profits only in projects with considerable potential to create value. Treating investors' money the same way they would treat their own is the best possible way for managers to earn investor loyalty, which constitutes an enormous competitive advantage in a business world increasingly challenged by the turbulence of investor churn.

BEGINNING THE JOURNEY

Every loyalty leader we've studied has found some way of addressing all eight elements of this loyalty-oriented business strategy. By aligning the interests of all the players, these companies have dramatically raised the odds that people will use their energy to increase the size of the value pie, not just to secure a larger slice for themselves. (One effective way of strengthening the incentive to work for the common good is to defer payment on some portion of everyone's individual share. Leo Burnett's system of paying out managers' stock holdings only upon retirement is a good example of such a device.)

By itself, of course, no set of incentives can generate loyalty out of thin air. Loyalty is a character trait; it cannot be created, only reinforced. As a result, loyalty leaders care deeply about the quality of the people who become their partners. They want people with character and integrity, people who will not run for the exit when something in the system goes wrong. Meaningful failure analysis requires a high degree of trust and the active participation of people whose inclination is to do the right thing for the right reason. Lacking either, it is hardly worthwhile to invest in the kind of scientific loyalty measures and failure-analysis tools that will allow a company to refine its value creation process and set goals so high that zero defections becomes a visible target.

While the journey toward that target has little real prospect of ever ending, it does need to begin. For most companies, the beginning presents the single greatest challenge, because it means a fundamental change in orientation from profit to value. A lot of practical executives want a list of things they can do first thing on Monday morning to set change in motion. What this usually comes down to is a list of marching orders for subordinates. But the essential first step on this journey does not involve the hands and feet of your subordinates; it involves your own head and heart. You need to consider carefully whether the pursuit of value and loyalty is truly consistent with your own aspirations. For most companies, this is not an exercise for one person but for the entire team that runs the business. Before you start trying to apply the eight-part strategy just described, there are seven critically important questions that you and your management colleagues need to ask and answer.

QUESTION ONE:
AGREEMENT ON PURPOSE

The first step in the process is for the real leaders of your company to sit down together and consider two fundamental points: Do you want to enter into a long-term partnership with one another? Can you commit yourselves to value creation for customers as a primary mission? At A. G. Edwards, it took two years of soul-searching for the remaining partners to decide that they wanted to devote their lives to a higher purpose than profit, and that that higher purpose was to serve their customers. Profit was an indispensable ingredient and a vital part of the reward for succeeding at that mission, but it was not the mission itself.

Reliable answers to these questions require some careful consideration of the challenges you have to overcome. Your company leaders need to develop at least a rough picture of the changes this new mission will demand, including possible shifts in strategy, investment, measurement, culture, decision making, organizational structure, bonus cycles (including deferrals), and ownership. Outside perspectives are valuable here, as are the opinions of core employees and customers about where your current system is out of alignment with the loyalty-based model we have described.

QUESTION TWO:
ECONOMIC QUANTIFICATION

Once your management team has reached a consensus on the types of change required, the second question is whether the shift makes economic sense in your industry and your business. Purpose and vision can energize your team for a while, but a sustainable mission must be economically rational. Loyalty-based management will not transform every business in every industry. Your company may face far more pressing problems, especially if your industry is one where the investment in customer acquisition is minimal, or where long-term employment offers little potential for learning and increased productivity. Commodity suppliers like oil companies and certain high-tech businesses where technological breakthroughs can overwhelm customer relationships are examples of companies where loyalty economics can make a difference, but probably not a decisive difference.

Making a rational case for loyalty on economic grounds requires you to construct for your own business the basic economic model described throughout this book, particularly in Chapters 2, 4, and 8. Until you know which specific elements of customer and employee loyalty are likely to improve the economics of your business—and by how much— you cannot know which loyalty investments make economic sense and which should have top priority.

QUESTION THREE:
OWNERSHIP STRATEGY

Next you must ask yourself if the changes you're considering are really feasible, given the current ownership of your company. Investors will have to understand and endorse your strategy and the time frame it involves. Many companies (perhaps *most* public companies) will find that they have to change their investor strategy if they're to focus on the long term. Chapter 6 offers a range of options, some conservative and incremental, some bolder and riskier. But it is a waste of time (and career suicide) to embark on a series of fundamental changes without making sure your owners agree with your plans. In other words, it's a waste of time to commit your team to the creation of lasting value if the owners would rather maximize next quarter's earnings.

QUESTION FOUR:
PARTNERSHIP INCENTIVES

Before you go any further in your analysis of necessary changes, you need to ask yourself whether you have an adequate system of partnership incentives, not only for your senior management team but for as many parts of the business system (vendors, employees, distributors) as makes sense. If you think your current incentive system is adequate, please reread Chapter 10 and its crucial advice about how to structure value-sharing arrangements so that individuals prosper only when the group prospers, and the group prospers only when the company serves the long-term interests of customers, employees, and investors. At many of the companies where senior executives' bonuses include stock options, a sudden and temporary rise in the stock market can enrich top management whether or not there has been a corresponding rise in customer and employee value—and in certain egregious cases, precisely *because* customer or employee value has been impaired.

You have to begin by understanding what drives loyalty economics in your business, then design your value-sharing partnerships to concentrate on those points of leverage. Very few large public companies today have value-sharing partnerships as effective as those at Chick-fil-A, Corporate Software, Leo Burnett, ABRY, or Accuride—companies that make sure that only the creation of lasting value is rewarded.

QUESTION FIVE:
GETTING THE FACTS

Once you have deciphered the economics of loyalty in your business and aligned your partnership accordingly, you are in a position to begin a systematic review of the changes needed to improve value creation in your business system. The eight components of loyalty systems listed earlier in this chapter provide a good road map for this process. Beginning with the value proposition for customers and working through the entire cycle (shown schematically in Figure 1-3), you can evaluate the current health of your business system. But this diagnosis demands facts—the facts contained in the balance sheets and value flow statements described in Chapter 8.

Many firms will find they must fill enormous gaps in their information about customers and employees—why they join and why they defect. In order to determine which flows of customers and employees represent the most important value sources and value leaks in the system, these gaps must be filled. For some businesses, this effort will highlight important oversights or inconsistencies in strategy. Some companies may find, for example, that there is no agreement about who the firm's target customers are, let alone how well the company delivers value to them and receives value in return. Comparing your own performance to the competition's on such dimensions will help you to determine whether you can rely on incremental improvements or will need to consider a complete transformation of your value proposition.

QUESTION SIX:
SYSTEM FAILURES

Once you've gathered the facts, you can begin to ask questions about the nature and the scope of your business system's failures. With a good command of defection rates, gain rates, yield rates, and the most significant flows of value to and from customers and employees, you can now turn back to Chapter 7 and apply the tools of failure analysis.

Because you want this analysis to lead to action, make sure that each part of the organization is digging into the root causes that it controls or can at least affect. If your company needs to think about a major transformation of your value proposition, it makes sense to perform this analysis at the most senior level. You need to consider strategic solutions, not simply incremental improvements to the current strategy. Focusing the organization on the right scale of failure is one of top management's most important jobs.

QUESTION SEVEN:
MEASURES, TOOLS, AND TARGETS

Finally, a question so important it cannot be overemphasized: How will you measure your progress? When you implement solutions, you need to track their effectiveness precisely, using accurate rates of value flow and human turnover. Great business ideas and visions don't become real because they're great; business people *make* them real with the help of measurement.

It has been said a thousand times that you can't manage what you can't measure. If you want to manage your business to gain the loyalty of key customers, employees, and investors, then you must strive to create so much value for the first group that there is plenty left over for the other two. The only practical way to apply this value-centered business philosophy is by carefully defining and tracking defection rates, then making sure your organization has the tools and training it needs to analyze failures and improve value—continuously. There is no other way to manage toward zero defections.

A FINAL REFLECTION ON LOYALTY

The messages in this book are mostly messages you've heard before. A business must serve its customers. People are your most valuable asset. Pick your associates carefully and make sure they share your most important values. Learn from your mistakes. You can't manage what you can't measure. Treat others the way you'd like them to treat you. Profit isn't everything.

These are certainly not fresh ideas. Some are ancient; many are self-evident. All are now clichés. Obvious as they may seem, however, the business world ignores most of them with increasing frequency. The tendency to regard short-term profit as the primary business objective has become more and more pronounced in both business schools and boardrooms. Job-surfing careers, quick-buck investments, disposable employees, and an emphasis on growth by means of slick marketing and massive new-customer acquisition are some of the norms of modern business practice. As for picking your associates with care, why bother? The odds are remote that you will still be colleagues a few years hence.

But while the ideas are not new, the principles on which loyalty leaders base their enormously successful businesses make more than common sense and moral truth. They make money—more money in the long run than the cynical and opportunistic strategies we see all around us. By managing the economic linkages between value creation, loyalty, and profit, the companies described in this book have generated consistently superior cash flow for decades.

For all the companies we call loyalty leaders, the road to zero defections began at the center. The CEOs never assigned a loyalty project to marketing or finance or even the board of directors. They never thought of loyalty as a project, much less as a project they could delegate. For them, loyalty was a matter of honor and integrity. They committed themselves and their organizations to a higher mission than profit—the creation of so much value for customers that there would be plenty left over with which to reward employees and investors. They recognized that loyalty was not only an important means of accomplishing their mission but the best measure of their progress. They understood that losing half their customers in five years would be very bad business—indeed, that as a test of value creation, it would be a failing grade.

These leaders aspired to build businesses that would grow and last. By concentrating on value creation and partnership, they helped their organizations to learn the fundamentals of loyalty-based management: partnership builds incentive; incentive builds value; value builds loyalty; loyalty builds even greater value. On this foundation, the employees, investors, and customers of loyalty-based businesses have generated ascending spirals of profit, growth, and lasting value.

Notes

Chapter 1

1. Carol J. Loomis, "State Farm Is Off the Charts," *Fortune,* 8 April 1991, 76.
2. Greg Steinmetz, "State Farm Will Increase Payouts to Aid Policyholders Hit by Hurricane Andrew," *Wall Street Journal,* 11 September 1992, sec. A, p. 3.
3. David Illingworth (speech at a conference entitled "Elite of Lexus," Carefree, Ariz., 16 March 1992).
4. Henry Ford in collaboration with Samuel Crowther, *Today and Tomorrow* (New York: Doubleday, Page & Company, 1926; reprint, Cambridge, Mass.: Productivity Press, 1988), 29 (page citation is to the reprint edition).
5. Hal Lancaster, "A New Social Contract to Benefit Employer and Employee," *Wall Street Journal,* 29 November 1994, Managing Your Career column, sec. B, p. 1.
6. Thomas Teal, "Service Comes First: An Interview with USAA's Robert F. McDermott," *Harvard Business Review* (September–October 1991): 127.

Chapter 2

1. John Case, "Customer Service: The Last Word," *Inc.,* April 1991, 89.
2. Scott Cook, "Life Cycle Product Line Extension" (speech at a conference entitled "Loyalty-Based Management," co-sponsored by The Conference Board and Bain & Co., Inc., New York, N.Y., 1 June 1994).

Chapter 4

1. Peter F. Drucker, "The New Society of Organizations," *Harvard Business Review* (September–October 1992): 100.
2. Bruce D. Butterfield, "Broken Promises: Work in the '90s," *Boston Globe,* 10 October 1993, 23.
3. John Holusha, "A Profitable Xerox Plans to Cut Staff by 10,000," *New York Times,* 9 December 1993, sec. D, p. 1.
4. Hubert B. Herring, "Xerox Takes Itself to the Gym," *New York Times,* 12 December 1993, sec. 3, p. 2.
5. John Case, "The Question We All Wonder About: 'For Whom Do You Work?'" *Boston Globe,* 29 December 1993, Business section, p. 44.
6. Ben Edwards III, telephone conversation with Fred Reichheld, 1 September 1994.
7. Ibid.
8. Ibid.
9. Michael Siconolfi, "Rating the Brokers," *Smart Money: Personal Finance Magazine of the Wall Street Journal,* December 1993, 100.
10. Ben Edwards, *1993 Annual Report,* A. G. Edwards, Inc., 5.
11. Dan Truett, interview by Fred Reichheld, Atlanta, 13 January 1994.
12. Carol J. Loomis, "State Farm Is Off the Charts," *Fortune,* 8 April 1991, 80.
13. Chuck Wright, "State Farm's Success Based on Loyalty," *Bloomington Pantagraph,* 12 April 1993, sec. D, p. 1.
14. Karl Schriftgiesser, *The Farmer from Merna* (New York: Random House, 1955), 234.
15. Ibid., 217.
16. Loomis, "State Farm Is Off the Charts," 78.
17. Phil Schaff, interview by Fred Reichheld, Jupiter, Fla., 25 February 1994.

Chapter 5

1. Henry Ford in collaboration with Samuel Crowther, *Today and Tomorrow* (New York: Doubleday, Page & Company, 1926; reprint, Cambridge, Mass.: Productivity Press, 1988), 44 (page citation is to the reprint edition).
2. Albert Karr and Susan Pulliam, "Streamlining Wave Is Sweeping Insurance Companies," *Wall Street Journal,* 19 February 1992, Industry Focus section.
3. Ibid.
4. Peter Kerr, "Northwestern Mutual: Frugal, Stodgy and Admired," *New York Times,* 30 August 1992.
5. *1993 Annual Message,* Chick-fil-A, Inc., 11.
6. Marshall Loeb, "How to Grow a New Product Every Day," *Fortune,* 14 November 1974, 270.

Chapter 6

1. Peter F. Drucker, "Reckoning with the Pension Fund Revolution," *Harvard Business Review* (March–April 1991): 108.
2. Kurt Moser, telephone conversation with Fred Reichheld, 3 January 1995.
3. Warren Buffet, "Track Record Is Everything," *Across the Board,* October 1991, 59.
4. *1989 Annual Report,* Berkshire-Hathaway, Inc., 14.
5. *1992 Annual Report,* Berkshire-Hathaway, Inc., 20.
6. David Illingworth, telephone conversation with Fred Reichheld, 21 September 1994.
7. Quoted by Peter F. Drucker in "Reckoning with the Pension Fund Revolution," 108.
8. Mitt Romney, interview by Fred Reichheld, Boston, 15 December 1994.
9. Alex Pham, "Corporate Software's Metamorphosis," *Boston Globe,* 20 March 1994, Business section.
10. Ibid.
11. Dyan Machan, "Monkey Business," *Forbes,* 25 October 1993, 184.

Chapter 7

1. Warren Buffet, "Track Record Is Everything," *Across the Board,* October 1991, 59.

Chapter 8

1. David Illingworth (speech at a conference entitled "Elite of Lexus," Carefree, Ariz., 16 March 1992).
2. Private conversation with Fred Reichheld.
3. *1993 Annual Report,* Berkshire-Hathaway, Inc., 6.

Chapter 9

1. Dick Chitty, interview by Fred Reichheld, Torrance, Calif., 17 June 1993.
2. George Borst, interview by Fred Reichheld, Torrance, Calif., 17 June 1993.
3. Carl Sewell, interview by Fred Reichheld, Dallas, 9 February 1994.
4. Ronald Henkoff, "Service Is Everybody's Business," *Fortune,* 27 June 1994, 52.
5. Chitty, interview.
6. Sewell, interview.
7. Borst, interview.
8. Chitty, interview.
9. David Illingworth, telephone conversation with Fred Reichheld, 21 September 1994.

Chapter 10

1. James Ericson, telephone conversation with Fred Reichheld, 29 December 1994.
2. Laura R. Walbert, "Shopping for Life," *Forbes,* 22 February 1988.
3. *Performance* (Milwaukee: Northwestern Mutual Life, n.d.), brochure.
4. Ben Edwards III, telephone conversation with Fred Reichheld, 1 September 1994.
5. Ibid.
6. Carol J. Loomis, "State Farm Is Off the Charts," *Fortune,* 8 April 1991, 77.
7. David Illingworth, telephone conversation with Fred Reichheld, 21 September 1994.
8. Thomas Teal, "Service Comes First: An Interview with USAA's Robert F. McDermott," *Harvard Business Review* (September–October 1991): 118.
9. James Ericson, interview by Fred Reichheld, 29 December 1994.
10. *1989 Annual Report,* Berkshire-Hathaway, Inc., 2.
11. William Lynch, interview by Fred Reichheld, Chicago, 23 December 1994.
12. Ibid.
13. Ibid.
14. Ibid.
15. Carl Sewell, *Customers for Life* (New York: Doubleday, 1990), 102.
16. Royce Yudkoff, interview by Fred Reichheld, Wellesley, Mass., 20 March 1995.
17. Ibid.

Index

315

About the Author

Frederick F. Reichheld is a director of Bain & Company, a leading strategy consulting firm headquartered in Boston with twenty-three offices worldwide. He is the leader of the firm's worldwide Loyalty Practice, and his pioneering work in the area of customer, employee, and investor retention has quantified the linkage between loyalty and profits. This work forms the conceptual foundation for the practice, which helps clients achieve superior results through improvements in customer, employee, and investor selection and retention.

Reichheld's views have been quoted in *Business Week* and *Fortune,* and his recent publications include articles in the *Harvard Business Review* and *The Wall Street Journal.* He is a frequent speaker to major business forums and groups of senior executives.

A graduate of Harvard College and the Harvard Business School, Mr. Reichheld lives in the Boston area with his wife, Karen, and their four children, Chris, Jenny, Billy, and Jimmy.